THE GREEN REVOLUTION

STANLEY JOHNSON

The Green Revolution

HAMISH HAMILTON
LONDON

First published in Great Britain 1972
by Hamish Hamilton Ltd
90 Great Russell Street, London, WC1

Copyright © 1972 by Stanley Johnson

SBN 241 02102 2

Printed in Great Britain
by T. and A. CONSTABLE LTD., Edinburgh

CONTENTS

Introduction
page ix

PART ONE
Latin America
page 1

PART TWO
Africa
page 71

PART THREE
Asia
page 145

Index
page 213

The illustrations appear between
pages 114 and 115

'And, he gave it for his opinion; that whoever could make two ears of corn, or two blades of grass to grow upon a spot of ground where only one grew before; would deserve better of mankind, and do more essential service to his country, than the whole race of politicians put together.'—*A Voyage to Brobdingnag*, *Gulliver's Travels*, by Jonathan Swift.

'The time is a quarter to midnight . . . if we hesitate or falter, the monster—rapid population growth—will destroy the world.'—Dr Norman Borlaug, winner of 1970 Nobel Peace Prize.

INTRODUCTION

I TRACE the origins of this book to a few days spent in Rome in November 1969, attending the Fifteenth Session of the Conference of the Food and Agriculture Organization of the United Nations (FAO). The delegates to the Conference were a strangely reticent breed. Rhetoric, emotion, hyperbole—these were absent from their deliberations. They sat hour after hour in Plenary or in Commissions I and II, fiddling with their earphones, passing messages to each other, sometimes sleeping. Of course, the sheer labour involved in being a UN delegate was enough to dull the edge of wit. They had come from meetings in Geneva and Paris and New York; they were flying on to other meetings in Bangkok and Santiago and Addis Ababa. They were, in a sense, in perpetual motion. Small wonder that the spirit sometimes flagged.

Yet this Fifteenth Session of the FAO Conference was in fact an important occasion. It was here that FAO's Provisional Indicative World Plan for Agricultural Development (IWP) had its first public airing. Altogether, IWP was 744 pages long, contained in three volumes. It embodied the results of four provisional regional studies: on the Near East; South America; Africa South of the Sahara; and Asia and the Far East, together with material on Central America and North West Africa. One delegate calculated that it took him $37\frac{1}{2}$ hours to read the study. On the bathroom scale IWP weighed five pounds.

There were those who contended at the Conference that IWP was not at all what its name implied. It was not Provisional, since the Director-General of FAO, Dr A. H. Boerma, emphatically denied any intention of thoroughly reworking the estimates. It was not Indicative: it did not denote—in the French planners' use of the word—targets mutually agreed upon after due process of consultation. It was not World, since it gave only a very cursory treatment of the agricultural prospects of the developed world and the communist bloc (the 'centrally-planned' economies). It was not a Plan in that it laid down no clear sequence of steps for further international action.

Yet, though the title might be a misnomer and though the whole exercise had from the outset aroused great controversy, IWP clearly had something to say. It was an attempt—the first ever—at long-range perspective planning. It presented the broad outlines of a strategy whereby the food/population equation could be brought (barely) into balance between 1975 and 1985. It could in a sense be seen as antidote to the many prophets of doom—the Paddocks, the Ehrlichs and the Snows of yesteryear.

The Director of the Study, Walter Pawley, an Australian economist, was fortunate early on in his six-year programme of research. While most of the world was still shuddering at the recollection of 1965 and 1966 when, following the failure of two successive harvests in India, only massive relief operations averted widespread famine, those who knew about these things, like the Ford and Rockefeller Foundations, were rubbing their institutional hands with quiet expectation. Successful experiments in Mexico and the Philippines had convinced them that a 'green revolution' was on its way, that technological possibilities existed for yields of wheat and rice far in excess of any experienced to date.

It is these high-yielding cereals which IWP sees as 'spearheading the production breakthrough', to use its own inimitable jargon. They would be grown on one-third of the area planted to cereals in 1985, compared with around five per cent in 1968. With the new varieties would come a 'whole package of complementary inputs'—fertilizers, pesticides, credit, land-reform, seed, agricultural extension and, above all, irrigation. For an assured water supply was vital if farmers were to be persuaded to adopt the new varieties on a large scale and if cropping intensities were to increase at the projected rate.

Closing the 'calorie' gap, i.e. quantity of diet, in turn made it possible to close the 'protein gap', i.e. quality of diet. IWP stressed the importance of this objective. With increased per acre yields of cereals, more and more land should be turned over to other crops.

IWP's agricultural scenario, to use a word much beloved of futurologists, looked like this. 1970-1975: increasing supply of vegetable protein on land released from cereals production, e.g. beans and peas and pulses. Also increased emphasis on production of meat from animals with a fast reproductive cycle, e.g. pigs and poultry. Need for massive transfers of processed milk from developed to developing world, if widespread malnutrition is to be avoided. 1975-1980: transitional period. By holding down the slaughtering or 'offtake' rate for cattle (except in India) IWP hoped to see a steady 'build-up of bovines and other ruminants'. 1980-1985: 'Vertically integrated production' from contented cows should lead to a tapering-off of food aid in the form of processed milk. 'Action in the field of fish' (especially pond culture) together with the development of semi- and unconventional protein foods (e.g. petroleum molasses) would add variety to a diet which should now include beef as well as pork, chicken and cereals.

There was a price tag, of course. There always is. Cumulative investments under the Plan added up to U.S. $112 billion, without taking into account the need for agricultural credit. IWP pointed out that sums of this magnitude could only be found if (a) developed countries opened their markets to the manufactured and primary products of the less developed countries and (b) gave more aid.

A few weeks after the FAO Conference, when I had returned to England, I formed the idea of undertaking a journey through the Third World in search of this so-called 'green revolution'. I took the phrase 'green revolution' in its broadest sense to · include not only the development and propagation of the new high-yielding varieties of wheat and rice, but also many other aspects of agricultural development. Field and forest; fish, flesh and fowl—the green revolution applies, or can apply, to all of these. The new wheats, the new rices are part of a much larger story.

Much of the literature of development has tended to be solemn, even heavy. Much of it has tended to emphasize urban and industrial aspects of the modernizing process, as opposed to rural and agricultural aspects. My aim was to write a lively colourful account of what lay behind the statistics in other sectors of agriculture as well as cereals, and on other continents as well as Asia.

There is a case, of course, to be made against the popularization of development problems. It can be argued that technical matters are best described at a technical level. Demographers should write about demography, educationists about education, agriculturalists about agriculture. I am certainly very aware of the hazards involved in producing a popular or semi-popular book about agriculture. However intensely one may feel that this is a lively exciting subject with immense implications for human health and happiness, it is only realistic to recognize that the 'general public' finds agriculture pretty dull. Few people turn to the 'Farming Notes' first when they open their *Times* on Monday morning.

I remember telling an Australian friend about the book and being saddened to see a look of total boredom and blankness come over his face. So I protested that agriculture was important because food was important. Food was what we ate. And he said: 'Great heavens, man! We eat with knives and forks, don't we? But you don't expect someone to write a bloody book about knives and forks!'

If this is a book about agriculture, it is about a good deal else besides. It is about 'experts' who toil in foreign vineyards and seldom see the fruit of their work; about people of different nationalities who travel thousands of miles at the behest of some government or international organization to do the kind of job which most of their compatriots would not understand or even care to understand; it is about friends and acquaintances, or just faces across a table, who were always kind and helpful to me and often amusing as well; it is about men and women (and they still comprise the vast majority of the world's inhabitants) who work on the land or fish in the sea for a living.

Lastly the book is, I suppose, a travelogue. To the extent that travelogues are rather personal accounts of journeys undertaken, this is a personal book. It contains dialogue and monologue, anecdote and episode. It wanders, like Satan in the Book of Job, both to and fro in the world as well as up and down in it.

Wherever possible, I have tried not to use many statistics. Sometimes, I have not used statistics at all. I undertook three eight-week trips altogether—first to Africa, then to Latin America and last to Asia. (For convenience of presentation, I have reversed the order of the first two.) By the time I had finished I had accumulated a roomful of documents. In March this year, when I sat down to write this book, I sorted all these documents out. I bought a labelling gun and printed out neat plastic labels, by country (e.g. India) and by subject-matter (e.g. rice). I put the papers in large envelopes and stuck on the labels. Then I put all the envelopes in a cupboard in my study and forgot about them.

I decided that, if I had not seen enough and read enough and taken enough notes in the course of the trip itself, it was too late to do anything about it now. So almost all the information contained in this book is information I acquired at first hand by actually looking at something or talking to someone. That is why there are no footnotes and no bibliography.

This book would not have been possible without the co-operation of the World Bank. I am especially grateful to William Clark, Lars Lind and Jim Evans.

Finally, I must thank my wife, Charlotte, who had to keep everything going during my long absences abroad.

June 17, 1971   S. J.

PART ONE

LATIN AMERICA

I

September 9, 1970. The Chapultepec Room of the Hotel Aristos, Mexico City, Mexico. The time is 9.30 a.m. and the Annual Board Meeting of the International Centre for the Improvement of Maize and Wheat (known more colloquially by its Spanish initials as CIMMYT) is about to begin. As is the case with most meetings, tables and chairs have been set up in the room. Sharpened pencils lie beside blank pads. There are glasses for water and short stubby microphones at each place.

But even if the trappings were familiar, this was no ordinary occasion. These were not ordinary men. Those who had guided the fortunes of CIMMYT over the last few years had, in a wider sense, guided the fortunes of a large part of the world. The 'green revolution', about which we have heard so much in recent months, began here in Mexico. The work of the Rockefeller Foundation in Mexico, and the partnership that was built up between the Foundation and the Mexican Government, was the principal factor in the development of those new seeds of wheat which have, in the space of a few short years, produced a truly global harvest.

This book is not intended to be a full chronicle of the 'Green Revolution'. That task must be left to agricultural historians who can expound far better than I could hope to the true significance of each genetic discovery, the advantages and limitations of each new variety tested, the tolerance factors, head weights, tillering characteristics and so forth. What I would like to do is to present, if I can, something of the flavour of a great enterprise and of the men who are, or have been, engaged in it.

The meeting that morning began on time. That was only to be expected. Plant breeders in the nature of their work have to operate to precise time schedules, so as to maintain the momentum of planting, transplanting, selection, crossing and yield-testing for literally thousands of different lines and varieties. The Mexican Secretary of State for Agriculture stood up before a

3

battery of flashing cameras and, in a brief speech, declared the meeting open. Dr Sterling Wortman, of the Rockefeller Foundation, responded. Then Robert Osler, Deputy Director of CIMMYT, took the floor. He referred to the illness of Dr Wellhausen, the Director of CIMMYT and a man who had been with the wheat-breeding programme in Mexico since its inception. Since Dr Wellhausen could not be with the meeting, he read out the first part of the speech which Dr Wellhausen had prepared.

There is a moment for members of the Board to express their sorrow and condolences at Dr Wellhausen's absence. Then Osler goes over to the wall where large maps of the different regions of the world have been hung. Coloured areas indicate the extent of CIMMYT's empire. Osler, an American in his early 40's, wears a greenish suit and a broad striped tie which matches the maps. He provides a commentary.

'One can say that 50 million hectares are involved in each crop, that is in wheat and maize. We think that CIMMYT is a unique resource for expanding the improvement in these two crops. We are talking about economic improvement in the nation as a whole, not just improvement in yield.'

Osler goes on to talk about the highlights of the past year where maize is concerned. 'All of us have heard a great deal about the need for improved quality protein in the diet. We have undertaken an expanded programme in the area of high lysine maize, largely financed by a grant from UNDP, the United Nations Development Programme. We have also extended our efforts to bring together the agronomic side and our breeding activities. We believe that CIMMYT has a role to play not only in helping plant breeders to develop more efficient varieties, but also in their application in the field. Our international maize nursery is leading to advances in international disease and pest control. . . . Briefly, then, in our maize programme, we feel we have the basic knowledge and ideas and we hope that we can continue to be a dynamic organization which can be flexible enough to respond to the real needs.'

Next Osler turns to wheat. 'Most of you know that, in the last five years, the international wheat programme has developed into the largest and most effective wheat programme in the world. It goes far beyond the coloured areas on the map. It would be hard to find a country in the world which has not benefited from the wheats which Dr Borlaug has developed in collaboration with the Mexican Ministry of Agriculture. In wheat, as in maize, we shall concentrate on agronomics. We find in many countries we don't have the know-how to make the best use of production possibilities. Many of you know countries that have benefited by, and are using on a large scale, germ-plasm that has been developed in Mexico—but almost all could do more. Dr Borlaug will be spending more of his time on this aspect of our work.'

I had, that morning in Mexico city, only the briefest glimpse of Dr Borlaug, Dr Norman Ernest Borlaug, who was a few weeks later to be awarded the Nobel Peace Prize for his services to agriculture. After Osler had finished speaking, he stood up to give us a ten minute harangue before leaving for the airport to catch a plane for New York *en route* to Algeria and then to Asia. Perhaps 'harangue' is the wrong word; I use it only to describe the intensity and conviction with which he spoke.

'Let me tell you first,' he began, 'what has really happened in the last three years of wheat production. In India, in 1965, 12·3 million metric tons of wheat were produced under near ideal conditions. Last year this had risen to 20 million metric tons. In Pakistan, in 1965, the harvest was 4·6 million tons and last year it had risen to 8·4 or almost double. There had, of course, been parallel increases in income. When this sort of money is injected into the economy, lots of things start happening. Any way you look at it, there has been tremendous change. Before the so-called "green revolution", tractors were parked around the place and no-one would use them. The payoff wasn't high enough. Now there's a black market in tractors. It makes the governments nervous, so they start trying to increase the output of the units. With mechanization, it suddenly becomes possible to grow two or three crops a year on the same piece of land. You can't do it with bullock power, because bullocks are threshing the wheat crop when they should be ploughing the land. But you can, if you have a small threshing machine or a small tractor.

'People talk about the unexpected consequences of the "green revolution". But I believe most of the governments of the world do take action in a time of crisis. The crisis in India came when the crops started building up and they were short of storage. So they tackled the storage problem. Now there are other problems, social problems, and the government will tackle them too. They say in the press that the "green revolution" only helps the big landowners, but millions and millions are growing wheat in these areas and this never comes through in what you read in the newspapers. I get sick of reading about the land-grabs and the green revolution leading on to the red revolution. The green revolution can't solve all the social problems which already existed before it.'

Borlaug ended with a quick résumé of the world scene. His summary was terse to the point of being laconic. It was hard to realize that a few words spelled the difference, literally, between life and death for thousands and hundreds of thousands of people. 'Iran and Afghanistan,' said Borlaug, pointing to the maps, 'need help. The Arab bloc—that is very frustrating. These countries are not concentrating on agriculture. Other things are of paramount importance. But there is progress in Syria in dry-land wheat production, also in Tunisia and Morocco. Algeria wants a crash programme. Wheats are growing widely in Rhodesia, South Africa, Kenya, Ethiopia. In Russia, they are growing some of the wheats in the south. But they don't know how to handle them on the dry lands and they are very short of fertilizer.

'As for Latin America, they are working in a modest way in Argentina. There's the breeding programme in Colombia. Brazil is tooling up. A surprising amount of Mexican wheat is being grown in southern USA. This will produce more kilos per hectare than the barley they've grown for 25 years in California. They will use it both for feed and food.

'Our main emphasis right now is increasing the scope of disease resistance. We want more stem-borer resistance, more mildew resistance and so forth. On balance I believe most of the effects of the "green revolution" have been good. There has been more food, greater bonds of understanding. But,' and here Dr Borlaug ended with his traditional plea, 'I never want anyone to say I am not concerned about population control. The time is a quarter to midnight. Produce more food, yes—by all means. But let us never kid ourselves that this is the whole answer.'

1970 was a good year to collect stories about Norm Borlaug. He was very much in people's minds. It must be the first time the world has witnessed the virtual apotheosis of a plant-breeder. Some of these stories had already acquired a kind of apocryphal quality. The chrysalis of legend was forming about the man.

Once, some months later, I was driving back late at night from Pantnagar Agricultural University to New Delhi in the company of an Indian agricultural scientist, called Rao. I recall the conversation vividly. It had an unworldly quality. The lights of the car were faint to the point of extinction. More than once we seemed certain to crash, as lorries hurtled out of the night towards us, buffaloes and carts veered across the road in the darkness or bicycles wobbled unsteadily in front of our wheels. But Rao, engrossed in the tale of India's agricultural revolution, ignored it all. He described how he and Norm Borlaug had travelled the country in 1965, looking at India's agricultural programme and prospects; how Borlaug had gone back to Mexico and had sent them seeds from some of his new wheats which they were able to multiply for the next year. 'Mexico was lucky,' Rao told me, 'she had the seeds; she had the water; and she had Borlaug.'

Or again, I remember sitting in Dula Navarette's house in Recife in the North-East of Brazil. We had flown down in the morning from Petrolina in the small plane which FAO and the UNDP had assigned to Dula's project, up in the interior. As with Dr Rao, the hazards of the journey seemed to inspire in Dula a streak of reminiscence. He was a Mexican. He talked about Mexico and about the new developments in the north of his country.

'As you go from Hermosillo to the coast,' he says, 'the first part is barren and bare, just like the Sertao where we were this morning. But then you reach this point—they call it Seven Hills. Actually, it's a chain of hills and the largest one has seven peaks to it. Go beyond this, and it's a different world. They have more than 100,000 hectares under irrigation—well irrigation. They call it "la costa de Hermosillo". Here are the

most progressive farmers of the world. The whole development
was private enterprise. The only thing the government did was
stop them opening new wells. Otherwise they would have run
out of water.

'My wife and I began our married life in Obregon, up there
in the north of Mexico. It's there in Obregon that the most
important research station was established. It was there that
Borlaug did his best work. Among the first varieties he introduced
was Cajeme. After that, there was a whole series of Yaquis
named after the Yaqui valley. There was Yaqui 54, 55, 56.
Then there was Lerma Rojo—that one has been very important
for Mexico.'

Mrs Dula, who is sitting with us, interrupts. 'In my family,'
she says, 'there are seven agronomical engineers. We all knew
how to recognize the different seeds. Lerma Rojo was easy—it
had a small beard and a reddish colour. The Yaquis were
yellow.'

Dula continues: 'Borlaug is a fan of baseball. He organized
the children's team in Obregon. He bought the balls and the
gloves and he used to go out on Sunday. You meet him in the
office and he's so serious and straightforward. But out on the
field, he knew all the nasty words there were!

'Borlaug's training, as I remember, was in parasitology. He
was called in to attack the rust. But he found out that the way
to attack it was through genetics. Now I doubt if there is
anyone in the world who knows more about agriculture.'

Borlaug, of course—at least to men like Dula who watched
the world they knew change before their eyes—is only a part
of the legend. 'That was a fantastic thing,' says Dula, 'this
Rockefeller team. Wellhausen used to go out to the field in a
Mexican hat. He would ask for a mule and plant the corn
walking behind the mule. Then he would watch it grow. We
Mexicans used to call the Rockefeller people "classified aliens".
They were mad enough to work alongside the peons. No-one
else would do that. They came and they stayed. Wellhausen's
daughter married a Mexican.

'The Rockefeller Foundation stayed more than a generation
in Mexico. In order to pass the programme into the hands of the
government, they had to train people. They prepared at least

200 Masters and I don't know how many Ph.D.s. Just bringing in the seeds wouldn't have been enough. Breeding is a constant, steady job.'

Mrs Dula joins in again. 'If you fly from Tucson, Arizona to Hermosillo, what you are going to see is a type of agriculture which makes you rich, so rich. You will see houses like you've never seen in Mexico City, swimming pools and everything. They have such a lot of money. Why do you go to Europe, they ask? Tucson is much better. Tucson is new. Tucson is the capital of Hermosillo. The Tucson stores advertise in the local papers. They say "this month you need give just 10 pesos for a dollar instead of 12." The ladies of these rich Mexican farmers like to save, so they get together and form a club and once a month they go to Tucson. Some saving!'

When Borlaug won the Nobel Peace Prize later in 1970, he received a good deal of publicity. I acquired, in the course of my travels, a number of potted biographies and press releases put out by different bodies with which he was in one way or another associated. I have them all somewhere. They contain all the relevant biographical data, colleges attended, publications, jobs and so on. But somehow none of the blurbs captures the man.

*

One of the paradoxes facing plant-breeders is that their efforts are often jeopardized by the very successes they have achieved. Perhaps the first step in any breeding programme is to learn what genetic resources are available. The best way to do this is to make collections and to maintain collections of plants from all over the world. Looked at from a distance, this is a romantic task. The collector sets out in his jeep or Land Rover looking for strange botanical treasures on the slopes of Mt Ararat in Turkestan, or in the Kurdish areas of Iraq; in the uplands of Ethiopia or the high Andes. He will harvest and classify the indigenous varieties, noting carefully their provenance and the climate and ecology in which they flourish. Sometimes he will return with seeds, sometimes with a whole plant.

These wild varieties, culled in distant fields, may not look much like the modern domesticated strains of wheat and barley and maize and so forth. (The bison does not much resemble a cow.) Yet they may contain essential characteristics, some genetic property, which when it is transferred to other varieties may spell the difference between success and failure. Put crudely, the plant breeder is always engaged in a race against time. A highly successful variety may suddenly show itself to be susceptible to a new kind of rust which has apparently emerged overnight from nowhere. The spores of the rust may have travelled on the wind, setting down as much as a thousand miles away from the place of their last appearance. Or the rust may have been present all the time, but at a very low or suppressed level. It may be the spread of the new variety produces a more favourable ecology, so that the disease increases with the popularity of the variety until it reaches a critical level. And the same process may apply to pest infestations of various sorts.

The existence, in the raw untrammelled state of nature, of a large number of indigenous varieties is a kind of insurance policy for the plant-breeder. He has something to fall back on. The jeeps and Land Rovers may come back from Anatolia with what looks like an unpromising clump of weeds; but screening and testing may show that this is precisely what the plant-breeder needs to build into his programme. If he is a year or two ahead of the rust or pest or whatever, he may have time to do the cross-breeding, the production of foundation seed and, finally, commercial multiplication and distribution before ecological disaster strikes. It may, like the battle of Waterloo, prove a 'close-run thing'. The plant breeder is working on the margin far more often than many people realize.

The danger today is that this natural insurance policy is being rendered null and void by the rapid spread of the new varieties, the so-called 'miracle wheats', over the face of the earth. Complexity is being ousted by uniformity and the consequence, in terms of the loss of valuable genetic material, could be serious indeed. This process was well described to me by the Irish scientist, Erna Bennett, who has spurred FAO into undertaking a world-wide search to collect and maintain these indigenous resources before it is too late.

'In Turkey, in 1965,' so she told me, 'along the south-west and south-central parts of the Anatolian plateau, one could enter any wheat field and take samples which showed enormous variations. One might find twenty varieties altogether. A year later, I went from field to field and the only variations I could find were impurities within species. Of course, the farmer's job is not growing raw material for the breeders. But in ten thousand years of agriculture, this is precisely what he has done.

'In Greece, in 1920, 89% of all wheat was local races. In 1930, it was 79%. In 1947, it was 53%; by 1958 it had fallen to 25% and, by 1966, the proportion was around 10%. Last year, I drove from Rome to Greece in my jeep and discovered that, even in isolated mountain villages, the local races were almost completely extinct. I mean even in villages where they were cut off for six or seven months a year. The problem of variation has now reached such a point that the breeder can now no longer rely on nature herself for his supply. Instead he must look to collections to find what he needs.'

It is Erna Bennett's judgement that CIMMYT has run the most helpful and successful programme in the world primarily because it has recognized the value of local resources. The germ-plasm bank—it is a bank which literally grows in the fields at Toluca outside Mexico City—was started by the Rockefeller Foundation country programmes and has been inherited by CIMMYT. Collection goes on continually. Two committees have been set up, one for maize and one for wheat. The object is to ensure that all the relevant germ-plasms are in the bank, or at least as many as possible. An international nurseries programme has been started, with the involvement of FAO. Schools for collectors are being established. This is a high priority activity.

Apart from its stress on local resources, another factor which has contributed to CIMMYT's success is its geographical location. In Mexico, there is a very wide range of habitats. In any one year, breeders can rely on finding several growing seasons. The CIMMYT people have taken full advantage of this fact. They have two primary sites. The summer nursery is at Toluca, near Mexico City. Mexico City lies at 7,400 feet. Toluca lies at 8,500 feet and, at 19 degrees latitude, is farther south than Hawaii. By using Toluca in addition to the main site at Obregon, 1,200 miles from Mexico City in the big wheat-growing area of the Yaqui valley, in the State of Sonora,

CIMMYT is able to advance a generation in the breeding process and thus make a crucial time-gain. In effect, the use of two sites in Mexico means that CIMMYT can achieve ten plant generations in the space of five years.

Soon after I arrived in Mexico, CIMMYT arranged for me to visit their Toluca Centre. I was asked to be ready to leave at 7.30 a.m. since it takes a good hour and a quarter to reach the site (there is a 10,000-foot pass between Mexico City and Toluca). Waiting in the hotel lobby, I found two other visitors to CIMMYT, a Mr and Mrs Rhodes from Oklahoma. Mr Rhodes told me he was Chairman of the Oklahoma Wheat Commission and was visiting CIMMYT out of professional interest. The wheat revolution is not confined to the developing world. Rhodes says that in Oklahoma for the first time ever they are feeding wheat to the cattle and he adds, apropos of Toluca, that 'this place has got to be something'.

Art Klatt, one of the CIMMYT people, is our escort for the day. He is a Texan. He wears a blue cap and a yellow jacket. As we pull away from the hotel, he turns around and says: 'You all should know I'm from Texas. Did graduate work at TSU. So if I start talking too fast or using phraseology you can't understand, just stop me.'

Spending the day with Art Klatt, walking through the fields of standing corn at Toluca, taught me something about the arcane mysteries of the plant-breeders' art. 'You make a cross,' Klatt explained, 'and you plant that seed in what is known as an F_1. F stands for "filial generation". One row of F_1, when you harvest it, gives you enough seed for your F_2, plus a surplus you can ship to thirty or forty other locations. Your F_1 is uniform. Your F_2 is the first segregating plant. You select out and go on to the next F.'

We walk on to a different part of the field to where the F_2's are planted. Klatt explains again: 'Here there are 600 different F_2's.' He looks critically at the rows. The plants have begun to head but they clearly are not yet ready. 'When the plants become more mature, Borlaug and myself and the trainees—we have trainees from 17 or 18 different countries—will go through and pull the plants. Then come the breeders and the pathologists. The plants we don't want, we don't harvest. Everything we plant is planted by hand. Everything we harvest is harvested by hand. Either we pull it out by hand or with a hand sickle. We select on a plant to plant basis. F3 is still too early for it to be uniform. There is still half as much variability as in F2. And there is half as much variability in F4 as in F3. After F7, you either put the plant into yield trials or you throw it away.

'We select for disease resistance, for good head type, for high fertility. We look for types which can set a maximum number of seeds across a spikelet, as well as good straw characteristics and dwarfing characteristics.'

We came to the crossing block. Crossing is the crucial operation. Without it, there could be no progress genetically. There are CIMMYT workers crouched among the rows of wheat performing delicate intricate tasks. We stop beside one of them. He was removing the centre floret of a female head with a pair of tweezers. Then he puts a bag over the head and waits three days. The bags are little white paper bags and as you look down the rows of green and yellow wheat you can see them catching the sun, or rumpling in the light breeze. Once he has doctored the female, the breeder has to decide which the male parent is to be. He makes a choice and he brings a head which is shedding pollen. He cuts across the spikelet and puts the head in the sun leaving the anthers to extrude. 'You get some good anthers out,' says Klatt, 'in good heads, they'll come out all over.'

The pollen is like sperm. The worker puts the male head in the bag and twirls it gently. The female has ovaries which respond to the pollen.

We went slowly round the crossing block. It was in its way like visiting Chartres, or some famous artistic or cultural collection. I was seeing in the flesh, as it were, the masterpieces of the breeder's art, landmarks in agricultural history, which previously had only been names on a printed page. There was Sonora 64, six years old but still going strong, grown today with amber grains because the Indians grind the whole grain in their chapattis and they didn't like red chapattis. There was the famous Inea, named after the Mexican Institute of Agricultural Research, a variety which is probably grown over about 40% of the wheat area in Mexico. It looks a poor and ill-favoured thing until the last two weeks when, as Klatt put it, 'it suddenly matures at a terrific rate. The yield pours out of it.'

There was Justin, which takes 120 days to head in Mexico because the days are short. Then suddenly, pushing up at us at the end of a row, came Kalyan Sona, the spearhead of the green revolution in India—and in Pakistan too, where a red-seeded selection was called MexiPak. Here, in Mexico, it is called Siete Cerros, taking its name from that seven-peaked hill outside Obregon. Except to those who know it and love it, Siete Cerros is not a beautiful plant. It has a squat blocky head and a crooked, almost corrugated, neck. An ugly work-horse, perhaps. But it has done a fine job.

Still new names, magic poetic names which may one day be common currency in men's language, spring at us out of the field. There is Ciano and Klein Rendidor, Saric 70 and Yecora 70. These last two have yielded between eight and nine tons per acre in trials in the last year. Saric 70 is an E3, which is one of the most exciting things going. For the triple-E's, as the E3 is known, have only recently been released in Mexico and there are hopes that these—and other new varieties—are going to boost yield levels higher than ever. E3 means that the wheat has three dwarfing genes and is about 65 centimetres tall, as opposed to E2 which means two dwarfing genes and a wheat about 85 centimetres tall, or E1, which with only one dwarfing gene, ranges from 100 to 109 centimetres.

It is this dwarfing characteristic which, taken together with the photoperiod insensitivity that enabled the Mexican material to be sent all over the world and the built-in disease resistance, has been the real engine of the 'green revolution.' Where the old varieties lodged, or toppled over, under even modest applications of fertilizers, the new short and strong-strawed wheats can accept it in generous quantities. This factor, amongst others such as the proper use of water, has made for the quantum leap in wheat-yields which the 'green revolution' has come to denote.

We go on to another field and still another. Morning turns into afternoon. Art Klatt talks about the journalists who have found the 'green revolution' a ripe target for barbed darts. 'Boy,' he says 'they ripped us up one side and down another.' But he says CIMMYT wheats are grown over 95% of Mexico, so it must be nonsense to say they don't reach the small farmer.

He sees something strange in one of the rows and exclaims: 'Good golly, Miss Molly! What do we have here?' Blue hat and yellow jacket bobbing among the plants, he has seen some leaf rust on a plant as a sparrow-hawk circling at a great height spies a mouse hundreds of feet below. He comes back, having pulled the plant, and shows me the damage. 'I don't know whether the leaf rust would have made it because the stripe rust has already been there.'

Then Klatt, the tall Texan, stands in the field, spreads his hands out wide and feels the wheat all around him.

'Open your eyes,' he says, 'and feel it with your hands and it will talk to you.'

★

If its geographical location is one reason for CIMMYT's success, and its imaginative exploitation of all sources of breeding material another, a third consideration is that CIMMYT has done away at one blow with the traditional barrier between the breeders and the producers, by integrating pilot field operations with the breeding programme. The Puebla Project, the first major attempt CIMMYT carried out along these lines, attempted to answer the question: 'why can't we make progress with the small farmers? Why can't we put together a package and test it in the field and evaluate the result?'

The Puebla Project, when it began in 1967, had three main objectives. The first was to increase the production of corn under rainfall conditions. (Puebla has an average annual rainfall of about 800 millimetres, some 80% or 90% of this falling between the months of April and October). The second objective was to establish what was referred to as 'a new methodology' for increasing production in maize, a methodology which could be applied to other crops like beans and wheats, in other areas of the country and in other countries of the world. The third objective was to develop a programme for training people.

What was especially distinctive about the Puebla Project was that it was conducted completely on the farmers' own land. It was not a case of some external agency owning a demonstration

farm and bussing the farmers in just when they were most busy
with their own operations and telling them 'see how good we
are'. On the contrary, there were 47,000 heads of families in the
Puebla Project district, a total population of 260,000 in farm
families and probably 300,000 people altogether in the area.
The project covered 32 *municipios* in Puebla State. When it began,
the average yield of maize under rainfall conditions was 1,300
kilos per hectare.

At the beginning, it seems, the people in the district were
hostile. The feeling was that anyone from outside the district
was either a communist or a government official come to tax or
otherwise harass them. They were reluctant to answer questions
about the size of the land they held and, having carefully
developed over the years techniques for avoiding change, they
were reluctant to co-operate in the spirit of the project. A bench-
mark survey, carried out in January and February 1968,
revealed that 38% of the farmers were 'ejiditarios', i.e. bene-
ficiaries under the Mexican land reform, 27% were small-
holders and the rest (more or less) some combination of the two.

Working in the project area were twenty-one agencies,
including banks providing credit for different agricultural programmes, seed companies, insurance companies, and state and
local government official bodies.

I drove down one day from Mexico City to the project area
with Delbert Myren. Myren had been with the Rockefeller
Foundation in Mexico since 1955 and, more than anyone else,
has been the heart and soul behind the Puebla Project. It was a
rather short visit. Myren had one or two other guests; wives had
been invited and, inevitably, a good chunk in the middle of the
day was devoted to a long and sociable Mexican lunch taken in
a wayside café. Before lunch we did, however, manage—as
agricultural enthusiasts are supposed to—to 'get out into the
fields' for an hour or so. We clustered around the back of a
pick-up truck, wives and all, while a young graduate from the
National School of Agriculture at Chapingo propped up some
diagrams against the vehicle and harangued us with a battery of
statistics and charts. It was an impressive performance because
he was able to present quite clearly what a complex technical
business the new agriculture was and how important the

extension service could be if the small farmer was to be able to profit by it.

'There are,' said our instructor, and the diagrams and charts bore him out, 'certain factors of production which are not easily modifiable by man. These are TEMPERATURE, RAIN, EVAPORATION, HAIL DAMAGE, FROST, etc. Then there are various factors which can be modified by man, such as PREPARATION OF SOIL, DATE OF PLANTING, VARIETY TO BE PLANTED, CONTROL OF PESTS, etc.' Our instructor told us that they were now getting good rainfall data. They had forty measuring stations whereas when they started there were only two. They were getting better information on soil qualities and deficiencies in the various parts covered by the project.

'We are trying,' he explained, 'different amounts of fertilizer, different methods of application. What we need is to get the interaction effect of different variables. We are trying, for example, different levels of fertilizer and different varieties of maize. We need to discover the optimal economic applications. This year we have 42 different experiments in 24 different locations. The idea is to integrate research and extension. We have field days for farmers throughout the zone.

'We haven't pushed a new variety until we are sure that we do indeed have one that is better. To obtain a good variety probably takes eight to ten years. Of course, you have to do it by selection. The plant is selected according to the number of ears per plant. We prefer more than two, either on the principal stalk or on the tiller. Then you need a short healthy plant to make lodging difficult. We select out, for breeding purposes, only the plant that is less than average height, measured at the base of the ear. And we only select plants with large kernels and a healthy ear. The characteristics of the local varieties are quite good, but they have a lodging problem. If you use fertilizer, the farmers could make a total loss.'

After lunch, we all piled back into the car—gringos on our errands of mercy—and headed off in the direction of the 'typical Mexican village'. The 'typical Mexican villagers' had been alerted that we were coming and had been lined up in what, for want of a better name, must be called the village square. For an hour or more they had been waiting for us to finish our meal.

Some of them had become disgruntled at the delay and had quite properly gone about their business. But a nucleus remained and, in a stilted fashion, we plied them with questions. What had the Puebla Project meant to them? Had they increased their yields? Why did they still plant the beans so that they grew up the maize? Did they not know that the optimum planting density was 55,000 plants per acre? Did they have a co-operative? If so, was it a production co-operative or a marketing co-operative? What kind of credit facilities were there?

Well, these were all keen intelligent questions which proved that lunch had, if anything, improved the eye. The Mexican farmers who confronted us, most of them barefoot, heads and hands gnarled with age and the weather, eyes red and weak from a lifetime of squinting into the sun, took them all seriously when they had been duly interpreted. Gringo questions, at least when the gringos are present, are meant to be taken seriously. They conferred amongst themselves. Yes, of course they planted the beans along with the maize. As the leader of the group put it, smiling broadly, 'If the rains don't come, at least you get some beans. And sometimes you get both.' No, they didn't really have a production co-operative, if he understood the concept right. 'You see most people are waiting for the rain. Then when the rains come, they all need the equipment at the same time. So it is very difficult to share equipment. It is very difficult for these people to help each other.' As for credit, yes, they did have a credit co-operative and 69 out of the 70 members of the group had paid up on their obligations. But even here there are problems. 'You see we have to spend too much money paying off the man in the Bank so that he will give us the loan to which the government says we are entitled.'

Still, the confrontation was not a total frost. We learned that the average yield had risen, as far as this could be gauged with accuracy, to 1,500 kilos per hectare from the 1,300 it had been when the project started. One of the group, warming to the occasion, says he had made 10,000 pesos from two hectares of maize, converting it through pigs. And he shows us the pigs, large as life, gobbling up the maize behind a low mud wall at the back of the village. Cameras click and, mentally, the pigs are already subtitled 'The Puebla Project in Action, 1970'.

But there is more to come. With the pigs, the man says, fed on Puebla maize, he has been able to buy an electric pump and, now that electricity has come to the village, he can use it too. We see that too, gurgling away in the forecourt of the man's hut, his wife washing the clothes beneath a real live faucet and his children marvelling at the success of their daddy. He has not finished yet. The other villagers know what is to come, but still they hang on his words. For they all, to a greater or lesser extent, share in one man's prosperity. He has bought a television, too, he says and everyone around nods and smiles. You can't do better than that. This is the ultimate.

One of our party says, somewhat unoriginally, 'It's like pouring gasoline on a fire when these people get an idea.' And Del Myren, who started it all, says, 'Maybe next year we should start an agricultural extension programme on the TV. We could show them evening programmes about planting and picking corn when they come in off the fields.'

*

Around 1965, certain workers in the field of plant genetics reported that some samples of maize showed themselves to contain a particularly high proportion of the amino acid, lysine. This was an interesting discovery since it is precisely in their low lysine content that cereals fall behind meat in protein value. The polynucleitid chain, which is protein, is digested by the body and the amino acids, which hang like labels on the chain, are broken down. When there is a high lysine component, you begin to approximate to meat protein.

The implications of this discovery were far-reaching. Maize is eaten as a staple food by over 200 million people in all parts of the world. It is a poor man's diet and it is the poor who, lacking the resources to purchase milk and meat and eggs, suffer most acutely from protein malnutrition. The distended stomach and swollen knee-joints are—paradoxically—signs of starvation, not of plenty. The question was: could a variety or varieties of high lysine maize be bred which not only approximated or exceeded present varieties in absolute yield (leaving protein values aside), but which also had acceptable characteristics where taste, grinding properties, etc. were concerned.

B

Maize, it had to be recognized, was not like wheat. It was much more sensitive than wheat to a difference in environmental conditions. Though the bulk is grown between 3,000 and 5,000 feet, maize is to be found in practically all ecologies from sea-level up to 12,000 feet. It is not easy to develop a uniform variety at, say, CIMMYT headquarters in Mexico City and then send it out through the mails all around the world. The Indian peasant, high up on the slopes of the Andes, may have grown used to a sort of maize whose ecological habitat extends no more than a few miles on either side, and a few hundred feet up or down, climate and temperature varying significantly with altitude.

Following the discovery of the high lysine possibility, CIMMYT immediately started—as a high priority matter—a collection and screening programme for a high lysine maize which might form the basis of a commercial programme. In March 1970 the UNDP, in co-operation with FAO, provided a grant of one million dollars to CIMMYT to permit the work to be accelerated and intensified. Today a technical breakthrough has been achieved with the discovery of an opaque variety, known as Opaque 2, which has the magic high lysine component and whose ultimate production potential looks at least as good as the present varieties. (In a situation where the average yield of maize grown between 3,000 and 5,000 feet is only one and a half tons per acre, this is not an impossible proposition.)

But, though a technical breakthrough has been achieved, a production breakthrough has still to follow. It is not yet a 'miracle' maize. There are many problems to be overcome before it reaches the bellies of the people. The chief difficulty is related to texture. Opaque 2, as its name implies, is opaque to transmitted light. The flinty type of grain, which is what we are all used to buying in the supermarkets or (sometimes) growing in our gardens, will let light through. You can lay an ear of grain on a viewing table and clearly see its internal structure. Other physical characteristics follow the same pattern of differences. In those parts of the world where maize is still eaten as a staple diet, the family will as often as not grind its own flour to make the corn-bread. If they use stones to grind the flour, they will have problems with Opaque 2. For Opaque 2, which has a floury endosperm, rolls instead of grinding. If it is wet, and sometimes they like to boil before they grind, it is even harder to handle. This is a case where technical know-how is in conflict with tradition and social customs.

Even in those areas of the world where they prefer the floury endosperm, such as some parts of Colombia, there may still be problems. If the farmer is already growing the soft-kernel variety of maize, he may have difficulty in distinguishing after a while between the high lysine variety and the indigenous sort. The nutritive value of the former may be dissipated through random planting. CIMMYT can run laboratory tests to differentiate between one endosperm and another. But this is hardly a practical procedure for the average peasant.

In spite of these problems, the CIMMYT people remain optimistic. Their attitude can best be summed up by the old story of Columbus's egg. The courtiers at the royal court of Spain were one day mocking Columbus, asking him how he could possibly maintain that the earth was round, not flat. The King, joining in the fun, said: 'I have an egg. It is round. How can I make it stand up?' And the courtiers said 'We certainly can't.' But Columbus came and bashed the egg on its head and said, 'That's how.' The courtiers complained that nobody had told them they could do that, so Columbus replied 'Who said you can't?'

In the same way the CIMMYT people don't for a moment believe that it is just opaqueness that gives a high lysine content, or just a high lysine content that gives good protein balance. There may be many other avenues to be explored. They stand the egg up on its head. Specifically, they expect to be able to develop—using their well-tried techniques of breeding and experimentation—a maize with as high yield as present varieties as well as improved protein content; a flinty type maize which looks like what people are used to; and a maize which will have a wide range of ecological adaptability, being relatively indifferent to day-length, altitude and temperature, and is therefore capable of being moved up and down in the tropical world as well as around and about in it.

The rewards from a successful lysine programme could be

very high indeed. Colombia is the first country in the world to have made a commercial essay of the new opaque maize. At the Inter-American Centre for Tropical Agriculture (CIAT) near Calli, nutritionists are working hand-in-hand with agronomists to develop a product, based on the opaque variety, which can be sold as baby food. As Dr Eduardo Alvarez, who is in charge of the maize side of the programme at CIAT, was later to tell me: 'These children may have come to the hospital to die. They may have kwashiorkor with the skin wrinkling and falling off. They may not be able to walk. In three months, you wouldn't believe the difference. One spoonful of the product, which is now on the market, in a bowl of boiled water is richer and cheaper than the old mixture of maize flour and milk.'

Another big possibility lies in the exploitation of opaque maize as animal food, and especially as pig food. CIAT's rationale for its emphasis on a swine-feeding programme is that a pig will eat virtually anything that man rejects. You can have a pig tied up under every house. Also they argue that pigs adapt readily to the tropics. As Eduardo Alvarez again explained: 'We are going to establish trials to see how we can best utilize Opaque 2 in feeding pigs. There is only one period of fifty days in the pig's life cycle of 250 days where Opaque 2 does not provide a full and adequate diet. Opaque 2 has a higher quality protein, so the overall biology of the pig is better because his vital needs are looked after by high-lysine maize.'

*

It is estimated that 100,000 cattle die each year in Mexico from paralytic rabies. Some 25 million head of cattle, or 60% of the cattle population of Mexico, are thought to be at risk. Though the accuracy of these calculations is open to question, there is no doubt that the disease takes a heavy toll, both in Mexico and in other countries in Latin America, as far south as the north of Argentina. The disease does not extend beyond tropical Latin America. It is not to be found on other continents.

In Mexico, as elsewhere, the disease is transmitted by vampire bats who live in thousands in caves. Most of the communities, though not all, are infected by rabies. The bats spread the disease among themselves by biting each other. Even if it was possible to find some means of providing immunity to the cattle population, the source of the infection would remain. For here, in the often remote and inaccessible caves, is a constant reservoir of disease.

The rabies virus is excreted in the bat's saliva. When the bats bite the cattle, they transmit the infection. It is fascinating to watch a bat's strategy as it attacks an animal. It approaches so quietly as to be unnoticed. Its teeth are so sharp that the cutting operation is, it seems, entirely painless. The bat sucks the blood from the animal, scooping it up with its tongue. It can remain in position for as long as half an hour. When the bat is full, it will retire to its cave or its tree. The wound on the animal will go on bleeding for one or two hours, or even more in the case of a young beast. The swelling may be as large as 30 or 35 cubic centimetres. The loss of blood, where the bites are numerous, can cause death. Often the bat will return night after night to the same wound. There is also a loss of milk.

This is a centuries-old problem. There are reports as early as the fifteenth century of rabies being transmitted by bats. Since the beginning of the 1950's, vaccines have been tried with only limited success. Around 1965, Mexico asked the UNDP and FAO for help.

UNDP/FAO determined first to find out the overall situation. In 1966, it sent out a mission which travelled through Argentina, Brazil, Venezuela, Trinidad, Mexico—amongst other countries —trying to assess the impact of the disease and the best place to locate a project. Finally, they settled on Mexico and, more specifically, on the National Institute of Livestock Investigations at Palo Alto, outside Mexico City. The Plan of Operations, the document which solemnizes all UNDP contracts, was signed in July 1968. After normal delays in the arrival of personnel and equipment, the project got under way.

The operation, which was still in progress at the time of my visit to Mexico, consists of three sections who work closely together. The first section studies the ecology of the vampire bat; the second studies the epizootiology, i.e. the outbreaks of the disease among animals; the third is concerned with biology and the development of controls.

The ecologists and the epizootiologists work closely together. They go on field trips together. They have night-vision equipment on loan from the U.S. Army and are able to observe the bat at night while it is drinking the blood. The problem is the bat can hide in any convenient place, hollow trees, caves— anywhere. To explore all the caves is virtually impossible, so it is very difficult to arrive at a reliable estimate of the bat population. The scientist can keep a check on the number of the attacks on cattle. This may give him some indication of the bat population.

The ecologists work with nets. They catch the bats, band them and release them. When a bat is caught for the third time, it is killed and brought back to the city (much of the field work takes place many miles from Mexico City) for study.

The epizootiological section is most concerned with the transmission of the disease. How and why is the disease spread among the animals? It is reported that even healthy animals can secrete the rabies virus. Conversely, not all bats are vampires though they may be mistaken as such. Some may be harmless insectivores, eating grubs and spreading pollen and performing other fruitful works of nature. It seems certain that the rabies virus is secreted in the salivary glands. It goes with the saliva into the wound. The 'street' virus, as it has been known since Pasteur's time, is usually transmitted by biting. But the UNDP/ FAO people want to know if there are other possibilities. Perhaps transmission through biting is not the only way. Perhaps the virus is also in the urine of the bat which flies above the cattle and, as it were, bombs them with rabies. There is indeed some evidence that there can be an 'aerosol' transmission of rabies. Animals can be sequestered in a cage which the bats are unable to penetrate, but still they may be infected. In Mexico, there have been occurrences of local people going into the caves to collect the guano of the bats for fertilizer and dying of rabies without being bitten. There could also be milk-borne transmission. A healthy bat, with no visible sign of rabies, could carry it in its milk and pass it to its offspring.

This hypothesis at least would explain the 'healthy carrier' phenomenon.

The task of the biology section is to develop better vaccines. The team has discovered that the potency of some of the vaccines currently in use in Mexico is zero. They give no protection. So they are moving away from the old crude methods of using chicken embryos or sheep brains to grow the virus, towards *in-vitro* multiplication. In the past, the problem with *in-vitro* multiplication was to reach high enough titres, or concentrations, but they have overcome this difficulty. The team went out into the field, visiting places where there had been outbreaks of the disease. They brought some bats back to the laboratory and found that 3% to 6% of them were infected by rabies. They selected a bat which had high titres in its salivary glands and grew the virus on tissue culture cells from the kidney of a baby hamster. Nourished by an appropriate medium and incubated in a CO_2 incubator with carbon-dioxide at 5% and air at 95%, the virus penetrates the cell—assuming the cell is susceptible—and multiplies in the cytoplasm. With five million cells per petridish and 100 to 200 particles per cell, it is now possible to reach a titre of 10^9 per millilitre.

It is hard to exaggerate the significance of this research. In the past, inoculation of the cattle has been a cumbersome and expensive method of protection. It has also been dangerous. When an injection consists of a massive dose of foreign protein in the form of sheep brain or chicken embryos, cattle—like human beings—can develop anaphylactic shock and die. Though mass production is still some way away, there exists today the possibility of producing from one laboratory enough vaccine in a single month to inoculate 15 million cattle. For the biologists at Palo Alto have found that they can dilute the titre 1000-fold and still have a very good antigen response. One millilitre diluted a thousand times, produces one litre and that in turn can produce 200 doses of five millilitres each. This is a perfectly manageable quantity. What is more, it is cheap. The likelihood is that the bottle will be more expensive than the vaccine.

The development of a vaccine will not, of course, solve the rabies problem by itself. The logistic and veterinary require-

ments of undertaking massive inoculation campaigns will be
formidable. Nor is it known how long immunity will last. But it
is certainly a huge step in the right direction. The alternative of
blowing up half of Mexico in order to destroy the habitat of the
bat, even if it could be achieved, seems somehow a clumsier and
less efficient method of proceeding.

2

September 20th. Driving down to El Triunfo. The name had a deceptive ring of magnificence to it and I was for a while under the impression that El Triunfo was the principal port of El Salvador, being to that country what, say, Marseilles is to France or the Piraeus to Greece. The scale would be different, of course. El Salvador is the smallest country in Latin America, its approximate area being 7,720 square miles. If you drive for two hours at a stretch you will almost certainly end up by not being in El Salvador at all but in one of its Central American neighbours, like Honduras. But still, however small the country was, however small the port, I thought it should be worth seeing.

It was a mistaken impression. El Triunfo is a port only to the extent that it does indeed lie on the sea. A rough and muddy track about six miles long links it with the main Central American highway. There is a fishing industry of sorts, a pier and a jetty. Apart from this, the most distinctive landmarks are the heaps of rotting shrimp heads, which rise out of the shallow festering waters of the various bays and inlets and infect the whole place with a strong and remarkable odour.

In this unlikely spot, anchored about a quarter of a mile from the jetty, the UNDP/FAO exploratory fishing vessel, *Sagittario*, slops at anchor. Pelicans—or at any rate birds which resemble pelicans—are fishing around the boat. They circle it, flapping slowly a few feet above the water, then plunge suddenly to rise with a short silver fish in their beak. In the distance, dominating the horizon, the volcano of San Miguel belches smoke into the air. There is a hint of red around the rim. I am told, though it is impossible to see any cultivation from this distance, that people farm the slopes far up towards the summit of the mountain. If, for a few years, the volcano fails to erupt, they forget about it altogether. Even if the volcano does finally show its fury at the encroaching settlements, causing—as has

B *

27

happened in the past more than once—widespread death and
destruction, the effect is felt only momentarily. The survivors,
chastened, may move away from the mountain, but in a year or
two they return to resume their old style of life. For the slopes of
the mountain are fertile, like most volcanic soil and, for these
people, the future is always at a high discount.

I was lucky to find the *Sagittario* in El Triunfo. Within the
next few days the boat was due to sail for Burundi, in the middle
of Africa. It would pass through the Panama Canal, then up the
Mexican coast to one of the Gulf ports in the southern United
States. Provision had already been made for the *Sagittario* to be
loaded upon a larger vessel before making the long journey
across the Atlantic.

The fact that the point of final destination, Burundi, was
totally land-locked and would therefore, on the face of it, have
little need for an exploratory sea-fishing vessel, did not seem to
bother the captain of the *Sagittario* unduly. The United Nations
and its agencies, he had learned from long experience, moved in
mysterious ways. Besides, he himself would be leaving the boat
when it reached Houston. He half suspected that the Burundi
story was a ploy by the United Nations and the FAO to make
sure they could get their boat away from El Salvador before the
Salvadoreans claimed it.

Not that there were any really fundamental objections to
leaving the boat in El Salvador, as long as the Salvadoreans
would make good use of it. The UNDP and FAO often did this
in the case of other project equipment. But the trouble with that
idea was that the Central American Fisheries Project covered
six countries in Central America altogether. Besides El Salvador,
there were Costa Rica, Guatemala, Honduras, Nicaragua and
Panama. The project on the other hand only had four boats and
these differed considerably from each other. You couldn't give a
200,000 dollar ship to Honduras and a 60,000 dollar ship to El
Salvador and leave two countries out altogether. That way,
sure as turtles' eggs (the size and consistency of squash balls,
turtles' eggs are a traditional Central American delicacy), you
would have another war on your hands in the Isthmus. So they
were getting the *Sagittario* out while the going was good.
Burundi, maybe, was just a name to put on the sailing papers.

It is a lazy afternoon. The pelicans, flapping after the fish, are easily the most energetic creatures in sight. Certainly, there is little sign of activity on board the *Sagittario* itself. The crew are nowhere to be seen. Either they are sleeping below-decks until the heat of the afternoon has passed its peak or they are off somewhere in El Triunfo exploring whatever meagre attractions the place has to offer.

Inside the cabin, three men are talking. The rhythm of their conversation matches the rhythm of the afternoon. It could not be described as hurried or excited conversation, nor one animated by any special sense of urgency. There are long pauses while glasses of lukewarm beer are drunk or refilled; other pauses where the occupants of the cabin stare out to sea or towards the tree-line of the shore where the brown margin (for there is a ten-foot tide in the bay) is already clearly visible. Besides myself (an observer more than a participant), there is Bruno Rosetti, an Italian who is the Captain of the *Sagittario*, and a large, burly American who is, like Rosetti, an employee of FAO and whose formal title is Fleet Supervisor. His name is Bob Carpenter. He has already been two years in El Salvador and, before that, has spent an extended period in Ecuador working for the Van Kemp Sea-Food Company. Carpenter's life is the sea and all aspects of it. The sea is what he mostly talks about. He is a fisherman and proud of it.

He feels frankly that there have been some inadequacies in the Central American Fisheries Project. It has been too elaborate, too complex. 'When these people see our boat tied alongside the dock day after day with electronic problems which prevent it from sailing, and we say "this is the kind of boat you should have" and they say no, they know better than we do. They go out every day, weather permitting. We're in dock most of the time. If you have to have the best captain, the best electronic equipment, the best nets before you can catch a fish, then what you are doing is no use to these people.

'We are living in the era of the fat turkey,' Carpenter continues, 'we don't have to skimp and save as far as fish resources go. The biologists waste far too much time by systematic exploration. But fishing is not a systematic thing. It's a matter of knowing how to read the charts, how to read the currents, a matter of hunch and intuition. You don't put your nets down according to some elaborate grid pattern you may have devised. You look for the logical spots. You don't go over all the dead areas. You do what you do in business. Maximize as soon as you can. You use different methods for different fish. Use what suits the culture. The set net culture in Italy goes back hundreds of years. The biologists want us to take bottom temperatures all the time, instead of doing exploratory fishing. They had a boat down on a project in Colombia, a beautiful thing. It cost 400,000 dollars and 350 dollars a day to run. And they just used it as a floating hotel for some Smithsonian biologist. They moved it from place to place so that he could fix his lunch and float a few fish in formaldehyde.

'Biologists argue that a negative result is as good as a positive result. I mean they're just as interested to prove that the fish are not there as to prove that they are. But that won't help these people to eat. We're missing the boat if we can't leave here saying "Here's the resource, here's the gear, here's the boat you need and it's one that can be built within this country's means." Don't try and teach them anything until they have taught you everything. Go out with your canoe and see if you can catch as many fish with one hook as they can. "Back home" is another world. Don't talk about it.'

Bruno Rosetti, the dark and lithe Italian captain of the *Sagittario*, interjects: 'For this project, the big problem is the biologists' bullshit. Once they put a biologist on board us—I think the first time they ever come on the ship. Was a woman. She started folding up the captain's charts, *my* charts, making them all—how do you say?—scrumpled up? She wanted to draw her lines on them. So I took the charts away and put them under my bed. She not know—that one stupid woman—that charts is never folded, not ever. Then she come and she say to me "Captain, put your net down there." So I say: "Look, there are bad rocks." But still she say "Put it down." So I say, "O.K." And the net when he come up, he is all shot to pieces.' Rosetti draws the moral of his little story for us. 'This is too much biologists' programme. I say to them, "You put another biologist on my boat and watch out he not go over the side." I have a tricky shoulder!'

Carpenter sums up the general feeling. 'These fellows', he says, meaning the local fishermen, 'can catch more playing with their Peters by accident than a biologist can on purpose!'

One tale is capped with another, for this is how fishermen spend their time before it is dark enough to put the lights down in the water and the nets around the boat. Carpenter, huge and sunburned, narrowing his eyes—as seamen do—to look into the blue distance and the birds dropping in the wind, tells us:

'We had the Norwegians and the Icelanders down here— the best deep-water fishermen in the world. And they said "Gee, if you can catch as many herring as this in shallow water, there must be millions of them out there at fifty fathoms." So they went out with special nets which they had bought in Norway, but they didn't catch anything. So people began to say, "maybe the fish aren't there." And they were right. This particular species of herring lived within twenty fathoms of the shore. "Back home" didn't apply.

'We don't need expensive nets from Norway. What we need are simple improvements. Build a crow's-nest and use it. You can see fish ten miles at either side. Watch the birds. The birds eat the little fish which the big fish feed on. Get out of the cabin. The windows obscure the view. When I was fishing, I'd see a bird dip its wings and so I'd swing the boat around. Follow the birds out of port. If they're all heading in one direction, that's the way I'd go. The others would say "How come you stay on the fish, Bob?" I'd say: "Well, you know it's just a kind of sixth sense."

'The only good fishermen,' says Carpenter, 'are those who get drunk and go to whore-houses. Fishermen work hard and play hard. You talk to biologists about whore-houses and see what kind of reaction you get! You don't fight the sea for 72 hours, stay out for 30 days under all kinds of conditions, without acquiring a kind of toughness. The language these people speak is a universal language. I started work in oil fields after the war. Within three days, we had killed a driller. Another lost three fingers. These people who work in oil-fields are the roughest toughest men in the world. Fishermen are just the same.'

The UNDP/FAO Project had established some new shrimping grounds. Most of the shrimp caught off the Central American coasts were found under 25 fathoms. But they had discovered shrimp and langostino between 50 and 150 fathoms. The langostino was half way between the spiny lobster and the shrimp. Its best weight rises only to 10 to 14 pounds of live weight, but there could be several thousand pounds of langostino in each trawl. This meant that the local industry had to improve their fishing vessels. They needed faster and stronger winches. If they had to spend half an hour setting their nets and another half-hour taking them up, that was too long. At the moment, they were fishing 12 to 15 miles off shore in shallow water. For deep sea ventures, they would need 400 horse-power engines, instead of 150.

Carpenter says: 'Sometimes you have to push these people into making money. Fishermen are stubborn. I went back to Iceland the other day and they are still fishing the same way as they did twenty years ago. We are not here to push big fish to rich people. We want to push small fish to the poor people. Something within their range. It all has the same amount of protein. I figure they throw away on this coast 240 tons of fish a day. And right up there on the hills,' Carpenter points towards the mountains, 'are people who are starving.'

Small fish to poor people. Jesus, long ago, had the same idea. One day some international civil servant, not afraid of the inegalitarian overtones of the phrase, will elevate it into a 'key plank' in some global nutritional 'strategy'.

Take, for example, the shrimpers off the Pacific coast of Central America. Usually most of the catch in the shrimp nets, if you weigh it, is fish. But the shrimp vessels are not equipped to deal with fish. They have refrigerated tanks for the shrimp, but not enough room to keep the fish in them as well. So they throw away nine or ten days catch of fish and only keep the last two or three days' worth. The word they use for it is 'moralla' or 'trash fish'. It denotes almost any kind of fish that is caught in the small-mesh shrimp nets.

Part of the reason why so much of the fish catch is thrown away is economic. There is no point in having larger refrigerating tanks on board the shrimp boats (assuming this was feasible) unless there exist marketing and distribution channels to dispose of it subsequently, and unless this trash fish can realize a price high enough to make the whole operation worth-while. Another part of the reason is cultural. When people in the market see fish with ice on it, they argue that it must be bad. Nobody puts ice on fish unless it is bad. In any case, frozen fish must be kept frozen until it is eaten. This means that it must be sold in refrigerated form somewhere near the final point of consumption and that it must indeed be eaten soon after it is bought. Even if the poor peasant from the hills can afford to buy the trash-fish when it reaches the market, it will not be much use to him if he has to take it on a three-day march back to his village.

Since canned fish is too expensive for low-income families, the UNDP/FAO project is trying to introduce salted dry fish as a staple diet. The first step was to develop special cheap driers. Drying in the sun is of limited use because the humidity in this part of the world is such that the fish rot before they dry. They have devised a mechanical system for reducing two tons of fish over a 24-hour period to about 28% humidity. Guatemala, which has one of the lowest rates of fish consumption per year (less than a pound a head), was selected as the country where the salted dry fish would first be marketed on a trial basis. At the time of my visit, the fish was being sold in 12 or 15 com-munities. The main questions were, how fast would people accept it (here the FAO people found that the secret was to offer an interesting sauce with the fish) and, related to this, how much publicity could be generated. (From the publicity point of view, the salted dry fish was poor material. In Central America, you can't bring a minister to open a drying plant which is only the size of a small room. Ministers, who tend to own huge estates themselves, lack the imagination to think in *small* terms. They like enormous plants and hundreds of workers.)

Bob Carpenter summed up the situation succinctly. 'In the present market, the big fish make a big profit and the small fish make a small profit.' If you could persuade the middle-men to handle the trash fish and sell it, suitably processed, at a price the poor people could afford, you could effect a revolution in the diet of hundreds of thousands of people in Central America. Says Carpenter: 'We have to get aboard those boats and tell the captains not to throw away the small fish. Maybe he has to turn over one of his shrimp tanks so he can handle it. If he handles enough of it, he can make a profit. He can make a profit at two cents a pound. There's no other form of protein so cheap in the world.'

*

On June 26, 1969, El Salvador broke off diplomatic relations with Honduras. Honduras followed suit. A few days later fighting had broken out between the two countries. It was known in the international press as the 'football war', because the immediate cause of the break between the two countries had been rioting over the results of two football matches played between El Salvador and Honduras. Honduras had won the first match on home grounds, but charged foul play when El Salvador won the second match in San Salvador on June 22. At the match itself, some violence was supposed to have been done to a Honduran girl spectator. Subsequently the crowd bombed the Grand Hotel in downtown Salvador, where the Honduran team was staying, with eggs and fruit.

On July 14, regular formations of Salvadorean troops moved into Honduras. Scattered air-raids took place, with both sides using antiquated fighter-planes of World War II vintage, or even private light aircraft. The Salvador oil refinery was bombed and there were rumours of paratroops landing. Military casualties on both sides were small—neither country had total armed forces of more than 6,000 men—but the affair was none-the-less bloody and proved highly disruptive of trade and good relationships in Central America. At the time of my visit there was still no telephone communication between El Salvador and Tegucigalpa. If you wanted to fly, you had to go via Guatemala or Nicaragua. Airmail from one place to the other took three or four weeks and cables three or four days.

If the 'football war' was the immediate cause of the war between Honduras and El Salvador, there were other more fundamental reasons. The population density in El Salvador is the highest on the American mainland. Throughout the hemisphere, it is exceeded only by the island states of Jamaica, Haiti and Puerto Rico. At the present rate of increase the number of inhabitants, which already approaches three and a half million

people, will double in under 25 years. These demographic
pressures, seen in the context of El Salvador's acute social and
economic problems (a third of the rural population lives at
subsistence level and perhaps as many as 90% of the peasants
are landless), have caused over the years a steady stream of
emigration. Predominantly, the emigrants have settled in neighbouring Honduras which, with six times the area, has only half
the population of El Salvador. Around 300,000 Salvadoreans
altogether had settled in Honduras at the time the war broke
out. Many of them, no doubt, were not even aware that they
were in a different country. The border is not marked. Few
people would be able to tell, short of a cadastral survey, where
the Salvadorean jungle ends and the Honduran jungle
begins.

In the period leading up to the outbreak of war, Honduras
embarked on a programme of agrarian reform and 'discovered'
that the Salvadoreans who had settled on their territory did not
have title to the land. There is some suggestion that an offer by a
US lumber company for the rights to exploit this particular
piece of jungle may have had something to do with this 'discovery'. At all events, the settlers were encouraged to return
home, a process which involved some violence, arson and the
occasional massacre. At one point some eight or ten thousand
Salvadoreans a day were being driven back into El Salvador,
causing immense problems to an already beleaguered economy.
The despatch of troops by Salvador into the border areas was
not so much to settle a football score as to staunch at its source a
flow of refugees which (had it been allowed to swell to the full
300,000) would certainly have overwhelmed the country.

One of the by-products of the 'football war' was intensified
pressure on the Salvador government to accelerate its programmes of land reform. To those who follow Latin American
affairs, this plea for 'more and faster land reform' is a familiar
one. Land reform slogans are espoused with an almost evangeli-
cal fervour as though, this problem resolved, all others would
pale into insignificance. There is more than an element of truth
in the claim. Take Salvador. Here 5% of the population owns
as much as 60% of the land—in holdings of over 20 hectares.
Thirty per cent of the land is held in little or medium farms,

between two and twenty hectares. The vast bulk of the population is crammed on to the remaining 10% of the land, working on what are classified as 'very small' farms of under two hectares.

Sixty per cent of all workers in Salvador work in agriculture. At best, they are employed for, say, 100 days a year. If a man works 100 days a year at a wage of two and a half colones a day, he will receive approximately 100 dollars a year. If he has a wife and three children to support, and no other sources of income, *per capita* income in that family will amount to 20 dollars per head per year. It is hard to overstate the grinding poverty in which these people can live, hard to deny the powerful logic behind land-reform programmes. Split up the latifundia (the big estates), consolidate the minifundia (the small bits and pieces of land), provide credit and marketing facilities, promote production and sales co-operatives so that economies of scale can be achieved even on small units. These are the typical planks of a land-reform strategy, whether it is published in Salvador, or Colombia or elsewhere on the South American continent. That there are political as well as economic objectives behind this strategy goes without saying. Ever since the Roman Senate paid off Sulla's legionaries with grants of land, the distribution of real estate has been an essential ingredient of any political power-play.

In practice, one of the hardest things in the world is to develop and implement a successful land-reform programme. More often than not, the political will itself is lacking. Those who run affairs of state in a country like Salvador are almost invariably members of the privileged and propertied classes. They will espouse a reforming platform if it is the only way of buying a further period in office. They will demonstrate their good-will and their proletarian sympathies by one or two dramatic gestures, seizing—for example—some lush estate on the outskirts of the city and doling out an acre or two, with accompanying fanfare, to some landless peasant families. But this is tokenism and little more. Once an election is safely passed, and vested interests secured, the programme will be returned once again to storage.

Even if the political will is there, the technical basis for a viable programme of land-reform often does not exist. The literature is full of statistics which purport to show, arguing especially from Asian experience in countries like Japan, that the highest per acre yields have been achieved on the smallest holdings. From this it follows, so the argument runs, that the way to increase production on a world-wide basis (or at least one of the ways) is to divide and intensify. But these are dangerous generalizations. What was valid for Japan is not necessarily valid for Salvador. There is a difference, clearly, in the relative availabilities of what are known in the jargon as 'the necessary inputs'. Capital may be lacking; credit; marketing arrangements. The institutional infrastructure, so vital for the promotion of the whole 'agricultural package', may not yet have taken shape. Water may be a limiting factor, imposing firm constraints on the intensification of the farming system.

Above all, though, it may be a question of human resources. However noble the goal, however lofty the ambition, the essential economic and political purpose of land-reform may be turned aside through the sheer impossibility of converting, virtually overnight, the peasant into a modern farmer. In its own way, the difference between the one and the other is as great as the difference between the man who is barely numerate and a computer-programmer. To say this is not to belittle land-reform as an object of policy in Latin America. It is merely to inject a note of caution.

Perhaps I can best indicate what I mean by describing a visit I paid, while I was in El Salvador, to the ranch of Roberto Aguilar, not far from the coast. Roberto was about 55 years old, a cattle-breeder and a cotton-grower. He was a Guatemalan by birth, but he had been thrown out of that country in 1920. He went to school in California, came to El Salvador on a vacation visit to Central America, decided he liked the place and stayed. For a while he painted children's portraits for a living, rich people's children. After that he painted the rich people themselves, including the President. When the supply of rich people was exhausted, he acquired a wife and a career.

Together with his father-in-law he cleared 1,000 manzanas of land (there are one and a half manzanas to a hectare.) It was back-breaking work. They would pull out trees with two-

foot thick trunks by hand before they had money enough to buy
a bulldozer. In time, he extended his holding to 3,000 manzanas. He built a house for his headman, then found as cotton
went through one of its periodic down-swings, he had to live
in it himself. But he stayed with cotton. Though he had, as he
put it, lost his hat and half his clothes, cotton was in his blood.

Roberto was a farmer, no doubt about that. He was always
looking for ways to improve his herds or his crops. He could
keep 100 calves on five manzanas, grazing half a manzana a day
so that every ten days they came back to the same place. He used
legumes to fix the nitrogen instead of fertilizer. Besides, Roberto's
cows under his careful system dropped 80% of what they
consumed in the place they found it. He had built a new milking
shed for his cattle and a circular standing-yard where the gate
swung automatically on rails behind the beasts, bumping their
ankles—as it were—and moving them steadily through. The
milk Roberto sold on the market was premium grade. There
were no fish or frogs in it; there wasn't even very much water.
The *E. coli* figures were entirely tolerable.

Yet all the while, so it seemed, Roberto was battling against
the forces of inertia and superstition. He had this beautiful
new standing-yard, but his drovers would run the beasts into the
shed from the wrong side, through rivers of mud, leaving the
yard virgin and spotless. The hosing and spraying equipment
Roberto had had installed stood unused. His men didn't like the
milking machine so they moved the cows to bad ground and
then, when yield had dropped from 2,000 lb. to 400 lb., said the
milking machine was the cause. He had electric fences which
made intelligent pasturing possible, but his men cut the fences
or turned off the current because they believed the cows should
graze all over the lot.

We sit at a rough table inside Roberto's ranch-house, drinking
coconut milk mixed with gin while our horses, tied to a tree
outside, swished their tails against the flies. Roberto tells me he
used to plant his water-melon with fertilizer and insecticides.
But his 'mandador' or foreman didn't approve. He wanted to
plant them in the traditional way. 'Yes,' says Roberto, 'my
own mandador, and he has planted 600 manzanas of cotton for
me! Well, I gave him the land and I let him do it his own way.

He got a very poor result indeed. So I said "That shows you need fertilizer and proper seed and insecticide." And he said: "No, the trouble was I planted them next to the cemetery and a deadly vapour came off it!"'

Another time, says Roberto, he tried to teach his mandador to plant maize six inches apart. 'But I found out he didn't know what six inches was. So I gave him a piece of wood six inches long so he could show the workers. But they just took the pieces of wood and stuck them in their belts and went on planting maize in the same old way. Finally, when I told him off, the mandador said "No, señor, this is not how to plant maize. This is the way to plant maize." And he scattered it in the old way. But in fact the new hybrids require different planting techniques.'

'Still another time,' says Roberto, 'I came by the mandador's water-melon patch and saw different-coloured flags all over the place. Gee,' says Roberto, lapsing into his Californian grammar, 'I think this guy has got me all beat. I think the different flags mean different seeds and different dates of planting. But then he tells me the flags are to ward off the spirits.'

Roberto shakes his head. 'Let me tell you something else. Near the ranch there is an estuary and this has an outlet which is opened up in the rainy season otherwise the floods can damage the corn patch. The mandador came to me and said: "Won't you lend me your tractor, Don Roberto, so that I can work on the canal?" Off he went and a few hours later I see him come back leading a band of men all armed with sticks. "What's wrong?" I asked. "Are you fighting someone?" And they answer: "We're looking for the pregnant woman who keeps on passing and filling up the canal with sand while we work. We're going to get hold of her and we're going to beat her up." Well, the third time they went back to work, no pregnant woman came past and, as it happened, they managed to get the canal dug. But it was an accident. They think a pregnant woman has got powers in her stomach. They won't let one near a water-melon patch, for example. They are afraid the melons will puncture.'

We get into a jeep and ride around Roberto's farm. He talks about cotton. 'There was a wind for 24 days one season and we couldn't spray. Then the communists down the valley decided I was one of the big land-owners and I'd have to pick cotton when they decided, not when I wanted to. As a result I picked the cotton off the ground and got the worst classification of all my time in cotton.'

We jump down and walk through some fields which Roberto has let out to a neighbour. Roberto handles the plants. 'It's the cheapest cotton I ever saw. He hasn't sprayed once. He's used natural control and it's been all right because it rained and kept the worms down.'

The sun has set, for it is already six o'clock. The elephant grass bends in the night-wind. I can hear a chorus of frogs over by a hedge and, from a long way off, the sound of shouting and the thud of foot against leather. People, probably the children of Roberto's workers, are playing football. He is father and friend to fifty families, a better and kinder boss—probably—than the government could ever be. Yet those who now play football on his land, in their hearts aspire to take it over altogether.

'The peasants have got their little plots staked out,' says Roberto Aguilar. 'Something is in the wind. You can tell for sure because all the big boys have put away their Mercedes and have taken to driving their battered old 1960 models. Do you know Cardinal Cushing gave money to a guy who went on to raise 350,000 colones and so was able to start a radio station. Every morning the station began by saying, "Wake up, country people. Pick up your machetes and go after the rich landowner." In time the message gets through—the war with Honduras has made it all seem more urgent. But you know,' says Roberto, and there is sadness in his voice for, after all, this is the farm which he made with his own bare hands and the sweat of his brow: 'what could you do without the rich? The Indians will get only 15 quintals of maize instead of the 80 or 100 I am getting. They will get three bottles of milk per cow, while I can get nine. Look at Argentina after Peron. It used to be the biggest producer of cattle in the world. But they divided up the land. People sold their cattle and went to the cities. Now, even in Argentina, they have meatless days.'

Roberto Aguilar summarizes his position for me. 'Get rid of the rich and you lose any standard to bring the Indians up to.'

Frankly, I don't know enough to contradict him.

*

Most of the coffee-growing areas in the world lie between 20 and 23 degrees either north or south of the equator. El Salvador lies at 14 degrees north, where the sun is so strong that it is impossible to grow coffee without shade. Unshaded, the coffee bean in these latitudes produces a blend that is tart and unpleasant.

The coffee trees are planted in the shade of other taller trees. This has been so ever since the turn of the century when coffee was first introduced to the country from Hawaii. Wherever you see trees at over 500 metres, there will be coffee planted beneath them. Below 500 metres pest damage is found and the coffee is of a lower quality which deters production.

There are 160,000 manzanas under coffee in El Salvador. Eighty per cent of this area is owned by 5% of the growers. These large 'fincas', as they are known, are organized impressive affairs, producing as much as 70 to 80 quintals per manzana. The trees yield from the age of about five years to about 20. Systematic programmes of weeding and replacement are carried out. A scientific approach is taken to methods of pruning the shading tree (which itself may be some productive citrus) so that it gives exactly the right amount of light.

The remaining 20% of the coffee-growing area is owned by 95% of the growers. Probably half of that 20%, or 10% of the total coffee area, is marginal. The yield may be as low as five or seven quintals per manzana. A few bushes on a hillside, growing almost at random, never fertilized and seldom pruned, may have to provide the basic sustenance for a family of seven or ten. So the cry goes up 'diversify away from coffee. Get the marginal farmer out of coffee.'

But it is easier said than done, as UNDP/FAO experts who are working in El Salvador on precisely this problem, have discovered to their cost. To diversify away from coffee means you must diversify into something else. There's the rub. Land suitable for one thing may not be suitable for another. Coffee is not interchangeable with maize. In any case, to plant more maize on these steep hill-sides is merely to aggravate the already serious problems of erosion. Nor, even if it was agronomically desirable, would it be easy to achieve. The likelihood is that if the peasant is marginal in coffee which he has been growing since the turn of the century, he will be even more marginal in a crop he doesn't know, a crop which requires unfamiliar techniques of cultivation and, worse still, a much greater degree of effort and attention than that demanded by the casual bean.

The coffee mountains of El Salvador will not quickly change their spots. The world price of coffee will have to fall a good deal lower yet before those steep slopes are returned to nature or turned over to some other use.

One such 'coffee mountain' rises up sheer behind the town of San Salvador itself. One Sunday afternoon, when nothing much else was happening, I decided to climb up it towards the famous volcanic crater which lies at the very top of the mountain. Until 1917, a lake had occupied the crater. Then one afternoon the water in the lake began to bubble; it boiled; it steamed and finally disappeared a few moments before the volcano erupted. Fortunately, the lava poured down the mountain on the side away from the city. Its track, half a mile wide, can still be seen today. The mountain side has been left bare of vegetation where the lava flowed. It is as though a strip of skin has been pulled from an orange. The sheer momentum of its fall has pushed the rock out for several miles into the plain, though the floor of the valley has by then flattened out completely. Finally, with a few last contortions, the track peters out and the land resumes a more normal aspect.

In fact, I never reached the crater. I found I did not have the time or the stamina. I was constantly being overtaken on the narrow path by ancient Indian women who—though hugely burdened with vegetables, furniture and even livestock—leaped up the mountain-side ahead of me as though the juices of youth itself flowed in the instep.

I, who have nothing to carry except a Minolta camera which I use (or pretend to use) whenever I need to catch my breath, am amazed and chagrined. I watch them dwindling into the distance as the path winds high above them. I see them disappear, like Elijah himself, into the swirling mists which surround the summit of the mountain. It grows darker and the city below grows faint. There is a moment when the path forks. One way leads on up the hillside, the other heads back down into the valley. I choose the latter, aim—as I think—unerringly for the city. But somehow my sense of direction lets me down. I become entwined in the foothills of the mountain, and snared among the shacks of the poor which thrust upwards through the overgrowth looking for light and air. Dogs run out at me and bark and one, more incensed than the rest, bites me in the ankle. It was a retribution I had deserved for being faint-hearted.

3

BOGOTA, CAPITAL of Colombia, lies on the eastern margin of a large, high (8,560 feet) plateau which is bounded on all sides by peaks. The city, in fact, is situated not on the floor of the plateau itself but on a sloping plain at the base of two mountains, Guadalupe and Monserrate. On the summit of one of these mountains stands a large and imposing church. At weekends and at holidays, access can be made by cable car or teleferique. At other times, the funicular has to serve.

The little red cars of the funicular start from each end of the mountain every half-hour and they cross at a passing-place in the tracks exactly half-way up (or down) the slope. A few feet above the passing-place the rail track enters a tunnel hewn from the rock. The visitor, ascending, finds his vision of the city and the plain below him suddenly obscured. When the car finally emerges from the tunnel, at the upper station and only a few yards from the peak itself, the scene is revealed in an entirely different aspect. Bogota now appears to lie at a great distance below.

This impression of distance is partly due to the haze of smoke in which the city is enveloped. Atmospheric pollution of one sort or another has in recent years become a characteristic of the major urban conglomerations of the Third World and Bogota is no exception. As he stands leaning on the low wall which bounds the small flat area in front of the church, the tourist may have some difficulty in recognizing familiar landmarks. There, slightly to the right, is the great 800-room bulk of the Tequendama Hotel, where he is probably staying. A little nearer to the foot of the mountain, the Bogota Hilton—still to be completed—rises sheer into the air (surely an easy prey for earthquakes). Roughly in the centre of the plain or the savannah, the airport may be seen as well as the straight wide road which connects it to the city of Bogota.

The tourist who has been up to this vantage point on more

than one occasion over the years (as I have) will note how each time the airport seems to have moved a little nearer to the town. The 'green belt' is thinner and great chunks of it no longer exist at all.

Of course, this is an optical illusion. The airport has not moved nearer the town; the town has moved nearer the airport. The same story, of human habitations filling up the interstices of empty space, is repeated to the South, West and North almost as far as the eye can see. The city is spreading out like a stain across the plain; it is climbing up the nearby mountains. The savannah is being engulfed in a tide of humanity and no-one yet can predict an end to it. In 1938 only 23% of the population of Colombia lived in urban centres of more than 100,000 inhabitants. In 1964 the proportion was 51% and by the time Colombia comes to undertake her next census (it is planned for 1972) the proportion will almost certainly be higher. For the population of the urban centres is growing at almost 6% per year, while that of the countryside grows at about 1·3% per year. Since the overall growth-rate of Colombia's population is 3·5% per year, the figures tell a tale of massive migration from the country to the town.

Why do they come? What Pied Piper entices them forth from the farm? How is it that the prospect of life in the *barrio*, in the *favela*, can draw them across the mountains, leaving behind land and homes and relatives? There are of course any number of complicated sociological answers to these questions. Questionnaires can be devised and, once devised, can be promulgated among the populace. Responses can be tabulated and conclusions drawn. But for this purpose the short and simple explanation must suffice. They come to the slums of Bogota, these migrants from the rural areas, not because—like Dick Whittington—they believe that the streets of the city are lined with gold. They are not naïve or stupid. There is some evidence that it is precisely the cleverest farmers, the most aggressive peasants, who seek their fortune elsewhere. They know that there are problems in the cities too; they have heard through the informal network of communication which always exists in countries like Colombia (and is probably more efficient than any radio station) that they will be short of housing and jobs, even of food and light and air. But they also know that they could not possibly be worse off than they are at the moment.

As Dr Ramiro Cardona put it to me (he is in charge of urbanization studies in the National Planning Department): 'Urbanization will finish when the conditions in the countryside are as good as the conditions in the city. Here in the city they have better health, better water supply, better education for their children, job possibilities. Politically, they are a force to be reckoned with. The government has to take care of them. That is why they come.'

★

If there is one single agency in Colombia whose job it is to improve conditions in the countryside (and, amongst other things, to stem this haemorrhage of the population from farm to urban slum), it is INCORA, the Colombian Institute for Agrarian Reform. INCORA, which was established by law in 1961, has two problems to deal with. The first is land without people. The second is people without land.

Sixty-four per cent of the population lives on 5% of the land and 2% of the population owns 30% of the land. There are ten million farms and 40% to 60% of these are farmed in the traditional way with primitive technology and at a level of subsistence which is barely marginal.

The Agrarian Reform Law of 1961 set out in its first article the premises on which agrarian reform was to be based. On the one hand there was too great a concentration of large estates in a few hands—latifundia. On the other hand there was too great fragmentation of land in minifundia. The primary object-ive was, therefore, to restructure private property in such a way as to eliminate and prevent *both* the excessive concentration of land in too few hands *and* its uneconomic fragmentation. Many of the farmers in the traditional sector were wage-earners or tenants, not owners. The idea was either to give the land to the poor peasants who would work it themselves or to find ways of protecting the rights of the small tenants and share-croppers and to secure their access.

Looked at as a whole, Colombia does not seem to be a densely populated country. It has around 19 inhabitants per square

kilometre compared with 164 for El Salvador. There are many
who talk of the huge potential of those vast tracts of land which
lie beyond the Eastern Cordillera. Open up the 'selva', they
say; cultivate 'los llanos' and there would be no more problems
of land pressure in Colombia. It is an attractive idea, one which
appeals to rugged pioneering minds. Certainly, there is a good
deal of political pressure for INCORA to concentrate its efforts
on colonization schemes in the far interior, out of sight and out
of mind.

The trouble is, colonization is much more expensive than
'parcellization', which is the word they use for the process of
sub-division of lands which are already farmed. To colonize,
you need communications, schools, health services, administration—in fact a whole infrastructure which, in the case of the
well populated areas, already exists. The land must be cleared.
Once cleared, the soil proves to be of low quality and subject to
recurrent flooding in which the houses and fences and property
of the settlers can be swept completely away.

Land reclamation schemes in the populated areas are also
complex and slow. But the process is less costly. The lands are
better; they are closer to centres of production and export; most
of the infrastructure is already there. What really attracts
INCORA though, at least in terms of getting value for money,
is land reform along the classical lines: splitting up the big
farms and sharing them out between the tenants and share-
croppers, the peasant farmers and the landless labourers.

At first INCORA directed its attention to lands which were
badly farmed. The law permitted the Institute to expropriate
land which had remained uncultivated for ten years continu-
ously. In this case, the land reverted to the state and the pro-
prietors had no right to compensation. It was also possible for
INCORA, by simple legal process, to take over lands which
were defined as 'inadequately exploited'. In this case, the
proprietor had the right to retain 100 hectares for himself. The
real political dynamite resided, however, in the proposition (still
being hotly debated at the time of my visit) that INCORA—so
far from placing the emphasis on uncultivated lands or on
lands which were badly farmed—should in fact concentrate on
the well-managed estates. How unfair, so the argument ran, to

locate the poor so-called 'beneficiary' of land reform on lousy land where he has to work as hard as ever for a living. Why not put him on the good land?

INCORA was well aware that there were technical as well as political hazards in this approach. If agricultural production was not to drop swiftly and disastrously, the agricultural extension service would have to do a competent job. The provision of credit and technical assistance, the supply of tools and fertilizer and water, the organization of marketing and communications—all this would need to be done if the standard of living of the peasant was to be raised and production sustained at an economic level. But the goals, the objectives were large. INCORA believed that the types of reform they were pursuing could make a radical change in the political and social structures—and this without violent revolution. INCORA believed that, by solving the problems of the countryside, it might be possible to solve the problems of the city. If the *campesinos* produced more, their income would be higher and they would consume more. This in turn would lead to more jobs, both in rural industries and in the urban industrial sector itself.

Politically, INCORA has to walk a tightrope. If it concentrates its resources and its energies on schemes of colonization and development, it lays itself open to attacks by the left for not being 'radical' enough. If it promotes land reform, especially land reform in the good well-farmed lands as a priority, it lays itself open to attacks from the right for being 'too radical'. It is only if they are being attacked by both left and right together, that the INCORA officials feel reasonably happy. It means they are following the middle way with some success.

Towards the end of my time in Colombia, I flew up to the north of the country, to visit the Magdalena region. I was met at Barranquila airport by Rafael Pacheko, a wiry dark-haired Brazilian who was in charge of UNDP/FAO's diversification project in the banana zone.

We drive at sunset through the Isle of Salamanca, a Colombian National Park, which lies to the east of Baranquilla on the way to Santa Marta. We have crossed the Magdalena river on one of the ferry-boats and are heading for a small town in the jungle, called El Prado. It is a town which owes its entire existence to the one-time presence of the United Fruit Company. But United Fruit, so Pacheco says, left El Prado when the banana market collapsed in 1965 and disease hit the crop; and the government wanted them out of the country anyway. FAO had been called in, with the UNDP's financial assistance, to help INCORA pick up the pieces and put the place back on its feet again.

To understand what INCORA and UNDP/FAO and Pacheco are trying to do, one must also understand the historical background. There are today five rivers in the banana zone and five separate irrigation districts. The area with infrastructure, i.e. irrigation and roads, is about 40,000 hectares, but the actual area under cultivation is about 22,000. The rainfall varies from about 700 millimetres a year in the north of the zone to about 2,500 millimetres a year in the south. The soils, basically alluvial, are very variable.

The first crop was planted in hilly jungle at the end of the last century. This was cocoa. After that the French, always enterprising, came in with bananas. They started in the north where there was less rainfall and where the lighter soils were more hospitable. United Fruit arrived during the first years of this century. At that time, there were three nationalities in the area—French and Americans and Swedes. By all accounts, it was a rough tough life. Gabriel Marques, author of *One Hundred Years of Solitude*—a novel which is based on his experiences of life in the Macondo area, a town only a few miles from El Prado—describes the General Strike of 1911. The *campesinos* took over the trains (every farm had its own railroad connection to the main south-north line which was used for getting the produce out of the zone to the ships.) They proclaimed that they were going to Santa Marta to 'kill the Yankees'. But the army stopped the train in Sienaga and killed between 500 and 800 *campesinos*.

When the First World War came, the Americans abandoned their farms. They, and their banana boats, were needed by the Army and Navy. After the war, they returned to find their lands had been occupied by the local people. They had to buy back the 'mejoras', the improvements which had been made or any crops which were already planted.

In the post-First World War period, the Company expanded and moved south to the Sevilla district, setting up its headquarters at El Prado, a town which it virtually created out of the jungle. The irrigation system expanded along with the banana area. One company's activities shaped the landscape. Houses, roads, railways, canals—everything you can still see today in the Sevilla region was once the property of United Fruit.

In 1939, at the outbreak of the Second World War, United Fruit pulled out of Colombia for the second time. After the war, when the company failed to return immediately, the local banana growers organized themselves and started exporting. This was especially true of the Sienaga area. When the Company did at last return, around 1948, they found that the farmers in the Sienaga area had no wish to abandon their farms nor to sell them to the Company. The Company put a brave face on it. It had no option except to extend its operations still further south in the zone, into the cattle country south of Sevilla where it owned land.

It was not an entirely satisfactory move. The soils were on the heavy side. It was a hurricane area, with high rainfall as well as high winds. The Company saw it as a holding operation. They moved south of Sevilla because they couldn't redeem their lands further north, yet at the same time they still wanted to grow bananas in Colombia. For Colombia had become a key element in the Company's forward planning. The 20,000 hectares they had at Sevilla, together with a further 16,000 hectares they leased on the Pacific coast in the Choco province, enabled them to retain their share in the banana market while their lands in central America, especially in Panama and Costa Rica, were recovering from the effects of an outbreak of Panama disease which had wiped out 40% to 50% of production.

Technological developments were also a critical factor in the decision. In 1950 the French came up with a new variety of banana, resistant to wind and resistant to Panama disease. Though taste and quality were initially inferior to that of Gros Michel, the traditional variety, the yield was four times as great. United Fruit, under conditions of great secrecy, started studying the possibility of switching its production into the new

variety, which was known as Cavendish. They undertook a
feasibility study designed to provide information about how to
grow Cavendish on a massive scale and how to handle it. One
feature of the new variety was that it bruised easily. This meant
that they had to modify their transportation systems and their
marketing arrangements to eliminate wherever possible any
rough treatment. Above all, they had to change the taste of the
housewife through intensive advertising. She was used to bananas which looked and tasted like the old Gros Michel variety.
The company had to persuade her that Cavendish, whatever it
looked like and whatever it tasted like, was the new word for
bananas.

Satisfied with the results of the feasibility study, the Company
went ahead with the colossal change-over to Cavendish. They
invested some 400 to 500 million US dollars in the process. But
none of this money was spent in Colombia. Colombia went on
growing Gros Michel. This was, as it were, a rearguard action,
a time-gaining manœuvre undertaken in order to permit the
main forces to escape and regroup. That the rearguard itself
would be sacrificed, or callously left to its fate, was not significant
in the view of the generals.

When the Company first made its decision to move south of
Sevilla and to start planting Gros Michel there so as to safeguard
its markets vis-à-vis its principal competitor, Standard Fruit, it
found that the lands it owned were already occupied—as
untended lands in this part of the world so often are—by small
farmers, *campesinos*. The Company, sensitive to the changed
political environment, refused to adopt the classical tactics of
arson, violence and harassment which are used by the rich the
whole world over to get rid of the unwanted poor. Instead, the
Company hit on a formula designed to protect its own innocence.

In the cities of the coast, like Baranquilla and Santa Marta,
there was a burgeoning middle class—doctors, dentists and other
professional men. These gentlemen knew nothing about farming
but they were quite capable, at the Company's behest, of hiring
the necessary thugs, and coming down to dispossess the *campesinos*. The Company then agreed to pay these gentlemen money,
but in return they were to recognize the Company's title to the
land, a strategy which avoided any counter-claims or counter-

C

pressures by the dispossessed *campesinos*. In effect the Company ran the farms and paid the labourers, while the *arrendatarios* (as those who received the Company's bounty were known) did precisely nothing except await the deposit of a monthly cheque in their European bank accounts.

By 1964, the Company was ready with Cavendish and it decided to pull out of Colombia. In doing so, it left a small problem behind. According to the books, the *arrendatarios* as a group owed the Company about 300 million pesos. In April and May each year, especially in the southern part of the area, the farms are knocked about badly by hurricanes. The Company would advance the *arrendatarios* money to finance the rehabilitation. When the Company pulled out and the hurricanes began, the *arrendatarios*—who suddenly found themselves the actual, not just the notional farmers of the land—were at a loss how to proceed. Even if they knew how to rehabilitate the hurricane-stricken farms, they could no longer find the credit. The Company, which had supplied credit so liberally in the past, had gone. So the *arrendatarios* abandoned their farms. There was a complete economic collapse in the banana zone, except in the northern area where there were still some good independent farmers.

It is hard to describe in words the full impact of these events. Here was an area which, under the United Fruit regime, had in a way reached the highest level of technical development possible in agriculture. There were paved roads, railways and electricity supplies all over the zone. Every farmer had a telephone. There were hospitals and health centres accessible to each farm. When the Company left, the schools stopped operating. Nobody wanted to live in the camps. The canals didn't work. The Company left behind the physical assets but it took its knowledge with it. And knowledge was the key ingredient.

Most of the 40,000 people who had previously been employed in the banana area left the area, many of them migrating to Venezuela. Children were left fatherless. Some died of hunger and malnutrition. In 1965, the *arrendatarios* petitioned INCORA. The then Director of INCORA, Dr Enrique Peñalosa, approached United Fruit and offered to buy out the debts which the *arrendatarios* owed the Company. In some cases, he obtained as much as a 95% discount on the debts. Debts of 300 million pesos were reduced to 14 million pesos. Initially, INCORA bought 5,000 hectares of United Fruit land and also the camps which United Fruit had constructed.

The evening I arrived in El Prado, site of the headquarters of United Fruit Company and now headquarters of the INCORA Project (called Magdalena No. 1), Rafael Pacheco and his wife gave a small dinner for me in their house. The tropical rain blasted down out of the black night, splashing into the swimming pool which lies in the middle of the circle of houses. The Company first built it for its staff. Today it is used by INCORA personnel and their FAO advisers (and wives).

One of the guests at the dinner in Pacheco's house was Dr Sergio Duran, Director of the INCORA Project. He was a young good-looking man. One suspected that somewhere he had some large *haciendas* tucked away and that his work in the dismal jungle could be taken as a kind of apology for his wealth.

'We came here,' he said, 'to do agrarian reform and economic and social development. The structure of the area was so centred around one company doing everything, that our biggest problem is to develop the human beings here, so that they have a change of values. To make the land produce, they must learn new skills. They all want to go back into bananas. But we have had a Dutch team here and they have made studies and they have shown that all we need is 5,000 hectares under bananas. Five thousand hectares of Cavendish give you as much as 20,000 hectares of Gros Michel. As long as it is good quality, Colombia might in the end go up to 10,000 hectares of Cavendish, without interfering with the world price. But not more.

'As part of INCORA's development activities, we are financing the change-over into other crops. We're distributing plots of land to each family out of the 5,000 hectares INCORA purchased. When we came, most of the camps were abandoned. The people had all fled to the cities. Some of them are coming back now that they know we're giving out the land. Up till now, 284 families have been settled on 4,852 hectares. Sixty families have been settled on 469 hectares of bananas, 97 families on 1,121 hectares of annual crops, 127 families on 3,262 hectares of livestock. Those are the exact figures. In general, a family doing bananas gets six hectares, a family on permanent crops gets ten hectares, and one doing cattle gets fifteen.'

Sergio Duran said that about a month after they distributed the first parcels of land, the farmers banded together and came and made a big demonstration at the INCORA offices. Duran described it. 'They came and made a petition. They protested "our salary is too low". So I had to explain to them they weren't getting a salary. INCORA was merely paying a subsistence wage to the *parcelleros* until they had their land back in shape and could carry a harvest. So they said, "Well, give us a salary anyway". The trouble is, they still think that they are working for the Company. The Company used to take care of all their problems. INCORA came and moved into the United Fruit offices and the United Fruit houses, and this makes us seem just like the Company.'

Pacheco summarizes the problem. 'These people are *jornaleros*, not *empresarios*.' Day-labourers, not entrepreneurs.

The next day I went round the banana zone with Pacheco and Duran. It was like visiting a ghost town, a place stricken by some nameless disaster so that overnight all the inhabitants fled. The houses United Fruit Company had built for the peasants were decaying and crumbling. The banana trees grew untended. The canals were clogged and the rail tracks overgrown.

The whole area was infested by a weed known locally as 'coquito' and, formally, as *cyperus rotundus*. The Americans deliberately introduced the coquito weed so as to stabilize the canal banks. One of its other properties is that it overwhelms and kills all other weeds. When bananas were the main crop, this didn't matter. Effectively, the coquito cleared the ground beneath the banana trees.

The coquito can be carried on the wheels of cars and tractors; it can be transported by river. Growing over three metres high, it is an aristocrat among weeds. Once introduced, it is almost impossible to remove. If the coquito kills the other weeds, it also kills most of the annual crops that INCORA is now seeking to foster. The bitter legacy of the United Fruit Company lies on the land itself, as well as in the minds of men.

4

September 26. Leo's birthday. (Leo is my youngest child and, for that reason, specially missed on these long absences.) I left Bogota at 6 a.m. in a DC 4. About 40 minutes later, we landed at Villavicencio, south-east of Bogota. All the passengers disembarked and went into the airport building to have 'tamales', a kind of maize pancake with chicken inside. Villavicencio lies at the beginning of that vast stretch of country which extends towards the Brazilian border in the south-east and across to the Venezuelan border in the east. Vast—and empty. For though they cover two-thirds of the area of Colombia, the eastern plains contain less than 2% of the country's population.

10.30 a.m. We have been flying for hours over the forests. The open savannah (*los llanos*) gave way to jungle soon after we left Villavicencio. Seen from the plane the dense rain forest (*selva*) resembles a green desert. The plane flies low and slow, but even with this advantage it is hard to distinguish signs of human habitation. The Indian groups who inhabit the forest do not give much notice of their presence, except for a clearing here and there among the trees and the beginnings of a path which, to aerial view at least, is rapidly obliterated by the thick foliage.

It is hard not to be overwhelmed by the immensity of it all. For the last several hundred miles we have been heading towards the Amazon. I knew from books that this was the greatest river of South America and the largest river in the world in volume and in the area of its drainage basin. I knew that the river rose in the snow-clad Andes in central Peru to flow for almost 4,000 miles across Peru and Brazil before entering the Atlantic on the Equator. But to realize what the statistics mean, one must go and witness the sheer scale of the thing.

We hit the river at Leticia, a small town which lies within Colombia, at more or less the point where the boundaries of Peru, Brazil and Colombia meet. There did not appear to be a single well-defined channel of water. Instead there were several mud-brown bands which threaded their way in and out a network of wooded islands. Some of the trees had fallen, or else been felled, at the water's edge. As they lay there, one gained some idea of their immense height. The clouds lay low on the river and over the sandbars where the water had etched a distinctive herring-bone pattern.

11 a.m. We circle anti-clockwise over the river, then fly in low over the trees to a dirt strip which has been cleared in the jungle. This, or so it seems, is the end of the road for most of my fellow passengers. In fact, Leticia could well be the end of the world. Shooting alligators on the Amazon seems to be the chief activity of the place and even that is pursued in the most desultory manner. The town, or at least what little I can see of it, reminds me of other places I have visited over the years. Other border towns, fly-blown and forgotten.

After an hour or two in Leticia we take off again for Manaus. I stand in the cockpit behind the pilot and watch the jungle roll beneath the wings of the plane. This huge bowl of greenery is one of the great oxygen-producing areas of the world. My layman's understanding of ecological interdependence is that air knows no international frontiers. On a clear day when the traffic has gone to bed and a soft night wind blows, one may taste the breath of the Amazon rain-forest even in places like Oxford Street. It seems so rich and so luxuriant that it is hard to believe this jungle, the ecological climax of the Amazon region, is only one step removed from a desert. But in fact the trees feed mainly on themselves. There is a perfect balance between growth and decomposition. Some still ill-defined relationship between mycorrhizal fungi and tree roots enables the trees to survive on very poor laterite soil. Abuse this resource through random exploitation and nature may wreak a hideous vengeance.

Towards evening, we landed at Manaus. Capital of the State of Amazonas, the city lies some 900 miles above the mouth of the Amazon in the very heart of the Amazonian rain-forest. I threw my bags into my room at Lords Hotel and rushed down to the river's edge before the sun set. The port of Manaus is still the commercial hub of the entire upper Amazon region. During the last century it was little more than a river anchorage. In 1902, when the rubber boom was gathering momentum, the British came and built wharves and warehouses and the floating quays which the rise and fall of the river demanded.

I stand on one of these quays and look upriver into the sun. At my back, men are unloading a cargo ship and their shouts mingle with the noise of the traffic on the river. The water front stretches ahead and, in the background, the twin towers of a church protrude above the line of roofs. The relative humidity here is probably over 80% and a clean shirt clings to my back. The sun dips suddenly into the river and it begins to rain.

A few minutes later, and considerably wetter, I had made my way from the water's edge into town, to the opera house. If I had not already known about the opera house in Manaus, I would—I suppose—have found its existence hard to credit. Operas are for Paris or London or New York. One does not expect to come across them in the middle of the Amazonian rain-forest. Even with fore-knowledge of what to expect, the scene was hard enough to absorb. Though the main doors were closed, a side-door was open and I was able to make my way, pushing aside the heavy curtains, onto the centre of the stage. I looked out onto rows and rows of gilded seats, the symbol of the wealth and luxury that the rubber boom had brought to Manaus. I looked up into the glittering cupola and was able, in my mind, to imagine the sounds it must have heard. Here, on opening night, the great Caruso is reputed to have sung. Here came the rich and the famous from two continents. But the rubber boom burst, as far as Manaus was concerned. Seeds from Brazilian rubber trees were despatched to the Royal Botanical Gardens at Kew and then sent on to the East where it was thought that climatic conditions would favour the production of rubber in plantations. By 1910, the production of rubber from countries like Malaya, the Dutch East Indies and Ceylon totalled 11,000 tons. Fuelled by the growing demands of the motor-car industry, plantation output was over 300,000 tons by 1920. By 1927, it was almost 400,000 tons and Manaus was dead—or certainly moribund.

I stood on the stage in the darkness, listening to the rain crash around the building. Somewhere above me, up on the balcony, some caretaker of the place was shutting windows against the storm. It was good to know that someone still cared.

I had dinner in the Hotel. The restaurant is on the roof of the building and looks out over the river. At a table next to me was a gaunt and bearded American. He told me his name was Steve Besuk; he worked for the US Government as an oceanographer but was taking time off to paddle a kayak, single-handed, 3,500 miles from the headwaters of the Amazon in Peru down to where the river met the Atlantic Ocean. He had begun his journey in June, he said. It was the end of September now and he hoped to make the Atlantic by Christmas. He was taking a few days rest in Manuas before the next and final stage of his journey. It had been tough at times, he admitted. He had been eaten alive by black fly and mosquito; scorched by the sun; chased and almost killed by Indians. But he was going on, and his wife would fly down to meet him at the end of it all. This was a journey he had dreamed about and planned for much of his adult life and he was not going to chicken out on it now. Sitting there, with the lights of the river below and the sound of the rain easing into silence, it was not hard to understand what he meant. This is still a country to dream about.

The plane follows the river down to Belem, then follows the contour of the coast. We touched down in São Luis, capital of the state of Maranhão and Ceara, capital of Fortaleza. Then, late in the afternoon, we reached Recife.

The principal city of the State of Pernambuco, Recife has 1·3 million inhabitants according to the latest census. Pernambuco itself has 4·7 million. The North-East region as a whole, which consists of nine states, covers over 600,000 square miles (or about 19% of Brazil's total land area) and contains some 27 million population (or about 30% of Brazil's total population.)

The region can be divided into three zones. There is, first, the Zona da Mata, a coastal strip with ample rainfall. This is the area where the density of population is heaviest. This is where the old sugar plantations are concentrated and employment levels highest. Next to the Zona da Mata, going inland, is a transition zone known as the Agreste. The rainfall here is moderate; the area is characterized by subsistence farming and the large quantity of minifundia. The Agreste, in turn, leads to the Sertao, a huge semi-arid zone which dominates the whole region. The Sertao, which is roughly coterminous with the 940,000 square kilometre area designated by law as the 'Drought Polygon' (because of its shape on the map) has a measured rainfall of from 500 to 750 millimetres per year; but this rainfall is highly uncertain. The total annual precipitation is heavily concentrated in a short time-period.

The North-East of Brazil is one of the poorest zones in Latin America. Less than half the population six years old and over are considered literate, compared with 76% in the rest of the country. Medical facilities and services are inadequate, often non-existent, in rural areas. The deficit in housing is estimated at 2·3 million units. The employment rate is estimated to be only 32% of the economically active population. *Per capita* income is about 40% of what it is in the rest of Brazil. It is an isolated deprived region. For years, investment has been directed away from the north-east towards the buoyant, rapidly growing centre-south, the Rio–São Paulo axis. A high rate of population growth has compounded the problems of hunger and unemployment. Poor soils, and a low level of technical accomplishment, have led to low agricultural output. Recurrent droughts—there have been six major drought periods already this century—have only made matters worse.

The last drought was in 1958. In 1959 the law establishing SUDENE (the Superintendency for the Development of the North-East) was enacted. The idea was to have a single body to plan and co-ordinate development in the north-east. SUDENE's five main objectives were: to assess the natural resources of the region; to increase industrial production—and here key legislation was passed providing for tax benefits for those investing in the north-east, with a view to reversing the flow of capital into the centre-south region; to create vital infrastructure—roads, communications, electricity; to improve social services, education, health, human resources, etc; and to develop agriculture.

As far as the development of agriculture was concerned, SUDENE had three primary strategies. The first was to improve production in the Zona da Mata, especially through diversification and intensification. The second was colonization of the State of Maranhao which, though it fell outside the Drought

c *

Polygon, was nevertheless within SUDENE's jurisdiction. The third involved improving the production of the Sertao. And here, in the Sertao, one of the main thrusts was to be the development of irrigation.

In 1959, the Brazilian Government asked FAO to study the possibilities for large-scale irrigation on the lower reaches of the San Francisco river. This mighty stream, known as the most Brazilian of Brazil's rivers because it flows for the whole of its 1,987 mile length within the borders of Brazil, rises in the Serra da Canastra, in south-west Minas Gerais, flows north-north-east across the great central plateau of Brazil, then sweeps through the Sertao in a vast right-handed bend before entering the Atlantic about 60 miles north-east of Aracaju in Sergipe State. The San Francisco river has a discharge about 15% greater than that of the Nile, averaging about 90 billion cubic metres per year. It has a fall, over its whole length, of almost 3,000 feet and is now, following the completion of the Paulo Alfonso Project, a major source of hydro-electric power.

Between 1961 and 1965, a UNDP/FAO team made a general survey of two and a half million hectares in the San Francisco valley. Half a million hectares were found to be of irrigable land in terms of soil characteristics. Later, after taking topographical considerations into account, the team identified 20 schemes covering 105,000 hectares. These schemes were studied up to the preliminary design stage.

The project area extends either side of the San Francisco River. On the north side, the Pernambuco side, red friable soils are to be found. These are the latosols. On the south side, the Bahia side, the soils are the heavy black clay grumosols. The second phase of the UNDP/FAO project, which began in 1965, involved the promotion of pilot schemes in each of the principal soil zones. Irrigation works have been constructed, pumps and canals and water courses, and farmers have been settled. How far and how fast the project progresses depends on the results that are achieved on these trial areas.

*

October 1. En route to Petrolina. Petrolina is the small town on the lower reaches of the river where the UNDP/FAO

Project has its field headquarters. The Project Manager, Dula Navarette, whose recollections of Norman Borlaug at work in Mexico I have already alluded to, is with me in the plane. It is a single-engined Piper Cub aircraft, belonging to the UNDP. It flies low. I watch the altimeter in the cockpit and notice that our cruising altitude is around six or seven thousand feet. Dula tells me what to look out for.

'When you see green, it's still the Zona da Mata. When you see brown, that's the Agreste. When it's all dead below, you know it's the Sertao. At the moment, you can still see part of the original *mata*, that's the wood which has not yet been cleared.'

We enter some cloud and rise to leave it beneath us. By the time the cloud has cleared, I can see that we are well into the Agreste. The land is already dry and brown, split into fields by the darker lines of the hedges and fences. A few minutes later we have reached what Dula calls the 'transition of the transition'. Here some of the land is divided up. Some stretches out bare and arid. Here each man puts his cattle where he will with a rough and ready agreement as to who owns what. Later on still, we are over the Sertao proper. No hedges, no fences. Just a great brown plain below us with the occasional rocky outcrop. From time to time, one can see from the air a small dam, with an accumulation of water backed up behind it. This will be the work of one of the government agencies, like DNOCS (the National Department concerned with Works for the Relief of Drought) who have been involved in this area for the last 40 or 50 years, usually with scant success.

We left at dawn. By 9 a.m. we are crossing the San Francisco river a few miles to the north and west of the great hydro-electric development at Paulo Alfonso where the natural fall of the river provides a 50-metre head for the turbines. We will hit the river again, having drawn a chord to its arc, at Petrolina. Dula, the Mexican, who is in a way part-missionary, part-farmer, shouts to me above the noise of the engine: 'Of course, large scale irrigation could be economic,' he says. 'What we need is a proper co-operative organization, inputs at a reasonable cost and a taxation policy that isn't overwhelming. We have plenty of water, the climate is right—wind, day-lengths are constant.

There is no seasonal variation. Any time of the year, you can grow what you want. This is a totally controlled irrigation situation. Why shouldn't irrigation be economic? It is in other parts of the world. Mexico has four million hectares of land under irrigation, because it has a proper irrigation policy. Look at Southern California, North Africa. Fifteen million inhabitants in this region could provide a market for staple crops if they were grown here. You can produce for industry all the preserves you need—tomatoes, onions, and soon you can produce for export—alfalfa, oil seed. You can raise cattle on irrigated pastures. Brazil imports a lot of things which could be produced here.

'These are wonderful sanitary conditions. The land is largely free of diseases. It is a wonderful place to produce disease-free seeds. The US Bureau of Reclamation has said that there is enough water in the river to irrigate three million hectares.' Dula grasps my arm and points across me to the river below. 'Look out of that window. Here the animals are starving now and the people as well. But look at the water. Three million litres per second. Are you going to sit down and let it go to waste? If I were not born a Roman Catholic, I would be an irrigationist. Look at the river. 800 metres wide. All that water just has to be used. I am tired of these sharp-pencilled economists who are always trying to kill this thing. We already have a canal—1,300 kilometres of canal. The river is the canal. It might not be economical to construct it, but it's already there. We have a natural investment already worth millions and millions of dollars. Why, for the sake of a few halfpennies spent on irrigation works, throw it out of the window? I'm always fighting with my economists. But I tell you, I've seen the place. I've seen the river crossing the desert. This is something special. You don't have this in every part of the world.'

To understand men like Dula Navarette, one must try to understand the vision that inspires them. Irrigation is indeed a kind of religion, an article of faith. A man, if he is lucky, may build three or four dams in his lifetime. I mean the big dams, like Aswan and Mangla and Tarbela and maybe Pa Mong on the Mekong. These are, in their way, the highest form of civil engineering human beings have yet devised. These are projects which are planned for 20 years, or 40 years; which begin as distant gleams in someone's eye, take another ten years or fifteen to build but, finally, transform a whole landscape and the lives of millions of people.

The men who build these great dams know that they must stand through history, our own version of the Pyramids or the Statue of Colossus at Rhodes. Of course, they hope and expect that the wonders of the modern world will prove to be more productive investments than the wonders of the ancient world. But, in the last resort, they do not concern themselves too closely with the figures. To dam the Nile or the Indus, to tame the Mekong, to draw the water from the San Francisco river across half a million hectares of north-east Brazil, these are challenges the engineer is trained to meet. When they occur, he has to welcome them. The engineer may be the servant of the economist but in his heart he is a builder who either doesn't understand what the economist is doing or else believes that his sums are usually wrong.

Flying over the parched country that morning, and looking down at the vast resource of the San Francisco, I had some sympathy with Navarette. I remembered a meeting I had had back in FAO headquarters in Rome with a man called Lucas. He told me he was the father of the San Francisco valley project. He had nourished it for ten years and now he believed it was going to be a success. He told me a story to explain why, when others were raising their voices against the scheme, he stuck with it. He said he had a background for the project which the others didn't have. He came from Arizona. There was an old salt river there. In 1892 people came and put the river under irrigation. It was rough, the dam washed out every year and had to be rebuilt. But they kept at it. Then, in 1906, along came the Bureau of Reclamation. He said he used to work for the Bureau. The Bureau authorized the construction of the Roosevelt Dam, for the then enormous sum of 20 million US dollars. Now they were irrigating an area of one million hectares. This area contained one and a half million people together with the industries which employed them—all paying taxes. An economist had estimated that the annual tax paid to the government each year exceeded the total cost of all government investments over all the years.

The San Francisco Valley Project, at the time of my visit, consisted of 16 families settled on 120 hectares of land. They have not had an easy time. They had to learn much that was new and they have probably had to work harder than they expected to make a living out of their plots. There have been technical problems. Sprinkler irrigation, in theory so simple and so efficient, has proved a complex technique for them to master. The remoteness of markets and the difficulty of communication has deterred the production of the high-value cash crops on which the economics of the project depend. But these must be seen as only temporary set-backs. The results of the trial stations, on both grumosol and latosol soils, are coming in and these results are encouraging. Grapes and tomatoes and onions are growing where none grew before. Cattle are being zero-grazed with grass grown on irrigated lots.

So the government is pushing ahead with massive irrigation projects in the San Francisco Valley. The cost no doubt is horrendous. But the cost of *not* doing something is probably greater still. Brazil is a country where urban population is growing at twice the rate of total population. Many of the migrants to the slums of Rio de Janeiro and São Paulo have come from the drought-stricken north-east. To solve the problems of the cities, you must solve those of the countryside as well.

*

October 2. I sit in the Archbishop's palace, in old Recife, talking to Dom Helder Camarra, Archbishop of Recife. His eyes are hooded and sunken. He has an air of gentleness. I am lucky to find him in Recife at all for, though he must be past 60, he is constantly on the move—usually abroad. We sit at an oval table in one of the reception rooms. In the background hover various members of the Archbishop's staff. Sometimes they come to the table with messages for Dom Helder. In the middle of our conversation a woman enters and stands behind the Archbishop for a few minutes while he speaks, her hands resting lightly on his shoulders.

I ask Dom Helder about the situation in the north-east, particularly as far as agriculture is concerned. He replies:

'I am not a technician in agriculture or in sociology or economics or politics. I am only a pastor, a man of good will. I have no wrath in my heart, but I believe we need a change in the mentality of our rulers. The Brazilian army has always had a tradition of being near the people. For three centuries in Brazil, we had slavery. The owners of the slaves asked the army to help them keep their slaves. But the army always refused. They were too near the people. But now this has changed. Since 1964, our chief concern has been the fight against communism. But in their fear of communism, our rulers are maintaining an internal colonialism.

'I am not against my government. I hope that one day my government will be able to understand that without the courage to face internal colonialism, no real development is possible. Once in the past we were worried that the great problem was shortage of water. But the problem was not really absence of rain. There are other regions of the world with just as serious problems. The government was constructing dams without the courage to expropriate the land. You need co-operatives, but not co-operatives which are controlled by the government. I am not a technician, I am only suffering with my people. I believe if you introduce new technology now into agriculture, without changing the structure of the land, the only people who profit will be the rich.'

*

Brazil today is in the process of 'colonizing' the Amazon region. The Trans-Amazonic highway is daily being pushed further into the great green heartland, from the coast deep into the state of Amazonas. There is no doubt that 'opening up the interior' has for many years been a principal plank of Brazil's economic strategy. It was a dream which inspired former President Kubitschek to build Brasilia—back in 1959 I had stayed in the shanty town at the edge of the jungle and worked for a few exhausting days on the roads of the new city. It is still a dream today. If Brazilians think of their country as the nation of the twenty-first century, part of the reason lies in their sense of great riches lying unexploited, and vast hinterlands waiting to be populated by entrepreneurial spirits.

Dreams have their price and, in the case of Brazil, the price is already high and will go higher still. Fly over the frontier zone today—the state of Maranhão, for example—and you will witness a scene of devastation which is, in almost every sense, tragic. It is hard to persuade the pilot of these small single-engined chartered air-taxis to fly down low over the trees. They like to keep at two or three thousand feet at least so that, if the engine fails, they have a few moments for manœuvre before plunging through the canopy. But even from a height, one can see the flames and the smoke as the path of destruction fans out across the green desert. This is 'slash and burn' cultivation on a gigantic scale.

As the road has pushed out from the north-east into the transition zone and then on into Amazonas proper, the people have followed it. Poor people, largely living in the Drought Polygon. For them, any change must be a change for the better. They build their rough houses by the roadside and set to work clearing the jungle. They cut and burn the natural jungle and plant crops, probably rice, in the clearing. After two or three years the fertility of the soil is exhausted. By then, the road has forged many miles ahead and other settlers have filled up the interstices. So the settler indulges in a constant leap-frogging process which, presumably, will only end when the road itself reaches its destination or there are no trees left to burn.

No one at present knows the exact rate at which this process of random destruction and despoliation is being carried out. It is certainly far in excess of the natural regeneration of the forest. It is enormously wasteful. Some of the most valuable trees in the world, teaks and mahoganies and ebony wood, are consigned to the flames without thought being given to their commercial value. It is inhuman. The plight of Brazil's Amerindian population, confronted with the wave of settlement, has been much publicized in the newspapers of the western world. But material assistance or moral pressure has been largely absent. And, finally, this process of 'colonizing' the Amazon region has all the makings of an ecological disaster on a gigantic scale.

For behind the little, poor peasants with their machetes

clearing a patch of jungle at the roadside come the big rich men with their cattle. The hard work, of course, has already been done. The cattle come and eat down the secondary growth of the jungle, trampling the bones of those *cabochos* who died before they had time to move on. The cattle, too, move in a great sweep across the country. The ground cover disappears along with the secondary growth. The texture of the soil changes. From being aerated and granulated, water-absorbing, it becomes hard-packed and dense. The water, delivered in tropical deluges, bounces back off the surface. Problems of run-off and erosion become acute. The jungle is half-way towards the desert.

This no doubt is an over-dramatic picture. We have not reached this stage yet in Brazil. But unless care is taken, the Amazon Forest as I saw it last October will not exist beyond the end of the century. Brazil may learn too late the value of its unique resource and the world, once this green Sahara has been destroyed, may find itself poorer, aesthetically and in every other way.

There are, fortunately, some signs that the Brazilian government is alive to the dangers of unsystematic despoliation of the forest. While I was in Recife I heard of a British group, sponsored by the Ministry of Overseas Development and SUDENE, who were trying to devise patterns of development which could enable settlers to capitalize on the productive potential of the forest while avoiding some of the ecological and environmental hazards. The object of the project, which is situated in the frontier zone at a place called Ze Doca, near Alto Turi in the State of Maranhao, is to achieve organized, as opposed to spontaneous, settlement of the jungle.

I flew down to Ze Doca in a chartered plane from São Luis, the capital city of Maranhão. We crossed the estuary of the Pindare river and then flew almost due west towards Alto Turi. About half an hour from São Luis we were over the forest proper and could see the havoc which was being wrought below. The jungle looked as though it was suffering from a form of leprosy. The burning had cleared great areas. Where the trees had not been felled, they had died in their places and now stood denuded of life and foliage. In the frontier zone, trace roads began to cut through the forest. Even though they were not much more than tracks, and the proper road would not follow for a year or two, the settlements were already taking shape along the way and the process of clearing had begun.

Ze Doca was a frontier town. The frontier, of course, is not the political frontier. That is still thousands of miles to the west. It is the agricultural frontier, the frontier of human settlement. The great thrust westwards which characterized the development of the North American continent is being repeated today on this continent of Brazil. I could not, in my heart, fail to admire the enterprise of the people who come here to try to hack a living out of the jungle. The heat beats down out of the sky, the canopy of trees looms hundreds of feet into the air, the undergrowth is so thick as to be virtually impenetrable. Every trunk, every stump, every twig, every sapling has to be cleared by hand before a patch of rice can be planted, or a pineapple or two or some fruit-bearing trees.

The SUDENE people at Ze Doca tell me that, together with the British team, they are trying to develop a new methodology. Whereas typically each settler lived more or less isolated from other settlers, now they are trying to group them together and to teach them how to manage their land in such a way that they can live permanently on the piece they have cleared, instead of having to be constantly on the move.

When a settler comes to the area, SUDENE allots him 50 hectares of new forest. Through a co-operative, SUDENE also provides 50 cruzeiros cash incentive and credit of another 150 cruzeiros. There are about three and a half cruzeiros to a dollar, so these are not extravagant sums. They are enough to keep the man and his family alive while he is clearing the jungle and waiting for the first crops to grow. The colonizer also receives loans from SUDENE. For every hectare of rice, he can receive 150 cruzeiros from the co-operative (60% payable at planting, and 40% at harvest). He sells the produce to the co-operative and, if the value of the crop exceeds the amount of the loan, he builds up a credit or receives cash.

In his first year, the settler will clear two hectares. In the next three years, he will clear four hectares a year, then he reverts back to his first cultivation. In essence, SUDENE is trying to provide the settler with a plot of jungle big enough to enable him to practise some form of shifting cultivation (which is probably the only form of agriculture he knows) while at the same time retaining a permanent base. In all, the settler probably uses about 20 hectares for crops. If he has the energy to clear the rest, he may keep some cattle. In any event, 10% of the area has to be retained for timber and for the cash income the settler should derive from it, provided he exploits it sensibly.

SUDENE has devised a circular pattern of settlement. Say 50 families are to be settled in a single area; SUDENE will mark out a nucleus zone in which the houses are to be built. The 50 houses will all face inwards around a circle which is perhaps of 200 yards diameter. The 50 hectare plots of land radiate out from this circle, wedge-shaped and elongated. The tip of the wedge comes right up to the settler's house in the nuclear village. The base is in the forest. SUDENE chose the circular pattern because it was felt that this pattern ensured a fair distribution of the good and bad soils, and also meant that each settler had precisely the same distance to travel from his house to the field.

So far 1,000 families have been settled by SUDENE in the project area. It is slow work. The major problem, as SUDENE will readily admit, is the lack of a proper farming system. Even with an efficient extension service, the low level of literacy and the general unfamiliarity of the settler with modern techniques creates considerable difficulties. SUDENE has plans to colonize another 30,000 hectares in the state of Maranhao, at a rate of 5,000 families a year. From a national and international point of view, this would be no mean achievement. Five thousand families a year settled on SUDENE schemes are 5,000 families fewer leap-frogging along the great road to the west.

PART TWO

AFRICA

I

SUNDAY MORNING is always a bad time to leave. Trains from Somerset to London are few and far between. You wait on the station platform at Taunton in total solitude. There are no porters to be seen. No railway officials. Occasionally the disembodied voice of an announcer will proclaim that such and such a train left Penzance in the early hours of the morning but no hint is given of its present whereabouts nor any prognostication made of its arrival time in the still dormant city. The lone traveller may pass some time reading the legends on the silver cups which the Great Western Railway won in its heyday and which are now displayed in a glass case on Platform One.

After that, there is nothing else to do except wait for the arrival of the newsboy with the Sunday papers. At about half-past nine he appears, unwraps the bundles of newsprint which will have been off-loaded at the station only an hour or two earlier and spreads his wares on a dirty trolley by the ticket barrier.

The papers say, amazingly, that Mr Heath has won the election. He has already appointed his new team. Maudling and Macleod are to have the top jobs. Anthony Barber is to drag Britain, kicking and screaming, into the Common Market. The inside pages are full of comment and analysis as to why the Opinion Polls were wrong or, alternatively, not as wrong as they seemed. Mr Heath has given a private interview to Kenneth Harris of the *Observer* (or perhaps it is the other way round); Nicholas Tomalin, of the *Sunday Times*, tracks down the most minute details of the Prime Minister's movements on the fateful night. Mr Crossman is to replace Paul Johnson as Editor of the *New Statesman*, thus (apparently) fulfilling a lifetime's ambition.

The papers, once the train finally arrived, kept me happy until Bristol. There, Sunday travel being what it is, I had to change trains for Reading and I took advantage of the moment

73

to leave an accumulation of rubbish behind. It was a moral as well as a physical gesture. Suddenly I had had enough. For four solid weeks, in fact ever since Mr Wilson announced he would hold a June election, Britain had loomed larger than life. The price of butter and margarine, of fish and eggs and chips, had been presented day and night—on television and in the newspapers, in Press Conferences and campaign speeches —as though these were in fact the transcending issues of our time. It was a shopping basket election, won by the housewife. As far as I remember, Vietnam and Cambodia were hardly mentioned at all. Apart from a single obscure allusion by Sir Alec Douglas Home (a 14th Earl whom the papers that morning reported as having been appointed—once again—Britain's Foreign Secretary), there had not been a mention of overseas aid or of the great international questions of world poverty and economic development.

No doubt there were sound tactical reasons for the omission. Canny British politicians, interested in audience response, know and fear the potential—as far as election campaigns are concerned—of any reference to 'international affairs' in general and 'foreign aid' in particular. 'Aid' is the great turner-offer of men's minds. It has no natural constituency and it never will have. Economic development, poverty and over-population —these are not issues for the hustings.

That was why I was glad to be leaving England that Sunday, June 21, 1970. Glad, in spite of the unanticipated Tory victory which might have done me some good if I had stayed around, to be free for a while at least of Britain's mind-boggling paro-chialism. Quite soon, I would be involved in other trivial issues (for at bottom all issues are trivial), but at least they would not seem so. The price of maize and sorghum and cow-pea in Africa is different from the price of fish and eggs and chips in England, if only because Africa is different from England.

*

The Third World begins at Heathrow airport. In Terminal Building 3, the airlines of the 'less-developed' countries main-tain their offices. There, opposite the BOAC counter, is United Arab Airlines. Strange squiggly writing invites the unsuspecting traveller to forget about the hostilities in the Middle East and fly UAA to a different world. Out on the tarmac, parked next door to a QANTAS jet, a plane from Saudi-Arabian Airlines is being serviced. Boeings, VC 10's, Caravelles—the machinery may be made in the West, but it has become an integral part of the trappings of independence. The national airline, like the national flag and the national anthem, is a symbol that the transition has been made. It is a visible argument that the great emotive cries of 'Uhuru!' and 'Kwacha!', which were heard throughout darkest Africa a decade ago, were not empty bombast. The Iranian, the Saudi-Arabian, the Nigerian jets landing at, or leaving, Heathrow can be seen as poker-chips held out by the LDC's to show they still have a stake in the game.

We crawl, nose to tail, along the runway. It is a busy afternoon. Immediately ahead of us in the queue is a Caravelle of Austrian Airways; beyond that, the front half of a BOAC 747 jumbo emerges from a hangar like an enormous whale. The long grass at the side of the runway suddenly keels over as the Caravelle opens up for take-off. A cardboard box is caught in the blast and blown forty yards across the tarmac. Cars whizz this way and that. Cranes point towards the sky. Radar towers blink and bleep. The muzak, which has been churning away for the past half-hour, is suddenly interrupted.

'This is your captain speaking. We now have clearance for take-off at this time. However, we have been advised that due to congestion in French airspace, there is no possibility of a routing across France. We are therefore exploring the possibility of a routing across Belgium and Germany. We will keep you informed.'

No space on the ground. No space in the air. That's the way the world spins. Fasten your seat-belts and no smoking.

I change planes in Rome and fly on overnight, in a VC 10 of Ghana Airways, to Accra. Actually, to be accurate, I should say *the* VC 10. In that first flush of enthusiasm which followed independence, Ghanaian Ministers dashed about Europe buying —amongst other things—gold beds and jet aeroplanes. The beds could be returned to the store, but with the planes it was another matter. Ghana ordered three VC 10's, then found they were only able to pay for two. In the straitened economic circumstances of the time, they couldn't even afford the cancellation charge on the third. However, after a long negotiation they persuaded British United Airways to take their place in the delivery queue.

The second VC 10 was axed in a cost-benefit analysis carried out by a United Nations expert from Syria. He studied the facts and figures—load-factors, schedules etc.—and concluded that all Ghana needed was one VC 10 for the international service. So they let out the other one to Middle East Airlines. It was sitting quietly on the runway at Beirut when the Israelis made their famous helicopter raid. So then there was one and the Ghanaians did not even collect the insurance because someone somewhere had forgotten to insure the plane against war-risk.

I am not a historian but I knew enough to be excited when, soon after dawn, there was sufficient light to see the long African coast several thousand feet below and the surf rolling on the shore. I remembered the old jingle and its warning to mariners:

> 'Beware the Bight of Benin
> Where many put out, but few put in.'

This was a corner of the world rich in lay and legend. The Portuguese traders were here even before Columbus visited America. The Danes, the French, the Dutch, the British—they all came in their turn seeking the rich prizes of slavery. As often as not, their bones remained to whiten the beaches.

Desmond Baker, the World Food Programme's representative in Ghana, met me at the airport. He was a kindly man who had lived in India for twenty years, a fact which had coloured both his language and his face. He confessed that he was 'extra-ord-inarily pleased' to see me, which was cheering news since I had rather imagined that the reverse would be true. Visiting firemen are always tiresome; when they have pretensions in the realm of literature or art they are almost intolerable. But Baker took it in his stride and, on the short ride from the airport to the Ambassador Hotel, settled down to impart a few of the essential facts and figures.

Amongst other things, he said that the United Nations and its various organs had 144 people in Ghana altogether. If I left my bags at the hotel, we could call on Gordon Menzies, who was 'head of the whole shooting match' without further delay.

Half an hour later I was sitting in Mr Menzies' office in the United Nations building in Accra. It was a large and impressive office. Menzies was a large and impressive man. His formal title was 'Resident Representative of the United Nations Development Programme' but this was abbreviated, colloquially, to 'Res. Rep.' In the hundred or more countries in which the United Nations maintains missions, the 'Res. Rep.' serves as a kind of ambassador for the United Nations itself and for all the agencies which shelter beneath that pale-blue umbrella. The agencies, admittedly, are not necessarily happy with the arrangement. They would probably prefer to have their own accredited representatives in each and every case. But they are prepared to compromise in these small matters if it means that, in a wider sense, they can still retain their precious individual autonomy.

Menzies, who was not an Australian for nothing, hadn't much time for protocol.

'When I first came here, they were calling the Resident Representative "His Excellency" or "Your Excellency" or whatever. I put a stop to that. If I had my way, I would waive all diplomatic immunity and privileges for the UNDP man. We are treated like an ambassador here. Big air-conditioned car. Flag fluttering on the bonnet. Tinted windows. But we shouldn't be. We ought to be able to show that we are on the level of the people.'

Menzies' last post had been in Malawi. 'Banda put his whole weight behind agricultural development. He knew it takes a big man to get the peasant farmer moving. I was involved in several agricultural projects. One night Dr Banda rang me up and said "I intend to open your project tomorrow morning. Please meet me at such-and-such a point on such-and-such a road." Well, he was there on the dot. He—Banda—went round from 8 a.m. in the morning to 6 p.m. at night haranguing all the people who were going to be involved in the project, telling them why it was good for them, and what they ought to do about it.'

In Menzies' view, there was nothing in Ghana which was

'acting as a catalyst. What agriculture needs,' he explained, 'is internal promotion. All the resources of mass media should be used to prepare people for social change. Both with farming and fishing you are up against terrific odds. They are both very conservative, very isolated activities and the traditional pattern of life has been going on for hundreds of years. There has been no attempt to identify the progressive farmer, to work with him. Instead, the development agencies have been concentrating on industry and almost everything has been a complete failure.

'Another impediment is the after-effects of paternalism and colonialism. People have had everything provided for them in the past. Our major objective should be to help these countries help themselves. You can find out what is desirable, but it's not always the same—indeed it is very seldom the same—as what is feasible.

'I was in China at the end of the war. I had 53 million dollars and 40 million refugees. I had to choose: Do I spend my money on feeding them directly, or do I use it to try and construct some project where they can feed themselves? Remember what Confucius said? "Give a hungry man a fish and you feed him for one day. Teach him how to fish and he will never be hungry for the whole of his life." We have to be realistic. A man from the World Health Organization came and said every village in Ghana must have tap water. Do you know what it costs to maintain a piped water supply for each individual? Probably as much as the average peasant earns in a year. If you do put in taps, people just unscrew them. If you have a night-watchman guarding the supply point, you have to pay him and still people will unscrew the taps. They may take the taps to their own home and push them into the wall, hoping that water will come out of them.

'We have to work with the traditions. If you take the traditions away, it's like a tree without roots. This job is bigger than all of us put together. And the trouble is we, the UN agencies, have never tried to put ourselves together.'

*

The symbol of modern Ghana is the Volta Dam. The Volta is the second largest stream in West Africa, after the Niger.

It has four major tributary rivers: the White, Black and Red Volta and the Oti, whose catchment areas cover roughly two-thirds of Ghana. The idea of damming the Volta River was an old one. A dam site at Akosombo gorge, about 60 miles north-east of Accra and about 100 miles from the river's estuary in the Gulf of Guinea, was first noted in a geological survey conducted in 1915. Numerous studies and reports were made over the years and in 1953 the Volta River Project Preparatory Commission was established. Sir Robert Jackson—who in 1970 published his crucial report on the Capacity of the United Nations Development Programme and its relationship to the whole UN system of economic and social agencies—took charge of the Commission which completed its work at the end of 1955.

The realization of the Volta Project was one of the first and foremost objectives of the new independent Ghana. The Volta Dam would provide power for the electrification of Southern Ghana and for a big aluminium smelting plant on the coast. Since most of the construction and service industries are concentrated in the south and most of the modern sector of the economy (in all over 70% of total value added), the scheme seemed to be a vital one.

The World Bank provided a major loan for the project. Other loans were made by the US and UK governments. Construction started in January 1962; resettlement of the affected population in July 1963. The dam was formally completed in February 1965 and the Volta Project officially inaugurated in January 1966.

The dam rises 244 feet above river level with a crest length of 2,100 feet. In the power station, four generating turbines were initially installed and commissioned, producing a maximum of 588 megawatts per annum. Two more units are to be installed by 1972, bringing the total capacity to 882 megawatts. The VALCO aluminium smelter at Tema has already reached full capacity and a second stage is being built. The construction of a high-voltage transmission grid, extending to Accra-Tema, Kumasi and Takoradi is finished; a branch line to Togo has been agreed upon and a further extension to Dahomey is being considered.

The lake which has backed up behind the dam covers at flood level 3,275 square miles or about 4 per cent of Ghana's total land area. It is about 250 miles long and about 50 miles wide at its widest point. Its northern half reaches deep into the savannah zone, whereas the southern part crosses the forest belt.

This colossal enterprise is the new nation's show-piece. Visitors take their drinks out onto the veranda of the Volta Lake Hotel and watch the water thunder down the spillway, racing its way over to eat away the very hillside on which they stand. They gaze down at the great orange penstocks or walk through the ultra-modern, incredibly silent, totally automated power-house. Inevitably, they are impressed. They are meant to be.

June 28. Standing by the marina upstream of the dam. Mike Gilbert is in the cabin of one of the lake transports. He is the master-fisherman on the UNDP/FAO Volta Lake research team and he is testing radio communications with the base at the Project headquarters. A hundred yards or so from the boat, a huge floating dock is moored. It is used to service the lake ferries and other large craft. They built it piece by piece on the lake.

Half a dozen Africans poke their heads into the cabin while Gilbert works. Something has clearly gone wrong with the electrical system. Gilbert leaves instructions: 'If you don't have it, make it. If you can't make it, steal it.'

I ask him, as we set out on the lake in one of the FAO speed-boats, if he is bothered by the prospect of bilharzia.

'Bill Who?' he laughs. Then he says: 'I usually wipe some diesel onto my legs if I'm going to wade in the water. Acts as a bit of a repellent. Cirrhosis of the liver is much more dangerous for us Europeans than bilharzia.'

We pass the President's yacht, out at anchor. It was brought up by road on a trailer from Accra and is used at most once or twice a year.

We drive upstream, the front of the boat lifting out of the water and spray rising at the sides. Gilbert says: 'I've only built one boat. A speed boat. A bit bigger than this. I got a Land Rover engine, fitted a marine gear-box. Worked like a

charm.' I get a good look at him. He has a bronzed face,
bronzed legs (he is wearing shorts) and a grey beard. He has
the slightly leathery look of men who spend a great deal of their
time near the water. When he is in England, which is hardly
ever for he leads a roving life like so many of his colleagues in
FAO, he lives in Lincolnshire. He talks about Lincolnshire a
great deal.

There aren't many villages, nor is there much fishing, in the
first part of the lake. The gorge is too steep. Too little algal
growth, too little oxygen. Later on, the gorge opens up. The
water spreads out on either side like the sea. In fact Lake Volta
is a kind of sea, an artificial sea. The overall impoundment is
120 million acre feet (a million acre feet—MAF—is one million
acres flooded to the depth of one foot). The annual flow into
the lake varies; on average 120 MAF equals about four years
flow. Judged by its surface area, Volta may be the largest
inland lake in the world. Its shoreline may be as long as that
of the Caspian and is probably longer than that of Lake
Victoria. It's hard to establish this kind of data with precision,
because it depends on the type of map you use. If you use a
map with a very large scale and (assuming the lake has been
flooded to the 280-foot level) trace the 280 contour, you can—
in the case of Volta at least—pick up a great many nooks and
crannies and squiggles to be added in to the mileage count.
The contour is more squiggly on Volta than on Lake Victoria.
Which means that at a very detailed scale Volta appears to
win the shoreline contest.

The fishing industry on Volta Lake is correlated more with
the shoreline than with the total area of the lake. There are
masses of slime and weeds in the drawdown zone, and also in
the slope just beyond the drawdown. There is more plankton;
more benthic organisms which flourish and multiply in the mud
and rotten wood. What happened on Volta, as the lake filled
up, was a sudden explosion of fish, a flash in the catch rate.
Not a single species of fish was introduced, yet 120 species have
been recorded in the lake and in the river system, 60 of which
are found in commercial quantities and can be eaten. (The
fishermen, and others who have the right ju-ju, will even eat
electric fish.)

It is a strange business. Bill Taylor, an Australian who was the Director for the UNDP and the FAO of the Volta Lake Research Project, described it to me. 'One of the critical things is the number of canoes. You go on this lake; you don't see any fishermen. You see the odd village, the odd canoe. But not much more. One of our people decided to map the shore-line. He covered it, found it was dense as hell. Hundreds of villages, He went to a part of the shore-line where there weren't meant to be any villages and found out that there were even more. The land at the water's edge hasn't been cleared of course. None of the land was cleared before they flooded it. It's still forest. That means, because of the trees, you can't go in a big boat and you can't go in a cabin cruiser. You've got to go in a work boat and even then you may be fifty yards from the shore. The villages are in the trees, set back from the water. They don't know how far the water may be coming. They don't know what the 280-foot contour is or where it runs.

'The average depth of the lake is 60 feet, but you've got to know where the trees are. Some of the trees they flooded were 120 feet tall. You can have a tree sticking up 30 feet above the water. You can see that one all right. But you don't know the tree below the water.

'The best way to find out where the villages are is to look for the landing place. Or the nets. They use gill nets, set at various depths. The great bulk of them are set in shallow water near the shore. Stationary nets. You can't use moving gear because of the trees. Most of the fish are caught in the gill nets, though they sometimes use traps and long lines to catch the great big Nile perch, or cast-nets which you throw over the fish and pull in. There's a bit of spearing too.'

Bill Taylor, in his drawling Australian voice, told me that FAO had sent in eight teams to do a survey of the fishing villages. They reckoned that there were 12,000 villages and may be 14,000 or 15,000 canoes. 'A white man can get this kind of information easier than a black man. The villagers don't suspect him for being a tax man.'

The survey teams asked three questions. Did you fish today? Did you fish yesterday? Did you fish the day before yesterday? They made a note of which fishermen achieved what results and weighed the catch on a random basis. At the end of 1969 FAO brought in a consultant, a Greek, who estimated from the data that the present yield of fish from Volta Lake was 60,000 tons per year.

'People from the traditional fishing-tribes have come back into fishing,' said Taylor. 'There may be 70,000 people altogether along the lake shore. The villages are very evenly spread. The best fishing is close to the shore; fish move towards the food in the drawdown level. The people move their villages to where the nets are. They don't want to have to paddle three or four miles. Naturally, you'll find some concentration in areas of good road access, especially on the southern arm of the lake and part of the eastern arm. There we estimate an average of ten canoes per mile; the average over the whole shoreline is about four canoes per mile. You can reckon that a canoe equals the fishermen, an assistant, a wife and the children.

'The traders walk in to where the villages are, buy the fish in a fresh state, walk away with the fish on their heads, process it—probably salting or sun-drying—then sell it to the market. At the farthest point of the coast, you will still find that five to ten per cent of the fish eaten comes from Volta. In nearby areas the proportion may be 30 or 40 per cent. It's cheap and it's good. Probably just as good as marine fish. Kwashiorkor in the area has almost gone.

'There are about 130 transport launches on the lake, mostly 40 to 50 feet long, six to seven foot in beam. Bloody horribly built. Damn dangerous. Built like a canoe. They carry five tons at six to eight miles an hour and go to any villages which don't have the means of selling their catch. There is now a schedule. Small villages take their catch to the bigger villages where the transport launch stops. On the launch will be four or five mammies who buy from the fishermen. The average price is a bit better than seven pesewas a pound. Most of the mammies will sell the fish again in the ports—there are three major ports on the lake and four minor ones. It will probably be processed again in the port and could be reprocessed several more times before it is finally consumed.'

What they needed to do now, Taylor argues, was help the fishermen on the lake make some small and not specially

D

dramatic improvements to their equipment. 'The outboard motor is designed so that it kicks up automatically if it hits anything, a submerged tree for example. But it is not economical. It chews up petrol. We need to develop an inboard motor—the steady chug-chug variety—but with some outboard character- istics. An inboard-outboard. Also, we need an improved canoe. Most of the villagers use plank canoes, not dug-outs. The lake has waves and squalls blow up just like that. In places it's 15 miles across. Fisherman are reluctant to venture too far out. But there are fish in the middle of the lake as well as inshore. So we are working on an improved canoe. Rome sent a man and some plans. We'll build it out of local wood and we must keep it in a price range they can afford.

'We are also doing testing on improved gears. Experiments on Lake Kariba showed that the effect of a net varies with how you set it. The nets we use at the moment are mostly nylon filaments, three or six strands twisted together and knotted by machine. Now they have developed mono-filament nylon, where the webbing consists of a single thread. It's much less visible than the multi-filament, but it's more difficult to handle and repair. It's springy, so it's difficult to load a great deal of net onto these small canoes. And it is inclined to get brittle over time. Also it kills the fish quicker, which is not a good idea since you want to keep them alive as long as you can before you process them.

'How can we solve whether the advantages outweigh the difficulties? We've brought in 5,000 dollars worth of the new netting and have started giving it out to the fishermen. We have given it to five villages, five nets each. They have to fish five mono-filament nets alongside five multi-filament nets. Their catch ratio so far has been four to one. Every time we go to the villages, there is a proper palaver. They try to beg or buy or steal the nets—the mono-filament ones—from us.

'We hope the mono-filament net will make a big difference to the total volume of the catch. Also, we hope that it will even out the catch over the year. The off-season at the moment is the period from July to February when the water in the lake is dropping. The catch falls at this time of year and one of the reasons is that, as the water drops, the fish are able to see the nets better. We hope that with mono-filament, they will be able to get a good catch even at low season.'

The man whose job it is to translate hopes into realities is Mike Gilbert, Master-Fisherman. It is almost an hour since we left the marina beside the dam. We have at last put the gorge behind us and are on the open lake. There are already a few nets to be seen, marked by floats made of logs and other debris. I ask Gilbert if fishing rights are demarcated between family and family and between village and village.

'No,' Gilbert replies, 'but horrible things happen, if you lift someone else's net. You may even find yourself caught in a net somewhere and drowned.'

The sun streams down; the spray rises from the bow; we sit in the back and shout to each other above the noise of the engine.

'Africa's a way of life. It's in your skin.'

'Do you like it?' I ask.

'It's where I am. I'm certainly no missionary. I do it for the money. A lot of the old hands are coming back. They know the Africans. They know their ways.'

Around mid-morning we pass a lake transport steaming slowly in the opposite direction. It will have left the northern end of the lake at midday the day before. That's 200 miles away. It is bringing yams down to the south and other vege-tables. One can see them piled high amidships and people crowded into whatever space there is left. There are lights on the islands in the middle of the lake, to help the transports as they chug on through the night. The navigational equipment is very primitive.

We pull up alongside a fishing canoe. The man is leaning three-quarters out of his boat and running his hands through the nets to find out if he has caught anything. They generally try to avoid pulling the nets up if they can. It doesn't seem as though he has. Still, he waves and grins at us. He knows Gilbert and Gilbert knows him. It looks like a good life anyway.

Gilbert says: 'You land at London Airport. You get on the bus. You drive up through Chelsea and you look around and wonder "are these blokes in London any better off?" '

We steer to the shore, tie up on a dead tree-stump sticking

out of the water and walk to a little village a few yards back from the water. Some stools are brought out for us by a young man, and shortly two or three of his wives appear with their children. Gilbert, using our driver (who works with the Volta project) as an interpreter, asks the man about the fishing. The man appears disconsolate and rather depressed. It doesn't seem as though he has caught much for a few days, but this is anyway the low season. His net is spread out on the ground before us, full of holes. Gilbert says it should have been thrown away a year ago, but they go on using it. That's partly the reason why they get bad catches.

A fire has been lit between stones built up on the ground into a rough square. Over the flames, in a large saucepan, two fish are being smoked. Other fish, maybe two or three weeks catch, are spread out to dry in the sun on the roof of one of the huts.

The man we spoke to on the lake has now come back in. That makes two men, four women and about twelve children. One on the back, one in the belly and one in each hand. This pattern is the rule not the exception. I ask, naïvely, about contraception.

'Contraception?' Gilbert scoffs. 'They prefer to buy a transistor radio.'

'You can get a hell of a lot of contraceptives for the price of a transistor radio.'

'Yes,' says Gilbert, 'but you can't get a tune out of them.'

Our friend from the lake tells one of his women to go and get us a present. So she goes to the water's edge and pulls up a cassava from a number which have been planted there and presses it into my hands. We drive off with the plant tied to the bow of the boat. Some of the children rush into the water to push us clear of the trees. We wave and smile. The visitation is over, but Gilbert says he will be back on the next of his rounds. Maybe he will come with a mono-filament net, or at least some good advice. He knows it takes time to achieve results.

'You can't rush into a village with American attitudes. You've got to know how these people think, adjust to their pace. Otherwise, you'll kill yourself. You can't come in just for a few minutes and expect to put anything across. You have to spend the first day getting to know them, the second day explaining the kind of thing you are doing and the third giving some real instruction. Four or five years in Africa is like a pin-prick on an elephant.'

Gilbert thought the headquarters of the UNDP/FAO project was in the wrong place. It should be up on the lake where the fishermen are, not at the end of a twelve-mile gorge. 'It's no good doing fisheries work unless you can spit in the water from where you sit.' He is also rather sceptical about the mono-filament net. 'Why make someone hungry for chocolate, when there is no supply of chocolate? The mono-filament net is much more expensive and anyway it's not available in Ghana.' His, like Taylor's, was a wait-and-see attitude. They might be on to a winner. Or again they might not. If you wanted to work successfully in Africa, you had to understand the mentality.

By way of illustration, Gilbert tells some stories. He says he met a woman once lying on the road without any clothes on and clearly in the last stages of pregnancy. So he stops the car and asks her what she is doing there. So she says she is waiting. 'What are you waiting for?' he asks. 'The ambulance, to take me to hospital to have baby.' 'But where are your clothes?' 'I've left them behind. In hospital they take my clothes away anyway and I not see them no more. So what for I come with my clothes to that old hospital?'

'Another time,' says Mike Gilbert, Master-Fisherman from Lincolnshire, 'I wanted to take my boat out onto Lake Nyasa. It was a rough day on the lake. I told the boys to get ready and they looked very glum. Finally, they came in and asked for long blue trousers instead of their usual shorts. "Why do you want trousers?" I asked. "Oh sah," they said, "if we goin' drown, we prefer drown with them trousers on, not them shorts." '

Gilbert sums it up. 'If a bloke will paddle three miles on a hot day to talk to you, that's when you know you're in. The Americans come in, they think: "show them the big flag and away we go!" But these people don't like being pushed. It may work for a day or two, but then they'll sit back and say, "now what do *they* want?" '

★

By mid-afternoon, we are back again at the marina. While Gilbert goes down to see whether or not his boys have been able to fix the radio, I wander around. The lake transport we passed earlier that day has unloaded its yams and the mammies are sitting cross-legged at the side of the road with piles of vegetables in front of them. A radio blares in the sunshine. An absurd English accent doing a spot commercial. 'YOU TOO CAN BE ONE OF THE HAPPY PEOPLE WHO BANK AT BARCLAYS! YOU ARE ALWAYS WELCOME AT ONE OF BARCLAYS 60 BRANCHES THROUGHOUT GHANA!' Then the radio breaks into a kind of care-free West African calypso, ending always with the refrain. 'HAPPY PEOPLE BANK AT BARCLAYS!'

A policeman wanders up and down through the piles of yams, engaging in occasional conversation with the mammies. He wears a red-and-black striped belt, blue-black shorts and a peaked cap, black socks and shoes. On the radio there is another voice and another commercial. 'GET PALUDRIN FOR THE SAFEST SUREST PROTECTION AGAINST MALARIA. DON'T LET MALARIA SPOIL YOUR ENJOYMENT OR YOUR CHILDREN'S HAPPINESS. BUY PALUDRIN NOW!'

Buy Paludrin now! Here, in Ghana, malaria remains endemic. The white man's grave. The United Nations people and the Ghanaian public health authorities were concerned that when the water level in the lake dropped, it would leave behind stagnant pools, favourable breeding grounds for malarial mosquitoes. But in fact the lake shore is mostly made up of sandy soils and the water drops evenly without leaving pools. Malaria is not a problem which has been altered by the lake. But the same cannot be said of other diseases.

Water in the tropics is always a public health hazard. This is especially the case with large man-made bodies of water. When you create large masses of water, you may increase the environment for certain vectors. By altering the water regime, you change the environment for other vectors. You probably force rapid changes in population. There are more people who are not used to the new environment. Their habits are not geared to avoiding infection. You bring people with disease in contact with people who don't have disease. Sometimes the plusses outweigh the minusses. More often, it is the other way round.

Trypanosomiasis—or sleeping sickness—is borne by the tsetse fly which has to spend part of its life cycle in the shade of the forest. The bulk of the gallery forest, i.e. the forest alongside the streams, has been drowned—as have the streams themselves—with the creation of the lake. The lake has greatly reduced this aspect of the tsetse habitat, almost to a critical point. This is one of the plusses.

The score, as far as river-blindness is concerned, remains hard to assess. River-blindness is carried by the simulium fly and is found throughout the world in temperate and tropical zones. Mostly, though, it is a tropical disease. There is a big belt of it in the Sudan zone in Africa, with an extension running down to the coast down the Volta River. River-blindness is associated with fast-running water, because larva development requires water super-saturated with oxygen.

Over half the people over 40 years old living on the Volta are blind. What happens is this. If an infected fly bites you, a worm develops, then another worm, then a nodule, micro-filaria under the skin. When these tiny little worms die, the body encases them in fibre. If they die in the eye, you can get a fibrous substance all over the eye. Europeans rarely contract river-blindness because their nutrition levels are better and the period of exposure generally not long.

With the creation of the lake, and the flooding of the gorge, the experts thought they had wiped out the breeding grounds for the simulium fly. In fact this is not the case. The people who were infected by flies developed on the breeding grounds of the Volta River are now being infected by flies developed on the breeding grounds of its tributaries. What is more, the installation of the turbines and tunnels in the dam itself has meant that there are, downstream of the dam, beautiful man-made rapids, a nice steady flow of 20,000 cubic feet per second providing ideal conditions for the simulium fly. River-blindness plagues are recurring. (In the old days, you put an African out with a pair of shorts on and if he received 20 bites in an hour that was a plague. Now there are more scientific definitions.)

The situation may not be improved until demand for Volta electricity reaches such a level that they have to install a second dam, to take advantage of the final 40-foot drop remaining in the river. In that case the river itself between the two dams would flood out the rapids and the simulium problem should be at an end. In the meantime, they are trying to use chemical means such as DDT to control the fly. The ecological consequences remain unevaluated.

If the position for river-blindness is ambiguous, the bilharzia story is not. The increase in bilharzia was one of the most serious side-effects of the Volta Project. Cen Jones, an officer with the United Nations World Health Organization, who was serving with the UNDP/FAO team, talked to me about it. He had had a great deal of experience of tropical medicine; he had served in Sierra Leone, British Guiana and Aden. He had been in the Colonial Medical service before joining WHO. He was a rubicund man, with spectacles and an acid wit. Research into the medical aspects of Volta should, he believed, have gone ahead years earlier. Some excellent consultants from England had recommended it in the 1956 Jackson report. But the suggestion was not accepted.

'Schistosomiasis—bilharzia—is of two forms. The rectal form and the urinary form. Let us forget about the rectal form because it is very patchy and not important from the medical point of view. Let us concentrate on the urinary form.'

I am not a medical man but, as I understood, the urinary form of bilharzia has more or less the following pattern. You step or swim in the water and a schistosome will or may swim towards you. When you get out, it may be on you. If you can, you rub yourself down with a towel, or with alcohol or take a shower. If you don't (and not everyone can), the schistosome may go into the bloodstream. Then it gets into the bladder and the urinary system and you bleed. In another stage of the schistosome's life cycle, you urinate its eggs, the egg gets washed down into the water, it finds a snail, creates an eruption on the host and from that eruption the disease continually escapes. When you urinate blood, you know you've got bilharzia. That is why the villagers call it 'piss blood'.

'Blood in the urine' said Jones 'is not necessarily more

significant than menstruation in women. It's just a dramatic way of stating the problem. But in the third or fourth decade of infection, schistosomiasis buggers up the water-works. X-rays on the kidneys show they are distorted and damaged. You get all this gubbins in the bladder; the bladder becomes fibrosed and smaller; this leads to back pressure so that the ureters are dilated and the kidneys injured.

'Opinions are still divided as to the true importance of bilharzia. In countries like this, where 50% of the people die before they are five years old, that is to say where a cohort of 1,000 is likely to be reduced to 550 or 500 before the end of the fifth year, you have to have the thing in perspective. Priorities aside, it is clear that before the lake came there were low rates for bilharzia on the river. Then, quite unexpectedly, although they rehoused the population from the flooded area, some 60,000 to 90,000 Ewe fishermen came up from the Lower Volta region where bilharzia endemicity was very high and settled on the lake. So an infected population moved into the lake.

'The attraction, of course, was —as you know—the biological explosion of fish who liked the slow-moving water and the rich weeds. But this was also the favoured environment of the vector snail. So when the infected population moved in, an intense cycle of transmission was generated. Infection rates started to rise enormously. At the end of 1966, there were 10% of children between the ages of 10 to 15 infected. By the end of 1968, the rate was probably 100%. By 1970 the rates were falling. We have not found any snails since January, or damn few. Either there is an intense seasonal fluctuation, or the snails have gone. Perhaps it's too rough for them. Usually, the schistosome thing likes relatively placid conditions. They can't stand waves. They've only got 48 hours to find a host. One could summarize it by saying "the ecology appears to be changing in a direction unfavourable to the vector snail." '

The interesting question is: why? Bill Taylor could offer no clear explanation. 'We have a weed control programme set up. By removing the weed, you can reduce the feed supply for the snail and thus the snail population itself. WHO were impressed because the infection rate had dropped from 90% to

D *

10%. They concluded that the weed control programme had worked; but in other villages without weed control programmes the infection rate had dropped even further.

'It may be that the fish population has reached stability with its food supply. There isn't much submerged weed any more. The fish may have eaten the snail and the food of the snail at the end of the low season. But we'll have to wait till the flood season when, with the drawdown covered with water again, there'll be lots of food for fish and snails. All we can say at the moment is that maybe God is on the side of the Ghanaians.'

★

The Volta Project, in its earliest conception, placed a strong emphasis on self-resettlement. Compensation was to be paid according to the value of the properties destroyed. This was the thrust of the Jackson report. But, by 1962, Ghana was independent and no government could afford to implement fully the self-resettlement idea. To get a fall of 300 feet at Akosombo, they had to go 200 miles up country. 3% of Ghana's territory, or the equivalent of half of pre-1967 Israel, had had to be flooded. 1% of the electorate was directly affected by the dam and that 1% was probably related to about 5% of the electorate. Self-resettlement was just not politically expedient. In any case, there was a danger, perhaps a certainty, that people would merely take the compensation money and go and drink it away all at once.

There were roughly 80,000 people in the area before impoundment began—in May 1964. They were spread out between some 750 villages. Sixty-seven thousand people were resettled by the government into 52 villages. The remainder chose cash compensation. A few—perhaps around 1,200 men or 5,000 people altogether, if you allow for women and children—came back to the lake as fishermen, to be joined there by the great inrush of Ewes from the Lower Volta.

The resettlement process was a difficult and complex operation. The Volta River Authority, who had charge of the resettlement scheme, had originally hoped to have fewer than 52 villages. But this proved impossible. Some villages, conscious of traditional feuds, refused to amalgamate with others. Others were debarred, whether through custom or taboo, from crossing certain rivers. Still others could only be resettled on ancestral land. If they moved, they took their gods with them and generous libations needed to be poured by way of expiation and propitiation. The project accounts indicate that the spirits were thirsty. There are frequent references to official expenditure on gin and whisky.

But the problems of persuading people to move to the right place at the right time were small compared to the problems which arose when they arrived at their destination. Polygamous for the most part, the settlers objected to the concrete houses which had been constructed for them by the Volta River Authority. It was not the concrete they minded. On the contrary, a concrete house back in his 'home town' is the average Ghanaian's idea of paradise. (The Tongu Ewes will never settle on the lake. They will simply stay there until they have made enough money to return home and start building.) No, what bothered them was the size. In the traditional village houses, the wives had separate rooms. The man moved round from one room to the other, changing monthly or weekly depending on taste or circumstances, on pregnancy or lactation for example. The new houses in the settlement area offered only one room for the man and all his wives.

Apart from the question of housing, there was the question of land. The settlement villages were often designated in what were already heavily settled areas. Competition between residents and newcomers was sometimes intense. The switchover from traditional patterns of shifting cultivation to stabilized agriculture, which was what the government intended, meant teaching the peasant a totally new system; required a complete change of attitude. The sheer labour involved in clearing and cultivating, surveying and demarcating vast tracts of territory implied a different sort of farmer, one imbued with a 'modern' set of values and a 'modern' approach to life.

I remember talking to a young English sociologist, called Dave Butcher. He was a fellow west countryman—from Bridgwater in Somerset. He had been working and studying in Ghana for virtually the whole life of the Volta Project. In his opinion it was absurd to think that changes of the magnitude required could be achieved in a generation.

'Quite honestly,' he said to me, 'I don't think it's any good trying to convert traditional farmers. I believe in getting hold of the youth. They've coalesced these 750 villages into 52 and as a result school attendance has grown from 34% to 71%, just between '62 and '68. That's more than double. I believe the thing to do is to introduce extra-curricular agriculture in schools. Why not begin in the rural areas, with agricultural training? Teach the children different ideas. Let them work alongside their parents and show their parents the new techniques. The trouble is, one of the hardest things to find in Africa is the dedicated extension worker. How do you teach an educated man to go into the bush and do a job teaching some country peasant, a job which has no prestige in his eyes or in anyone else's?'

I also remember talking to Kan Akatani, the Director of the United Nations Information Centre for West Africa. He was a Japanese. He didn't like the way his own country was going and he didn't like the way Africa was going much better. The initial fault was largely the West's, but the mistakes had been perpetuated by the developing countries themselves. 'Development is always thought of as building dams, generating electricity, building roads—they think that this is development, because that is how we have taught them to think. But I say if you can get an idea into the brain of a child, that is development! People think that earthquakes and lightning are astonishing natural phenomena. But I think a blade of grass pushing through the ground is much more important. Education is the crux of the whole business. If we can get away from the old colonial pattern, with its emphasis on the colonial language, the white-collar job, the urban environment—we stand a chance. But that means we must go into the villages. And stay there.'

Going to the villages. Staying there. Doing a job. Perhaps the best example of what it means that I saw during my time in Ghana was that of an American Peace Corps worker, Judith Marshall. She had been living and working in one of the resettlement villages. Her concern had principally been to teach the women better nutrition habits, how to conserve rather than waste food; where to find proteins; the meaning of a balanced diet. Her time was up and she was being given a unique honour. The villagers of Nkwakubew had decided to rename her with one of the traditional names of the Dodi people.

Dave Butcher and I arrived at the village of Nkwakubew in good time for the ceremony. We paid our courtesy call on the village chief, sitting in his hut and drinking a glass of beer each. An inch or two off the top of each glass must be spilled on the floor as a libation to the ancestral gods, even though it is an encouragement to the flies. Others in the hut were offered palm wine out of a green plastic bucket. A little boy with a shaved head sat at the chief's knee. Over his shoulder he carried a ceremonial sword with a gold hilt. We talked through an interpreter, mostly about the problems and prospects of the resettlement programme. Finally the chief gives us his blessing and the interpreter translates. 'May you increase your salary and achieve your aims in life.' He is clearly a realistic man.

We offer him a ride in our car to the Nkwakubew Middle School grounds, where the ceremonial renaming of Miss Judith Marshall is to take place. But he prefers to go on foot. His umbrella, symbol of his chieftaincy, is too big to fit in the car and he won't be seen without it.

The ceremony has been organized by the Christian Service Committee of Nkwakubew. It starts, a mere hour and twenty minutes late, with the arrival of two huge tom-toms which are carried on broad shoulders and set down in the middle of the square. We all stand up. Those who know Twi, the language of the area, blast away with the vernacular version of 'Now Thank We All Our God'. The Reverend Odame, Chaplain, recites a prayer—again in Twi; the wife of Chief of the Volta River Authority makes a speech; a girl in front of me reads a James Bond novel with undistracted attention; the pupils of Nkwakubew Middle School sing some songs; and—at last— Chief Nana Appiah II (he of the too-big umbrella) comes to the great moment itself.

He strides forward to the middle of the square and a loyal

claque comes forward with him. Their job is to shout with vociferous enthusiasm at all appropriate moments in his speech —a kind of Amen corner; and at many inappropriate moments besides. Chief Nana begins (the speech being interpreted for our benefit):

'Today is a grand day for all the people. Welcome to all who have come here to the settlement dwellers. Government has not forsaken us, has been feeding us all the while. We have been helped especially by a woman from America. In every part of our daily life she has helped us exceedingly.' Pause for cheers and the beating of tom-toms.

Then the chief, referring to Judith Marshall's nutrition classes, goes on: 'If your wife can cook well, you love her well. And this woman has helped us to achieve this. Everything', he says with rising excitement, 'that makes a housewife admirable, this woman has helped us to attain. Her courage in this reminds us of one of our own women, Nana Ohenewa, over 260 years ago. So we plan to rename her after Nana Ohenewa. That woman, Nana Ohenewa, was a militant woman. After she had left this place, she advised every one of her subjects to go to the forests and work. So they left their arms and turned to farming and tried to establish markets along the shore. . . .'

When the Chief has finished speaking, it is Judith Marshall's turn. She is a plain girl, but her spirit shines forth. She wears an African robe and, so she tells us, treasures the knowledge that she too is part of the Dodi people. She sticks to her brief to the end. Agriculture, horticulture, education, nutrition— this is what she is there for. She reaches her peroration, an ordinary bespectacled American girl, probably from somewhere out west. 'All the Dodi people and the people of Nkwakubew will be known everywhere as fine farmers. Your children will become fine farmers. We see the spirit of Nana Ohenewa at large as we look at the fine Nkwakubew Middle School. And so in the days to come I am sure that her spirit will continue to guide you in this place. Every time I put on this beautiful trinket you have given me'—and here she holds up a golden brooch that Chief Nana Appiah has thrust into her hand—'I shall think of the hard work you are doing.'

For the moment, though, thoughts of hard work are far away indeed. There is an hour of tribal dancing and drumming. Then it is time for the final item on the programme, an item dear to Judith Marshall's heart and, no doubt, to the spirit of Nana Ohenewa. It is a play, a little village drama, about the importance of mass education.

Two girls are dressed up as husbands. They are clearly well known in the village and their appearance, backsides bulging out, the trousers fit to burst, sets off a great wave of laughter in the audience. Then there are two real women. One of them is obviously a lazy woman, who doesn't cook properly for her husband (heinous crime) and who, in spite of the remonstrations of her friend, has no wish to attend the mass-education programme. Trumpets announce the arrival of the magistrate, another woman dressed up as a man, with a bowler hat to signify his/her legal office.

The husband wants to bring the wife before the magistrate, so that he can give judgement as to whether his wife's crime in being a lazy woman and in not attending the mass-education classes is bad enough for him to divorce her. At about this point in the drama, a great quiet descends on the square. The villagers are following every point closely, not missing the slightest nuance or innuendo. What grips them is that they see people they know, acting out roles that are not far removed from their own lives.

In the end, the woman asks the magistrate: 'Is it true that Mr Kofi will divorce me unless I go to the classes?' The magistrate, with mock sternness, says yes. 'OK, then,' says Mrs Kofi simply and cheerfully, 'I will go to the classes.' Mr and Mrs Kofi walk off arm in arm to wild applause. Judith Marshall, alias Nana Ohenewa, returns to America.

*

High up above the gorge at Akosombo, several hundred feet higher than the crest of the high dam itself, stands the Presidential chalet, built in 1964 for President Nkrumah. To get there you drive along the road which runs across the top of the dam, before zig-zagging up the hill. There are two or three security checks along the way because, even though Nkrumah is in exile in neighbouring Guinea, the house has been taken over by the Volta River Authority for the use of the Chief Executive of the Authority.

It has been renamed Executive Chalet. But the smell of Nkrumah is still powerful. I saw the rooms of his children, Gamal (named after Nasser) and Yaaba. I looked over the kitchen. It was equipped with the finest ovens and refrigerators and cooking utensils. Nkrumah spared no expense. There was beer in the fridge and the caretaker opened a bottle and brought it out to me as I sat on the veranda looking out, as Osagyefo himself must have once looked out, at the great dam below with its huge orange penstocks, at the swirling water beneath the power-house and the pot-lines swinging south to the smelter at Tema.

Thinking about Tema, I remembered Mr Zei, a Yugoslavian fisherman, I had met down in the port a few days earlier. He was involved for FAO on a complex project aimed at improving the sea-fishing industry off the coast of Ghana. He—and his assistants in the laboratory—were studying the habits of both pelagic and demersal fish, in order to find out where the fish spawned, at what depth and temperature the greatest catch took place and what correlation there was between catch and geographical and oceanographic features.

It was difficult slow work, necessitating the most careful procedures of tagging and sampling and, where information about spawning was needed, the removal of the gonads for inspection. (From the female gonads, it was possible to tell whether the fish had spawned or not). Professionally, Zei was a scientist and, in everyday life as well, he looked about him with a very scientific eye.

He told me the story of how he had been at a party and a guest had come in late and had parked his car at the top of the drive, away from all the other parked cars. When he came out after the party, he found that his car had rolled down the hill and had collided with the other cars. He asked the night-watchman about it and after a while the man admitted that he had taken the handbrake off and let the car go. Why? the guest asked. The night-watchman replied that he had done it because he thought the car would be lonely so far from its brothers.

'They want development,' said Zei, 'and they want it now. But they don't want to work for it. If they don't like to work, they should stay on in the jungle instead of asking for new cars and washing-machines. They also want Benz—that's what they call the Mercedes-Benz. One day I gave a lift to a girl. She asked for a smoke so I offered her a cigarette. She said: "No thanks, I only smoke king-size." In twenty years, you can't change this country. In fifty years, you might be able to.'

Sitting there, on the veranda of Nkrumah's house, and looking out over Ghana, a phrase came back and stuck in my mind. It was Dave Butcher's, pungent and powerful as the man himself.

We had been discussing, inevitably, the whole business of development. I was full of excitement, having lately attended a weird and wonderful ceremony at Kumasi, where a new Asantehene had been installed as paramount chief of the Ashantis. Why, I asked, could not Ghana build on these tribal patterns and values? Why, I said, remembering down-town Accra, did they have to opt for a hideous form of cultural suicide? And Dave Butcher had replied: 'They want development because that's what we've taught them to want. We want to shove 2,000 years of western history up their arse-holes.'

2

I sit in the airport lounge at Kotoka airport, Accra, waiting
for the flight to Cotonou to be called. There is a delay and I
manage to write three letters describing some of the events
during my time in Ghana and letting my wife and children
know, in retrospect, something about my movements. There is
a boy behind a desk in the lounge who purveys stamps to
customers such as myself. I am interested to note that, even
though all the letters are of the same weight, he uses stamps of
different denominations.

'But what is the *real* price of a stamp for an air-mail letter
to England?' I ask.

'12½ pesewas.'

'Then why have you used one stamp of 9 pesewas, one of
12 and yet a third of 16?'

He shrugs his shoulders and gives a great wide grin and says:
'The average, sir, that is what matters.' Then he adds, as
an afterthought, 'Anyway, they won't get there.'

There is a missionary from Kumasi, an American, sitting
next to me on the sofa. He is waiting for the Swissair flight
to Zurich. His luggage seems to consist solely of a huge General
Electric portable (barely) radio. He pulls out the aerial until
it touches the roof of the lounge and tries to tune in to the
BBC. But the interference defeats him. He says to me suddenly,
apropos of nothing, 'There is more typhoid around than people
will admit. You get it from the water or the food. You should
have jabs. The other day I carried a dead boy—16 years old.'

On my other side is a girl from the French Cameroons. She
is going for a holiday in France, which is what your upper-class
Francophone African tends to do at the drop of a *chapeau*. I ask
her if she has visited Cotonou and she says yes. So I chip in
with a 'Qu'est-ce qu'on fait là-bas?'—all very idiomatic. She
shrugs and says 'le même qu'ici'. It is as good a reply as any.

It is a short casual flight down the coast from Ghana to

Dahomey. Air Afrique didn't bother to use the loud-speaker system. One of the Ghana Airways girls, neat grey uniform bulging as always over the hips, walked through the departure lounge and identified, as if by intuition, the half-dozen or so passengers bound for Lomé and Cotonou.

A DC3, that most versatile of planes, with the dark green colours of Air Afrique, is waiting for us. We are taken across the tarmac in a minibus. We stay in the bus while two mechanics amble off to find some steps so we can enter the plane. Several minutes later they return pushing the steps in front of them. Fans whirr inside the plane and there is no door between the cabin and the cockpit. There is some Scotch tape over some cracks in a ceiling light.

A judder and a puff of smoke as the starboard engine starts up. Then the port. A man in white overalls waves some ping-pong bats. The pilot doesn't notice so he waves them again, then puts both bats in one hand and gives a brief limp salute with the other. We take off toward the sea, before curling round to fly along the coast. Out of the window, only a few hundred feet below (the pilot doesn't bother to gain altitude) I can see the surf rolling thunderously onto the beaches.

After about half an hour in the air we land at Lomé. It is time for a beer. I sit in the airport bar with the captain, a broad grey-haired Frenchman, and his navigator. We drink out of large glass mugs inscribed 'Bierre Benin'. The liquid foams over the top of the mugs onto the table, attracting flies and other insects. A notice on a bulletin-board in the bar announces 'Le Centre Culturel français et le comité d'organisation présentent FESTIVAL DE CHANT CHORALE DE LOMÉ avec la participation des Chorales Catholiques et Protestantes de la ville'. It turns out that Lomé is the capital of Togo.

I am the only passenger left for the onward flight to Cotonou. The navigator jokes: 'With him flying,' he points at the captain who is well into his third glass of beer 'all the others are frightened. They prefer to go by road. If they want to go at all.' As he says this, he makes a face.

'Why? Isn't Dahomey a good place to be?'

'Non,' says the navigator. 'C'est un désastre.' He puts a hand behind his back and wiggles it, palm upwards, in the traditional manner. 'Toujours les cadeaux. They don't do any work.'

'None?'

'Sometimes they sell pea-nuts.'

Carl Wright, the Resident Representative of the United Nations Development Programme, met me at the airport and drove me to the Hotel du Plage. We arranged to meet later in the afternoon, so I had a few moments to myself. I sat at the desk in my room looking out of the window at the sand and the sea beyond. The new port of Cotonou was to the right, half a dozen ships of different sizes and nationalities being moored behind the breakwater. Directly in front, growing on the beach itself, was a row of tall palm-trees. With the high wind that blows almost constantly on the shore, they have developed a permanent list. In among the trees, an African squats with his shorts around his knees. Another comes to join him and they squat together. I must remember not to walk along the beach.

The main international highway, linking the countries on the Gulf of Guinea, runs outside the room, serving at the same time as a board-walk for this West African Atlantic City. There are no cars on the road, however: first, because there aren't so many cars anyway in Cotonou; second, some construction work has been going on (or rather not going on) for months with the result that the road has been closed and a diversion has been posted. Arrows point to TOGO in one direction and NIGERIA in the other. Unfortunately, a mistake has been made and the true directions have been reversed.

My meeting with Carl Wright had been arranged for four o'clock and I was an hour late. We seemed to have travelled so short a distance that morning (allowing for the bar-stops) that I had not imagined there could be any time change. I had forgotten, of course, that it was not just a question of going from Ghana to Dahomey. One was, also, going from Greenwich Mean Time to Continental Time. Ghana—with precocious loyalty to the ways of her former masters—has retained GMT long after those same former masters perfidiously abandoned it.

Carl Wright, who knew a lame excuse when he saw one, eased my embarrassment by explaining the Ghanaian mentality.

'Yes,' he said, 'they know it's a relic of the old days. But they don't see why they should change in a hurry. They still drive on the left, you know, in Ghana. One day Nkrumah's opponents attacked him for permitting it. They said it was a monument to imperialism. "Very well," said Nkrumah, "we will change over to driving on the right. But let us make the change gradually." '

Carl Wright is a tall aristocratic Dane. As a Scandinavian, he is a member of the most advanced race on earth. The Danes, the Swedes, the Finns, the Norwegians have left their mark on the world in a way which no other group of nations has been able to emulate. Whereas the British, the French, the American, the Russian commitment to 'internationalism' is at best lip-service and at worst merely a device to mask the naked play of self-interest, the Scandinavian race has elevated a belief in 'the international community', and particularly a belief in the United Nations, into the cardinal tenet of their political philosophy. The United Nations, as something that works, would not long survive without men like Carl Wright and his Scandinavian colleagues. There are photographs of U Thant and Dag Hammarskjöld on the wall behind his desk and you know at once that, unlike so many of these office photographs, they did not come with the furnishings.

Wright's wife served as Denmark's Ambassador to Ghana. At weekends, or whenever he had a chance, Carl Wright drove along the rough coast road to Accra. He was, he said, past retiring age (though he looked as though he still had 20 years to go) but he would stay on in the post as long as his wife was still in West Africa. We talked into the evening, moving in due course from the office to his house on the sea-front. I asked, inevitably, naïve journalistic questions. Had they struck oil off-shore? How much? What were the French doing? Did they still run the place? Was voodoo important? What was the power of the fetish? Seeking the flavour of the place, the enquiry was random, disorganized.

Finally Wright said: 'Talk to Rentjens. He's probably the best man we have here. He'll show you something. I met him first in the Congo, when we were on opposite sides. Go up north and see what he's doing. They have 500,000 head of cattle in the north, but it's a resource which is very badly utilized. There is no water in the villages. The pasture is very primitive. The cattle is not used for draught or for transport. It provides neither meat, nor milk. Five years ago FAO sent in Rentjens. He's a Belgian. He's transforming the situation. He's teaching them how to use the cattle, instead of slaughtering it for festivals or counting it for prestige and nothing else. They dig wells and the cattle draw water. They build carts. The farmers get two crops a year instead of one; they pay their debts ahead of time. The rate of repayment has been 140%; 1,500 farmers have paid up. Some have even bought additional land. The whole thing is growing like a snowball.'

I drove up north to Parakou with Charles Koerber, an American who worked with the UNDP in Dahomey. It was a memorable journey. Dahomey is a country where the women, once you leave the city, wear few clothes. This is a land where the word 'topless' must have been first invented. Progress was an endless succession of torsos, of women with bundles of wood or gourds of water on their heads turning towards us as we passed and sometimes putting one or both hands up to steady the load. They will walk miles in a day, fetching and carrying. Or else run, with a quick shuffle step. I have seen women harnessed like oxen to a cart, while their husbands walk lightly along the road ahead of them, carrying nothing except a twig. I have even seen husbands sitting on the cart itself, along with a mountain of baggage and produce, while the wife labours in the traces.

The road is a living affair, shifting, shimmering, full of events. There are villages at the side of it. Houses with conical roofs of reed or thatch tied up into a bubble like miniature Kremlins. Little shrines dotted here and there among the houses, a witness to the power of the fetish. Chickens scrabbling and darting around in the dust. Women bent double washing clothes in a stream or in a bowl of dirty water.

We ran over a snake at one point, turned around and went back to make sure it was dead, for snakes are sacred; had a puncture and changed wheels, finding the tyre slashed to pieces on the rough road. In the early afternoon, I felt desperately ill and vomited, groaning, by the roadside. But I slept for an hour in the back of Koerber's Volkswagen with a hat over my

face to keep out the sun and found I was much improved when
I awoke.

There are rivers and water-courses to cross. Sometimes the
same bridge serves for both rail and road. You bump across
on the sleepers. The rail ends at Parakou, about 400 kilometres
from Cotonou. Goods going further, to Niger and Niamey, go
by road. About 250 kilometres from the coast, cattle country
begins. Rentjens' country.

*

July 10. Sitting on the terrace outside the Hotel Routier in
Parakou, talking to Jan Rentjens. He is a man about my age,
wears shorts, a white shirt and spectacles; has a wicked wit
and is driven by some fierce inner energy. He tells me what he is
trying to do.

The farmers in the region, it appears, own cattle but they
don't or can't keep them in the dry season. So they hand them
over to the nomad tribesmen, the Peul, who take them up to the
rivulets further north and to the Niger. In return, the nomads
are paid with the milk from the cows. Also, the beasts are kept
around the nomads' huts and their droppings used as fuel. Or
else, sorghum is grown on the manure.

Rentjens' idea is to bring the cattle back from the nomads
to the farmer. He wants to persuade the farmer to use the
draught power of the cattle to improve his agriculture. Wells for
water, simple tools for making hay and silage, two-wheel or
four-wheel carts built to a standard pattern—this is the kind of
improvement which, so Rentjens thinks, can revolutionize the
way of life of the Bariba tribesman.

The trouble is, the Bariba tribesman 'n'est pas un éleveur'.
He doesn't like raising cattle. He thinks it is a low-caste pursuit.
As far as he is concerned, there are three sorts of cattle. Cattle
for eating, cattle for milking, and cattle for counting. And the
greatest of these, as St Paul might have said, is counting. Oxen
are like a bank. (The Romans felt the same way: hence the
word 'pecuniary'). It's not what he can do with them that
matters; it's knowing that they are there and that, when the
need arises, he can go to the Peul and write a check on his
account. The fact that the Peul will let the Bariba's sucking

calf die because he, the Peul, is taking all the milk; the fact that he probably cheats in other ways too, isn't considered relevant. As long as the Baribas have enough cattle to slaughter for a festival or a celebration, for the marriage of a daughter or the death of an uncle, they are content. The wastage is phenomenal. Overnight seven hundred cows may be slaughtered in a village. People who are used, perhaps, to seven or ten kilograms of meat a year suddenly find they have a whole cow to eat by themselves.

After breakfast on the terrace of the hotel (if this is not too grand a description of what was little more than a way-side stop), we drive out to Belefougou. This is a small village where Rentjens has established one of his training centres. It has rained in the night so there is a 'barrière de pluie' across the road to prevent lorries and other heavy vehicles going through before the mud surface had had a chance to dry out.

Rentjens has a three-year-old Peugeot which looks twice its age. He pushes it constantly to the limit of its performance. He drives with one hand on the horn and with the other gesti-culates to make some important point yet more emphatic. His safe progress from A to B is a small miracle. They know him up in these parts; indeed he is a familiar sight throughout the whole of the Borgou and Atacora regions of Dahomey. They know him and, at least when he is on the road rushing from one encounter to the next, they avoid him.

With the dogs, the pie-dogs scrabbling around in the dirt of the villages, it was another matter. Rentjens said his record was 17 in a single 150 kilometre stretch (a score which included three deaths at a single blow). When I remonstrated feebly, Rentjens explained that this was a public service, not an act of cruelty. The more stray dogs that could be exterminated, the less rabies there would be.

It was a remark I came to appreciate a few weeks later when I was bitten by a dog while walking through some village in the bush. I had been sufficiently deterred by the prospect of 24 jabs in the stomach on consecutive days with a probably dirty needle to conclude that, no, the dog wasn't rabid but was just some household pet which had taken a fancy to my

trouser-leg. But it was a nasty decision to have to take. Over
the next several weeks, as I moved from country to country,
I wondered whether the dreaded symptoms of rabies—hydro-
phobia, paralysis, dementia—would appear. If they do appear,
of course, it is already too late. The man to consult then is not a
doctor, but a lawyer.

Belefougou is a training centre for the whole Atacora region.
The peasants are offered land to cultivate. They are offered
animals and implements so that they may learn the techniques
of ploughing. 'But,' says Rentjens, 'tools are never a gift to
the farmers. They are always reimbursed. Now I make 15
million CFA francs of *recettes*. We are building the tools locally,
but it is difficult to build the plough-shares. We scrounge old
leaf-springs from cars and forge them into what we need. The
golden rule is "standardize, standardize". There are only two
kinds of bolt we use, eight millimetres and 40 millimetres. When
a farmer wants a cart, we give him timber and iron to take to
his local blacksmith and we train the blacksmiths ourselves in
the centre to follow a model.'

The main problem, Rentjens believes, is the lack of credit.
'Normally, we won't give credit unless the farmers are organized in "groupements". The "groupement" applies for fertilizers
and implements as well as for cotton to plant. We believe in the
co-operative approach. For us the object is to give value to the
earth. Some of these foreign companies come in and say to the
farmer "grow cotton and we will pay you such and such". They
don't tell the farmer about the need for fertilizer and a proper
system of rotation. They have no interest in the long-term
viability of the soil, or in what the farmer will do for a living
once the fertility of his land is exhausted through growing
cotton for the company year after year. The CFDT, for example,
which is the big French company operating in Dahomey, will
simply go elsewhere once it has finished with Dahomey. But
the Dahomeans themselves cannot go elsewhere.'

As far as Rentjens is concerned, the most exciting prospect
is meat production. 'We tell the farmer, "if you want to sell
your cattle, you can keep the younger ones and fatten them,
and then sell them." You have to have a marketing organization.
If the farmer is to receive a fair price, he has to avoid the

middleman. I'm trying to set up a butcher's shop in Cotonou to handle the animals direct. Of course, you can't sell pig-meat in the same shop as cow-meat. If you don't know the problem, you can make a mistake and blow up the whole business. 70% of the population in the North is Mohammedan.'

Apart from his other activities with 'animal traction' or 'culture attelée', as it is known in French, the government of Dahomey has put Rentjens in charge of a cattle fattening scheme. Some twenty miles from Parakou he has a corral with several hundred head of cattle. The night Koerber and I arrived in Parakou, there had been some trouble with an elephant. Jan Rentjens explained the problem:

'We had 400 cattle in one of the pens and an elephant sniffing around outside. The animals were disturbed and our boys, the boys I keep on guard at the corral, were frightened. They didn't want to stay in case the elephant came back. I have to explain to them there's nothing to worry about. It's only an elephant.'

Next night the elephant returns and stampedes the cattle so that 200 of the fattening steers are lost to the bush. Rentjens and I visit the corral early the following morning. We find that all the boys have run away except one who hid up a tree. We discover him lying on the ground with an injured back. But the injury had nothing to do with the elephant. He had fallen out of the tree, in fear and exhaustion, several hours after the elephant had left. Now he was waiting for the witch-doctors, 'les sorciers', to come and make him better.

My third morning in the Hotel Routier at Parakou, I am woken at five o'clock by Rentjens. He bangs on the door and I jump out of bed to find him, in white shorts and shirt and a big gun over his shoulder, standing like a ghost outside. He says he believes the animal may have returned a third night running and that we may catch it red-handed.

It is still dark, but there is a moon. We drive without head-lights through the bush, stopping to listen from time to time. The road degenerates into a track and the track into a path as we near the corral. The Peugeot crunches against trees and undergrowth. Apart from the noise of our own passage, we hear only birds and mosquitoes—a full-throated dawn chorus.

There is no sign of any lurking elephant, though broken-down fences and uprooted trees tell a clear enough story.

Rentjens says that before he can persuade his people to come back to the corral, he must track down the beast and kill it. The 'sous-préfet' has already given an authorization. But that won't be the end of the matter. They will need to slaughter some sheep and some chickens and indulge in 'some other little bits of sorcery' before the boys at the corral will feel completely reassured. Quite apart from this, he has to find 200 cows somewhere in the bush. God knows where. By now, they are probably scattered to the four winds.

We are back at Rentjens' house in time for breakfast. For a man who has lost half his herd, he seems remarkably cheerful. He shovels out a plateful of fried eggs and sausages and turns on the BBC Overseas News. The announcer tells us of 'Riots in Ulster as Bernadette Devlin begins her prison sentence'. Rentjens suddenly looks shaken, utterly compassionate. He puts his hand on my shoulder and shakes his head: 'Voilà, ca c'est un vrai problème!'

He drives me back to the Hotel when we have finished the meal. Charles Koerber and I have to be back in Cotonou by mid-afternoon. It is 8.20 a.m. and a car is going slowly through the streets addressing the early morning crowds through a loudspeaker mounted on its roof. Rentjens tells me it is making publicity for the National Lottery. The lottery is like football or the bull-fight. Even a poor boy can become a Pelé or a Cordobes. Even a poor boy can win the big one. The lottery provides hope and excitement, a chance—perhaps the only chance—of making a quantum leap into a different future.

Besides ourselves and the lottery-car, there is another vehicle on the streets that early morning. It is a fire-truck, bright-red with the words SERVICE INCENDIE painted on the side. It drives in front of us towards the roundabout in the centre of the town, then comes to a deliberate halt. The driver gets down from the cab and on to the back of the truck. He unwinds a hose and turns on the water to spray a small bed of flowers which has been planted in the middle of the circle.

'Yes,' says Rentjens, 'after all, there is progress.'

★

The principal river in Dahomey is known as the Oueme. In the old days—and in Africa the old days are never more than a few years ago—there was a great fresh-water lagoon where the river met the sea. Sand, constantly washed down the coast by the prevailing currents, had formed an isthmus, a barrier between salt and fresh water. The lagoon yielded a catch of some 20,000 tons of fish a year and supported a substantial population.

With the construction of the port at Cotonou (the same port I had observed my first day in the country from my room in the Hotel du Plage), the isthmus disappeared. No new sand was being washed down the coast to build up the barrier. Instead the current, its direction modified by the port and its breakwater, was diverting the sand out to sea. The disappearance of the isthmus was catastrophic. The salt water was able to penetrate into the lagoon with the result that the whole ecology was changed. When the Oueme river was in flood, and holding back the sea with its own water, it was a fresh-water lake. But in the dry season, it changed into an evil briny affair— neither sweet nor sour.

As far as the fish were concerned, the mixture was lethal. The catch fell to 3,000 tons. The people who lived on the lagoon found themselves without a livelihood. They migrated to the near-by cities of Cotonou and Porto Novo, looking for work. Politically volatile, angry to have been losers not gainers from the process of 'development' (if they understood the cause of their misfortune at all), they had a clear claim on the attention of the government. It was this fact, as much as anything else, which induced the government of Dahomey, together with the UNDP and the FAO, to give renewed attention to the Oueme Project.

The Oueme Project had in fact been kicking around for a good many years. The concept, like that of many agricultural schemes, was basically simple. Wide flood-plains extended at either side of the Oueme river. Sometimes this land was inundated; at other times it was not. There was other land, still low-lying, which was not flooded but which nevertheless benefited from the proximity of the river in the sense of being readily irrigable. Grow food on the flood-plains and on the adjacent land, feed people (the Oueme valley is one of the most populous regions in Dahomey), create employment in the valley and

ancillary employment in the towns, and you may find you have
made a giant leap forward on the road to self-sufficiency.

But, if the concept was simple, the execution was complex.
There were studies and more studies, first by one firm, then
by others. There were studies of the studies. The people of the
Oueme valley grew sick and tired over the years of seeing the
well-fed experts arrive with their theodolites to measure the
contours of the plain and the slope of the land and ask questions
of such intricacy that they could scarcely understand their
meaning, let alone answer them intelligently. Finally, they said
'Enough of this bally-hoo. Put up or shut up.' Or words to that
effect. If they saw another surveyor in their vicinity, they said
they would have him for breakfast. And they probably meant it.

It was this kind of reaction, amongst others, that finally
convinced the government and the aid-giving agencies that the
time for action had come. They had talked a good game. Now
they had to deliver. In January 1968, the Oueme project was
declared operational. In the event this was a meaningless declaration. The project as formulated had two fundamental
objectives: first, to find new land to grow rice on; second, to
persuade the farmers in the valley to switch from maize to rice.
At the start, both objectives seemed unattainable.

Part of the problem was that, in spite of all the surveys that
had been made, it turned out that a far higher percentage of the
land in the valley was already owned or cultivated than had
originally seemed the case. Property in these parts of Africa
is a strange business. Rules and customs of land tenure vary
from country to country and even from village to village. Sometimes it is a question of going to the chief with a bottle of gin
and a pregnant wife and saying 'Look, chief, I need a spot more
land'. So he looks around and says 'All right, you can have
that patch of ground over there among the mango trees. But
you can't have the fruit, mind you, because the trees don't go
with the land. They go with someone else's piece of land two
miles down the path.' Sometimes ownership is established by
use. Sometimes there is no ownership at all: all land is the
property of the tribe's ancestors, loaned temporarily to the
living on certain strict terms and conditions.

Not all of these complexities were apparent to the theodolite men. They had reported that only 40% of the valley was cultivated; in fact the figure seemed to be nearer 90% or 95% when the UNDP/FAO team at last started work in 1968 and 1969. It began to seem as though there might not be a project in the Oueme valley at all. And how could they persuade the farmer to change from maize to rice, when they couldn't even find enough spare land to make a pilot farm and demonstrate the virtues of growing rice under flood or irrigated conditions?

At this point, enter Grigori Lazarev. A tall energetic talkative man 34 years old, he spends his life travelling around the world on behalf of a strange institutional hybrid known as the FAO/IBRD Co-operative Programme. (Like many hybrids, the FAO/IBRD Co-operative Programme tends to outyield traditional varieties. Based in Rome and forming a division of FAO itself, though it is supported to the extent of 75% by the World Bank, the Co-operative Programme is concerned to identify and 'appraise' projects suitable for financing by the World Bank and other capital-supplying institutions. It does a good job and must be reckoned, on results alone, one of the most successful performers in the whole UN system.)

Though French, Lazarev lives in Rome. He is by training a sociologist-cum-economist, a rare breed in the world of international banking where sociologists have a habit of being suppressed at birth. He told me he became interested in Oueme a year or two previously, when he was in Dahomey on some other work for FAO.

'The project was in a desperate state. They had no land, nothing to do. They didn't know where to look. There was one possibility and that was to clear some of the old canals which had been blocked up years ago and drain some land that way. But the engineers said we could do nothing without a detailed topographical survey. And that would take months, if not years. We couldn't afford to wait. The people in the valley wouldn't stand for it.

'I went into the villages. I found some of the old people. I asked: "Do you know how to clear the canals?" Well, they thought about it and when they came back to me, they said: "We do not ourselves know how to clear the canals but maybe we know people, the very old people, who still know how to do it." I said "Find them and try." My maxim is always: Follow the farmer's wisdom. One must be extremely subtle. One must learn every day. Only after three years experience with the peasants should one say "this is what we will do".

'There was a fantastic result. In 15 days the land was completely drained. This is a very good instance of the farmer's wisdom. We had enough land to begin rice cultivation.'

The first year they drained 100 hectares of which 65 was planted to rice. They planned to drain 150 hectares the next and 500 the year after that. At the end of three or four years, they expected to be up to 1,800 hectares. But success was creating new problems.

'Even though the land was flooded and useless,' said Lazarev, 'it still belonged to someone. When the landowners see the value of the rice-crop, they want to take the land back again. There is strong pressure from the land-owners and also pressure from the animists. The land-owner puts a palm-branch in the fields. Apparently, this frightens people away. The Project Administration has to go and remove the palm-branch.'

This was why the Administration of the Oueme Project was at the moment pressing the government to publish a decree, an 'arrêtée' relating to land tenure in the Oueme valley. They wanted to take a flexible approach. The arrêtée would establish that, where land was not being worked, it could go to a man who was prepared to work it. After a certain period of time, the owner would be given the option of taking over his own land. If he chose to take it over, he had to work it himself. In that case, compensation would be paid to the previous tenant. If he failed to work it, the land would be forfeit. Ultimately, the techniques of drainage and irrigation developed in the pilot project might be applied all over the Oueme Valley.

Most of the villages in the Oueme Valley are to be found on rising ground mid-way between the river itself and the low plateau which encloses the valley on either side. However, along the river itself is a strip of land which is higher than the normal level of the plain. Taking advantage of this fact, groups and sub-groups of the Oueme people have settled next to the waters. Their houses are built on stilts, so as to be protected from the seasonal floods. The cattle too, when the waters rise, are fetched in and tethered on pallets which are also constructed on the top of tall stilts. The villagers go out in their boats across the flooding water to cut fodder, bring it back and feed it to the cattle as they stand on the high pallets. (This must be one of the earliest examples of zero grazing.)

These people are traders, plying back and forth between the river and the villages on the slope of the plateau. And they are fishermen, a favoured technique being to dig a hole in the ground which is then swamped by the rising of the river. When the waters fall, they go out to see if anything has been left behind in the hole.

Grigori Lazarev had lived for several weeks in the village of Mitro a year or so previously. This was the time when he was engaged in the great drainage project and he had felt it necessary to be permanently on hand to supervise and to exhort. He had become firm friends with the people of the village and went back to visit them whenever his travels took him to Dahomey. What he learned in Mitro, from people he knew, told him a great deal about the feelings of the Oueme people as a whole towards the UNDP/FAO project and towards possible future developments in the valley.

I went with him one day. We drove off the plateau in our jeep, down through the tall trees of the forest until the land began to open out ahead of us. This was the Oueme plain. Now a virgin swampy tract it would, if the project was successful, blossom with rice. Where the water rose too deep for the normal irrigated varieties, they would plant floating rice—a plant whose stalk grew as the waters rose. When the time came, the farmers would come out in their boats. They would harvest the ear and cut down the straw to build paths of straw through the waters so that they could work on foot in the fields as well as by boat. What we were able to see that morning was simply the first experiments, a few acres of greenery, a few progressive farmers already enthused with the new possibilities.

We sit in the house of the customary chief of Mitro village. It is a concrete house, not a mud house, as befits a man of his status. We are surrounded by a plenitude of children. The chief offers us beer, which we refuse. We have not come to drink the old man's beer. One of the women pours water

Dr. Norman Borlaug, winner of the 1970 Nobel Peace Prize,
examines grains at the International Maize and Wheat
Improvement Centre (CIMMYT) near Mexico City (*see p.*5)

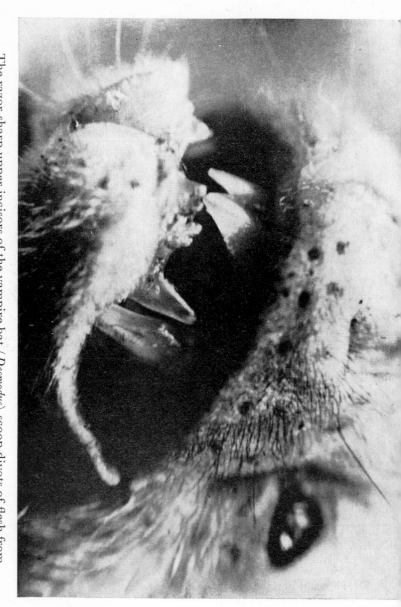

The razor-sharp upper incisors of the vampire bat (*Desmodus*) scoop divots of flesh from its victim (*see p.23*)

Photo: FAO

(*Above*) A well drilled by
SUDENE in a drought-stricken
area of north-east Brazil (*see p.*59)

Photo: *FAO*

(*Left*) An irrigation channel at
the Benedouro experimental
farm in the San Francisco River
basin, north-east Brazil (*see p.*64)

Photo: *UNO*

(*Left*) A shrimper unloads shrimps from the hold of a trawler at Puerto El Triumfo, El Salvador (*see p.*32)

Photo: UNO

(*Below*) A fisherman mends his net in one of the several thousand new fishing villages which have sprung up around Volta Lake (*see p.*82)

Photo: FAO

(*Left*) 'They dig wells and draw water' (*see p.* 104). A co-operative farm near Save, Dahomey

Photo: UNO

(Right) A 10000-ton grain silo, one of the biggest in India, at Hapur, Uttar Pradesh. The target of 'self-sufficiency in food-grains' is within reach (*see p.*185)

Photo: FAO

The 'green revolution' in action . . . 'the young progressive Punjabi farmer' (*see* p.178)

Photo: *COI London*

Government of Thailand is rehabilitating the irrigation network' (*see p.*194)

Photo: FAO

'There are night-schools in the villages all over the country' (*see p.*208)

Photo: UNO

Rafael Salas, Executive Secretary of the Philippines Cabinet and author of the 'rice miracle' (*see p*.189), seen here (first from left) inspecting rice harvest in Camarines Sur province, Philippines.

Photo: UNO

instead and we in turn pour it (or at least most of it, for we are not anxious to take too copious a draught) on the floor in a libation to the spirits of the place. There are three faded photographs on the wall, ornately framed. One of them shows a woman, ancient indeed, sitting stiffly beneath an umbrella which is being held up over her head by some unseen hand. Perhaps it is the Chief's mother.

The first few minutes of our talk are spent on small politenesses. The Chief tells Lazarev, in his engaging idiosyncratic French, how happy he and all the people of Mitro are to see him return to the village. Lazarev replies that he is certainly happy to be back and wishes he could stay longer but unfortunately he has to catch the plane to Rome that afternoon. This puzzles the chief slightly. He remembers that the last time Lazarev was in Mitro, his home was in Paris not Rome.

'Oh,' he says, 'so now you are an Italian!'

Lazarev replies that no, he is not an Italian; he merely lives in Italy. But the distinction between residence and nationality is hard to make. The talk moves on.

The Chief tells Lazarev that what they did with the drains had a big effect on the whole region. Lazarev in turn says he wants to discuss with the chief the question of the *arrêtée*, which they are now in the process of drafting. He wants to test the Chief's reaction, to see if he thinks the idea is realistic and what problems there will be.

In principle, the Chief favours the scheme. But he is worried about the political aspect. He explains that he personally, in the village of Mitro, faces a difficult situation. A former minister of the government, who still has important influence, originally came from Mitro and, now that he has seen the big developments in the Oueme valley and the good rice prospects, has returned to the village. This Minister, or former Minister, is laying claim to the Chief's own title as Head of the village, a title which he inherited from his father and which his father inherited before him. What is more, the Minister has laid claim to all the lands and wants to have his title to them officially inscribed. The Chief thinks that the *arrêtée* will encounter opposition in the government, incited by this former Minister and by landowners who feel similarly threatened.

E

This is not a matter which can be resolved this morning. Perhaps it can never be resolved. Politics lie at the root of everything. All development schemes must take politics into account. What happens in the Oueme valley depends as much on the interplay of personality and faction as it does on the technical possibilities for the production, marketing and distribution of rice.

After our talk had been going on for about half an hour, someone came to the door to announce that the 'sous-préfet' was on his way to the village. It is obviously time for us to leave. We go outside. The Chief quickly changes into his full tribal uniform and rejoins us. We give him a ride down into the village square where we meet the 'sous-préfet' coming in the opposite direction in an official Land Rover of the Dahomey Government. The Chief leaves our vehicle for the other. He, and the 'sous-préfet' (old order confronting the new) exchange bows and drive off together.

Lazarev and I spend a few more minutes in the village of Mitro. Looking back, I can remember the scene vividly. A circle of huts set amid the palm-trees; boys playing in the dirt; a path leading off down towards the plain; our United Nations car with its blue medallion parked next to the open stalls where cloth and food and small useful articles of various descriptions are being sold; a building with three fetishes depicting the humiliation of the enemies of Mitro; another building, its roof crumbling, which contains the long tom-tom which summons men to festivals or war; a goat; a bicycle. What, I wonder, will the village of Mitro look like ten years from now, when the Oueme Project is in full swing. It will have changed certainly. Will the changes be for the better? I am inclined to think so. It seems to be a scheme which fits quite naturally into its context.

*

On the way back from Parakou to Cotonou, Charles Koerber and I stopped in Savé to have lunch with a Frenchman, Monsieur Martin, who ran the affairs of a French tobacco company, CAITA, which operated in that part of Dahomey. Monsieur Martin explained his work to us. The company gives the tiny red-brown tobacco grains to the farmers. The farmers take what they grow to market, the loose leaves of tobacco folded into panniers. CAITA representatives come to the market and buy the tobacco at prices which range from 40 to 80 CFA francs per kilo. It is brought back to CAITA headquarters at Save where it is sorted and stacked for drying and fermentation.

Martin took us round the sheds. He employed about 120 girls altogether, mostly about 14 or 16 years old. They worked bare-breasted in the heat, lifting, sorting, measuring, rotating the stacks to ensure an even temperature. Once the tobacco is fermented, it goes to the grading shed. Then it is packed in burlap boxes and shipped. Eight hundred and fifty tons of Dahomey tobacco were sold in 1969, 500 tons in Accra and the rest in France. No home-grown tobacco is sold as cigarettes in Dahomey. The government receives more revenue by placing high duties on imports.

M. Martin and his Ghanaian wife fed us royally. The French know how to live, abroad as well as at home. I never expected to drink wines and cognac or smoke such good cigars so far from 'civilization'. We sat and listened to Martin talk about Africa.

'If one's honest,' he said, 'one has to admit that these countries have no chance of ever catching up with Europe, let alone America. What is their advantage in production? Cotton? The US can grow cotton cheaper. Maize? The French would laugh at the yields we get here, even with fertilizer. Oil-palms? Everyone is growing oil-palms now, even in South America. Maybe these countries can raise some cattle where the land is high enough to avoid the tsetse. But, au fond, the best they can hope for is a modest competence. The best way to achieve this is with a viable subsistence agriculture.'

A hundred miles or so before Cotonou, we stopped at Abome, site of one of the ancient African kingdoms. Perhaps 'ancient' is the wrong word. In fact, if not in theory, there is still a king of Abome—or at least someone revered as such. There is a king in Ouida as well, and two in Porto Novo (the old capital), one for the Day and one for the Night. Sometimes, you can see these high personages, carried on their thrones along the streets beneath a canopy of umbrellas and capable of being addressed only through their appointed spokesmen.

Dahomey, as a kingdom, goes back to 1625 A.D. Literally, the name 'Da-ho-me' means 'on the belly of Da'. Da, king of a small state, was killed by Ouegbadja, a more powerful neighbour and buried in the foundations of Ouegbadja's new palace at Abome. Hence the phrase 'on the belly of Da'. It became apparent, as we were shown around the palace, that Da was not the only sufferer. All the mortar used in the construction of the external wall had been mixed with blood instead of water and the royal tea-set was fashioned from human skulls.

The same palace at Abome contains the thrones of the later kings. They were evidently a blood-thirsty lot. One would not have believed, until one has seen the graphic art of this ancient kingdom, that there are so many ways to kill a man. Heads were being lopped off all over the place; bodies were dismembered in the most macabre way. Bows and arrows, spears, muskets—anything would serve, blunt or sharp, as long as it could pierce the skin or crush the skull.

The last king formally to occupy the royal throne was King Ghezou. He died in 1910. It was he who introduced the oil-palm to Dahomey, planting it so as to have something to trade with the West.

Back once more in Cotonou, looking out for the last time at the trees and the ocean, it struck me as ironic that the oil-palm, so much a symbol of this humid land, is about as native to it as rubber is to Malaya.

3

I FLEW overnight to Nairobi *en route* for Dar es Salaam. We were delayed in Nairobi (one of the aircraft's tyres being punctured by a stone on the runway as it was taxying for take-off) and so I had a chance to go through the East African papers while we waited in the transit lounge. The big story was the Tan-Zam railway. A delegation from Tanzania had been in Peking and the Chinese had come forward with a large and generous offer of credit. The papers also reported that Bruce McKenzie, the Kenyan Minister for Agriculture and the only white man in Kenyatta's cabinet, was ill in London. The paper proposed the 'Africanization of Bruce McKenzie', which apparently meant handing over his portfolio to a native Kenyan.

In fact, the whites are going out all over Africa. A few hundred miles south of Nairobi, the small town of Mwanza (which lies on the Tanzanian side of Lake Victoria) was preparing that very evening to celebrate the final departure of the official British 'presence'. The British Council was closing down.

It was a strange and moving occasion. I had not come to Mwanza to attend the ceremony. I had not known that there was to be any ceremony. But the bar of the Hotel Mwanza was full of men with flushed faces saying that they'd better have another before the show started, so I realized quickly that something was afoot. Towards eight, the bar emptied and a roisterous contingent of 'expatriates' (as the breed is known in United Nations jargon), headed for the last time for the British Council building.

By the time I arrived a film-show was already in progress. More than 100 people—at least half of them Africans—were gathered in the court-yard of the building; a screen had been fixed to the far wall and, upon the screen, the last flickering symbols of an alien culture were projected.

The British Council had exercised great care in making its

presentation for this historic night. I arrived in the middle of what was clearly a fashion-film, depicting the rise and fall of the British bust and the British hemline. Somehow the choice seemed inevitable. Butterflies are imported from England so that children in East African class-rooms can learn the biology of the Cabbage White. Ovid is still a sixth-form subject. The English Sunday papers can be, and are, bought on the streets of Dar the same day. Africans stay up all night, listening to the results of British General elections. Why not a film about British fashion?

Attention wanders as one style succeeds another and as the commentator matches his voice to the period. 'The corsets now were short at the top and lower over the hips . . . Edward was dead and George reigned in his stead. London became the brightest capital in Europe. Then the curtain fell.' The famous Kitchener poster flashes onto the screen. 'Your country needs you.' The Africans in the audience laugh at the huge moustache and at the finger which points at them in the darkness.

The commentary goes on. 'So many were killed. The song spoke of "two million surplus women". Inevitably a certain craziness followed the Great War. . . . But now prosperity led to senseless abandon and the clothes were made to match. Men and women all over England are dancing the Charleston. Charleston! Charleston! Cha-ar-ar-ar-arleston!' But then—yes, wait for it!—'the curtain fell again. Kerplonk! Boom-boom go the guns of the Second World War.'

Fortunately, a few seconds later the shadows lift and, following the return of Mr Winston Churchill for his last period of office, controls are cast aside. Fashion takes on a new abandon, a new release. We are about to plunge headlong into the Sack and the Empire Line when the screen is lit up by the headlights of a motorcycle and the sound-track drowned out by the noise of its engine. A despatch rider strides down the aisle through the centre of the audience and hands over a message to a man who is sitting immediately beside me.

He is about 35 years old, with dark hair and thick-rimmed black spectacles. It turns out that he is the retiring Director of the British Council in Mwanza. This is his party.

Doug Pickett, representing the official British 'presence' on the Tanzanian shore of Lake Victoria, rises to his feet with the message still in his hand. It is the signal for general movement. The whites, who have come in from the highways and by-ways of Northern Tanzania for the occasion, follow Pickett into the library which abuts on to the court-yard. The shelves of the library are bare; the books have either been sold or distributed to other British Council libraries in Tanzania. But though the shelves are bare, the cupboard is not. In a moment, the whites have drinks in their hands, by no means the first of the evening. The gin and the Scotch has been flowing freely for a good few hours on this famous day. The blacks, who cluster together at the far end of the room, seem to prefer beer and there has obviously been plenty of that as well.

Pickett, whose next posting will be in the Middle East if he survives his departure from this one, calls for silence. At this, there is an outbreak of cheering—a kind of baying sound—which resounds through the sleepy town of Mwanza to signify the mighty thrash which is gathering momentum.

'I have here in my hand,' begins Pickett, in the time-honoured way, 'a telegram which has been sent to us all at the British Council here in Mwanza from . . .' But they do not let him finish. There is a great upwelling noise, like hounds before a cornered stag. Glasses are raised and emptied, or raised and tossed to the ground.

'God bless her!'

'The Queen!'

'Rhubarb!'

'The Queen! God bless her indeed!'

Suddenly I am punched in the tummy and pushed firmly against the wall. 'You going back to England?' The voice belongs to a middle-aged white doctor who has come in from Ukiriguru, about twelve miles out of Mwanza.

'Yes,' I say.

'Well, then, you take this message back. And bloody well remember it. You tell Mr Heath, and Mr Powell too, when you next see them, that up there in Ukiriguru we celebrated the Tory victory with a champagne party that lasted two days. You tell him that.'

I have time to talk to Doug Pickett. I asked him what he

thought the occasion meant to the non-British who were present. I expected some sort of elegiac response but Pickett replied, frankly enough: 'A booze-up. That's what it means. Lure them in with drinks. That's always been one of the British Council's most unfailing strategies.'

I have time to talk to Les Holdgate, a red-faced cheerful man who, as I understand it, is in real life responsible for the town's electricity supply. He says he lent Pickett the Mwanza Yacht Club's Union Jack, so that the British Council could lower the flag ceremonially for the last time. He adds: 'Have to have it back by Trafalgar Day.' Les Holdgate is Commodore of the Club. Its members are a hardy breed. Apart from the hazard of drink, there is the danger of contracting bilharzia as they mess about in their boats on the lake. These are men who might have blood as well as beer in their urine.

Pickett is calling for silence once more. The evening, it appears, is not yet at an end. It has scarcely begun. The next item of entertainment is, ladies and gentlemen, another film. Tonight, yes, for positively the last time, the British Council in Mwanza, Tanzania—or, should I say for the benefit of all the old hands who are gathered here tonight, Mwanza, Tanganyika—more baying and braying—is proud to present the famous classic . . . pause . . . pause . . . GENEVIEVE! And a few who have had too many burst into song as the lights go out once more on the courtyard and the curtain (metaphorically speaking) rises again for this, the supreme moment of British culture. 'Oh Genevieve!' they sing, 'sweet Genevieve!' Then, with gusto, memory for detail fading with the years, 'ti-tum-ti-ti, ti-tum, ti-ti-tum!'

The last recollection I have of that evening in Mwanza is of Kenneth More, pipped at the post by Dirk Bogarde, attempting to cross Waterloo Bridge with his wheels locked in a tramtrack headed the wrong way.

★

But, even if the British are leaving Tanzania, others are filling the void. Bilateral aid from Britain is being replaced with multilateral aid given through the United Nations.

I was still sitting over breakfast in the Mwanza Hotel,

recovering from the night before, when Professor Yuri Vishnyakov arrived to find me. Vishnyakov, a Russian about 45 years
old, was in charge of the UNDP/FAO/UNESCO Adult Literacy Project which had its headquarters in Mwanza. I had, I
must confess, only the vaguest idea of what Adult Literacy
meant before I arrived in Tanzania. I had even less idea of
how one could make an 'Adult Literacy Project'. Most of the
projects I had encountered so far had clearly quantifiable
components like tractors and cement and fertilizer, all of which
were mysteriously termed 'inputs'. The fact that the official
descriptions of the projects in question were generally rather less
precise about what the 'outputs' were meant to be was a minor
consideration.

Yuri Vishnyakov, over a period of several days, made good
this deficiency in my education. He was a man who believed
profoundly in the concept of adult education in general, and
in its application to Tanzania in particular. His enthusiasm
resulted, I believe, in part from the fact that he himself was a
relatively new recruit to this field of work. Only a year or two
previously he had been Editor-in-Chief of the State Educational
Publishing House in Moscow, an enterprise which published
5,000 titles and approximately 250 million volumes a year.

More or less overnight, Vishnyakov had decided to throw up
his job. There was a danger, even in Moscow (or perhaps
especially in Moscow), that life for a man in his position could
become too predictable, too bourgeois. He felt the call of the
wild. But instead of sailing a coracle round the Horn or trekking
overland to Ulan Bator, he joined the UNDP/FAO/UNESCO
project in Mwanza. His title at first had been Book Production
Adviser. In January 1970, he had become Chief Technical
Advisor and *de facto* controller of the Project. 'I used to have
1,000 people under my control' was his wry comment. 'Now
I have five.' But he looked as though he thrived on the change.

The Project area covered four regions in the vicinity of Lake
Victoria. Each region has three or four districts and each
district has three or four divisions. They had selected one
division in each region for 'sub-pilot activities'.

'We have had a big training programme,' said Vishnyakov,
'we have trained 1,000 teachers. This year, we have done

E *

cotton, banana, fishing, homecraft and sometimes we have taught rice. It depends on the primer. Next year, 1971, there should be about 4,000 classes with 100,000 students. This means that we will be covering the four districts as fully as possible. Our aim is to change the illiteracy rate from 85% to 25%.

'Functional literacy means integrating literacy with vocational training. The main importance from my point of view is to make them literate in such a way that they feel the necessity to read more about farming. The problem is lack of reading material, lack of interest. We see them lapse back into illiteracy very quickly. But when the farmer learns step by step how to grow cotton, all the technical details about how to apply fertilizer, how to make insecticides, how to pick cotton, how to store cotton, how to sell cotton—then you have a chance of interesting him.

'The course is arranged in three six-month periods. June to November, the dry season, is for class teaching. November to April or May is the rainy season. There are no classes then, but there are practical demonstrations in the field. We have a special booklet for teachers on how to conduct demonstrations. Then, from June to November, we have another series of classes which includes two weeks of refresher courses.

'The classes meet three times a week for two-hour sessions. After 18 months we hope to be able to consider them as functional literates. At the end of 1970 we will evaluate progress. Certainly there are problems. The quality of the teachers is one of them. We have 1,500 teachers at the moment, of which 450 are primary school teachers. A lot of the other teachers are primary school drop-outs. This may sound unpromising but it is in fact one of the ways we can find manpower to do the job. We expect to have 3,500 to 4,000 teachers next year, of which about 1,000 will be primary school teachers.

'There are other problems, too. Drop-out rates, attendance, the irregularity of the sessions—all these make our work difficult. Another thing is that there has been little comparative international experience. We can't draw any conclusions yet about the validity of the approach, the concept. We are going to make an analysis of one sub-pilot area in the Mara region.'

Vishnyakov said that one of his main concerns was with the

follow-up programme. He was planning a list of follow-up books and pamphlets (the Project wrote, designed and printed most of the educational material it used), dealing not just with agriculture but with a whole variety of topics such as co-operatives, rural construction, civics (which Vishnyakov explained meant politics, local government and TANU, the Tanzania African National Union), nutrition and so forth. His idea was that UNESCO and UNDP should help the government establish a radio transmitter to serve the whole lake region. They would use it for in-service training for teachers and supervisors; to support the teaching programme in the class-rooms or in the fields; and to support the follow-up programme, the broadcasts being geared to the follow-up books. He foresaw special follow-up groups, listening groups and discussion groups or both. Vishnyakov did not believe you could use radio in the abstract; you had to use it in conjunction with the literacy material. A survey had shown that most villages already had medium-wave receivers.

The distribution of this literacy material was a major diffi-culty. With only a few classes, the problem could be overcome. But where there were many classes (as he hoped there would be), it was impossible to distribute the books individually. They were now using community centres and the whole TANU net-work as a means of distribution. Each village had a literacy committee and each class had a class committee. There was a TANU leader for every ten houses. This was the framework, these were the people to involve, if you wanted to get your material to the right place at the right time.

'You can't use the Post Office system because in the bush there are very few Post Offices and in any case you don't get mail delivered to your door. You have to go in to pick it up, and people don't go in to pick it up unless they are expecting a letter. In any event, even if we did post the literacy material in Mwanza, it would probably never even leave the town.'

Besides his plans for radio, Vishnyakov said the project had started a rural newspaper which was being produced in each sub-pilot area. He showed me some copies of it. Each issue contained about three or four foolscap pages of stencilled material. Items of local news were mixed in with 'small ads'.

The objective was to interest people in the idea of reading itself, to acquaint them with the printed word.

The rural newspaper was one of the aspects of his Project which seemed to appeal to Vishnyakov the most. 'I want to make it a tool of motivation. I shall print news about who is the best farmer, who has grown the best crops. We will soon run a special page, printed in extra large letters, for neo-literates and semi-literates. In the time-table of the literacy classes, special hours are allotted for discussion of the things written in the rural newspaper.'

The Swahili language, perhaps more than any other, is based on syllables. Vishnyakov's principle was to start with known words learnt parrot fashion, then to split them up into syllables, then to come to the construction of new words out of these known syllables. It was a new system of teaching.

'You are coming to the end of the book,' he said, showing me one of the primers and leafing through it, 'and still you can't find the alphabet. But here you have a table of syllables. From 120 syllables you can construct about 2,500 words. And this covers 85%—or thereabouts—of the communication needed for reading and writing in every language, including English. It's much more difficult for them to make up words from individual letters. It helps, of course, that in Swahili there's no difference between spelling and pronunciation.'

In a quiet unspectacular way, the UNDP/FAO/UNESCO Project is a controversial one. There are those who argue that, in seeking to promote functional literacy in the rural areas, you will achieve neither better farmers nor a higher degree of literacy. They argue that, if you want to make good farmers, you don't need to teach them how to read. If you want to make people literate, there are better ways than boring them to death with information about cotton and bananas and fertilizer which may be of dubious relevance to their immediate situation. They go on to maintain that if, by some stroke of luck, you do happen to create a neo-literate farmer, that is as good as giving him a one-way ticket to the big city. Once a man is 'educated', he no longer thinks of himself as a farmer. 'Educated' people, everyone knows, live in cities and sometimes run big fast cars at government expense.

The Tanzanian experiment, when it is properly evaluated, will no doubt shed some light on this controversy. It is too early at the moment to predict results. The programme is only now gathering momentum. It is hard to believe that, in a country where 95% of the population still lives in the rural areas and where production is still largely in the hands of adults, an intensive programme of adult education based on agricultural training will not make some impact on overall agricultural output.

But the importance of the Tanzanian experiment goes beyond this. Literacy can be seen as a tool to change men's minds and attitudes. It opens the eyes and broadens the perspective. All sorts of improvements—in nutrition, in health standards, in environmental sanitation, in contraception—are possible when a certain degree of literacy has been reached among a population. The significance of what Professor Vishnyakov is doing is that, conceivably, Tanzania may be able to reap the benefits of education while avoiding some of the costs—such as rural/urban polarization and the growth of the 'educated unemployed'—which in so many other parts of the developing world have seemed an inevitable concomitant of development.

My last afternoon in Mwanza, Vishnyakov and myself and two of his colleagues on the Project drove out into the bush to try to see some classes in operation. Vishnyakov said, optimistically, that we would see a good many classes along the route. A friend of his had come not long before and they had observed a dozen or more sessions in three miles of driving. (With Serengeti so close, it was understandable that Vishnyakov should use the language of the naturalist or big-game hunter, referring to the literacy class as though it was a species of wild animal.)

In the event, we were unlucky. We visited several likely spots where, according to the Project schedule, literacy classes should have been in progress at that very moment. The first three or four classrooms in the bush were totally deserted, only the blackboard and a pile of primers remaining to tell the tale of absenteeism. Finally, towards evening, a hundred miles or so from Mwanza, we came to a hut set in a clearing in the bush and went inside. Like the others, it was empty. No functional literates were being fashioned from rough unpromising material. But while we stood there a youngish man pedalled up on a bicycle, wearing a broad-brimmed hat against the sun and a wide smile.

Through an interpreter, Vishnyakov questioned him. Where was the teacher? The man smiled and said with evident pride that he was the teacher. Then where was the class? At this the man smiled again, an even broader smile, and said: 'Saba saba, sir. They all home sleeping. They drink too much. Maybe they come back class next week, maybe next month. Maybe they come when their heads feel better.'

So I said: 'What does "saba saba" mean?' Vishnyakov explained that "saba" was Swahili for "seven", and that "saba saba" meant the seventh day of the seventh month, or July 7, which is the day of the Great Tanzanian National Festival. All the students were still recovering from the festivities. When I mentioned that, by my reckoning, July 7 was already a week ago, Vishnyakov lifted his shoulders and shrugged.

'Awa,' he said in his best Russian.

'And what does "awa" mean?'

' "Africa wins again." '

*

The traveller who arrives in Dodoma in the heart of the central region of Tanzania at the end of a protracted dry season is witness to a scene of devastation no less appalling, in its own way, than the aftermath of a cyclone or earthquake. We do not think in terms of deserts south of the Sahara, apart from the Kalahari itself. Yet the word 'desert' can be applied, almost accurately, at least at certain times of the year to this part of Tanzania. You can drive for miles through the bush without a sign of grass. The soil for the most part is bare and barren, ground-cover non-existent. If anything flourishes at all, it is the spiky green thorns which the people of the region use as hedges or wind-breaks, the ubiquitous acacia or other trees of the euphorbia family.

Between 1850 and 1963, the period for which records are available, famines occurred more often than not. The immediate cause of these famines was drought, the average annual rainfall in Dodoma district being 22 inches. On occasion, the drought has been made worse by the ravages of animals and pests. The area has been a constant recipient of emergency relief, so much so that those who live here have come to feel that their efforts at self-betterment are largely futile. Anything they can do, the government can do better.

This kind of nonchalance (or fatalism) is a deeply ingrained characteristic. The notion of thrift is relatively alien to the Gogo tribesmen who comprise a majority of the inhabitants of the region. In the old days, the District Commissioner would travel from place to place and say 'You here fill this grain-store, you there fill that one.' When the stores were filled, he would lock them and take away the key until the food was needed in some emergency. But the old days have gone and no-one has taken the District Commissioner's place. Instead they leave the maize in the field until they need it, with the result that the rats eat it before the people.

As for making hay, the idea is foreign to their nature. Besides, they like to burn the grass when it is dry, so that they can shoot the cane-rats with their bows and arrows as they, and other animals, run before the flames. They have fruit trees of course, but not so many. If a man cannot reach an orange from where he sits, he will cut the tree down rather than climb to get it. This tends to deplete the number of trees.

The combination of natural adversity with human inertia can result in suffering of appalling dimensions. The government is not always able or willing to provide timely and adequate relief. When the rains fail, people scratch around for roots and tubers. Each man, who knows the region, will have his own tale of hardship. I remember best what an FAO Range Ecologist, David Thornton, told me one evening as we sat at our camp-site in the bush, a hundred miles or so out of Dodoma.

He had arrived, he said, after driving up from Dar in the middle of the severest drought ever recorded for Dodoma. That evening three small children were brought into the town. They had been found, several miles outside Dodoma, eating grass by the road-side. 'The father had died,' Thornton said, 'and the mother had gone off three days before. The eldest, who was nine, apparently said to his brother and sister "let's walk in".

Well, they were fed with whatever was available and left to sleep with hundreds of others at the Dodoma railway station. Next day they were taken back to their village, but still their mother had not returned. Somebody gave a local missionary some money and asked him to look after them. What happened to them after that, nobody knows.'

Human beings die. Cattle die. The water-holes are dry. The stock can be seen in the last stages of emaciation clustered around reservoirs and drinking troughs supplied by bore-holes. When the rains do at last come, the appearance of the country-side changes overnight. The bushes sprout leaves and the bare ground produces a sudden dramatic growth of grasses and weeds. But the cattle often remain too weak, too emaciated to profit by this change in their surroundings. They suffer from intense scouring as they eat the softer vegetation, and can die of it.

For human beings the onset of the rains brings no instant release. A cow may eat in two or three days after the rain has fallen. A man, lacking a cow's capacity to digest cellulose and other fibres, must wait till he has grown a harvest. And if he has eaten out his seed-corn during the time of drought, this can be a long wait indeed.

But the ultimate cause of famine and disaster in central Tanzania is not drought, but cattle. However bare and empty it can seem, this is an over-populated land, at least as far as its animal load is concerned. A vicious circle is set up. Over-grazing destroys the ground-cover and leads to erosion. The rains, when they come, compound the damage. Not only are they notoriously unreliable; they vary considerably in length and intensity. Sometimes, they peter out before any crops can be harvested. At other times, they are so prolonged and heavy that they can wash seeds and plants out of the exposed sandy soils. The carrying capacity of water rises with the square of its velocity. The combination of wind and rain is lethal. Without good ground-cover to stabilize and protect the soil, the rain-drops will literally blast the earth away. The run-off is immense. Water, instead of being conserved as ground moisture, streams to the swamps where it eventually seeps or evaporates away, or else it flows down river-courses out of the area entirely.

Under these conditions, the ecological balance becomes still more precarious. Problems of cattle-overpopulation grow more acute without (necessarily) any rise in numbers. As with human populations, the key question is not density itself but the relationship between resources and the demands which are made on those resources.

The control and proper distribution of livestock is essential to the prosperity of the Dodoma region; if prosperity is not too extravagant a word. But this concept, so easy to set down on paper, in fact implies a social revolution among the cattle-owning tribes. To ask them to restrict the number of their cattle, however ecologically sound the reasoning may be, is like asking them to go to bed one night speaking Kigogo or Kisukuma and to wake up the next morning speaking a different language altogether.

Sociologists and anthropologists have, of course, spent years studying patterns of cattle-owning and kinship among tribes like the Gogo and Masai. Their conclusions very broadly are that cattle in this part of Tanzania, as in so much of Africa, are regarded by the peasant as a security factor and as a prestige factor. What matters is quantity, not quality. If a beast is paralytic and has to be carried past, no-one will care. As long as it draws breath, it will be valued.

The relationship between families is strengthened, so the sociologists and anthropologists aver, through the mechanism of the bride price and, for the most part, the bride price is a gift of cattle. If a daughter-in-law is unfaithful to her husband, or if she is lazy, the father-in-law (i.e. the man in whose house she resides following her marriage) may throw her out and ask her father for the cattle, the bride price, back again. As many as 60 cattle could have changed hands in the course of the transaction. Under these circumstances, cattle can be a very illiquid asset. How can a man reduce his herd through intelligent culling when in fact ownership of some part of that herd is predicated on the good behaviour of his daughter or daughters?

There is evidence to suggest that, of the ten million or so cattle in Tanzania, perhaps 60% are effectively illiquid. They cannot be used on a commercial basis. Either the bride-price relationship intervenes, or some other taboo precludes commercial exploitation. The Tanzanian short-horned cattle of

Zebu type for example, especially the older ones, can be regarded as holy.

Over the course of the years, numerous schemes have been tried to combat the constant recurrence of famine. In each case, the government has eventually been forced to distribute emergency relief. In 1964 the Range Development Act was passed. The hope was that at last progress would be made towards achieving a permanent solution to the problem.

Under the Act, the Ministry of Agriculture declared seven range development areas. Within each area a Range Commission was established. The members of the Commission include local farmers, local politicians, the regional water engineer, the Area Commissioner himself, etc. Their purpose is to encourage and approve the formation of ranching associations with a view to 'rationalizing' the production and management of cattle.

The procedure laid down by the Act for the formation of a ranching association is long and complex. The first step is the identification of a suitable area. The association can be established only where sufficient water is available to make it independent of the vagaries of the weather. In effect, this means that there must be enough water to maintain the irrigation of a small plot of some high-producing fodder crop, which can be cut and stored against the dry season, and—besides this—of another plot capable of growing (ideally) two crops per year suitable for human consumption. Large-scale irrigation being considered uneconomic, water sufficiency could be secured by the construction of small dams, valley tanks, deep stock ponds, contour ditches and collecting tanks, wells, underground reservoirs, bore-holes and so on.

Once an area has been identified, the next step is the creation of the association. All the people who live in the area of the prospective association come together and decide whether they are in favour of the idea or not. If 60% are in favour, the association can be formed. The Act allows for a three-month period for all those who voted against the association to change their minds and join after all. If they stay out, the association may charge them for any facilities it provides.

With the area identified and the association established, the quiet revolution is in theory well under way. Boundaries are fixed. There is no going out and no coming in. Quotas are also fixed. Each association, and each individual within an association, will run no more than the prescribed number of cattle. At the same time, the process of range improvement proceeds apace. The idea is to eliminate the main bottlenecks. The association will provide more water. It will provide better veterinary services including dips in the areas where tick-borne diseases are prevalent. Since cattle will no longer graze wherever and whenever they want to graze, the land will have time to recover and it should be possible to set aside some grazing for reserve. The wider introduction of perennial grasses and the intelligent use of legumes should lead to a general upgrading of pasture, even without the (expensive) application of fertilizer. Better management and disease control alone should raise production by 30% and permit the commercial off-take rate for cattle to increase from a level of 3% to 25% or 28%.

All this is only the beginning. If you grow more cattle, you have to be able to sell what you grow. This is a broad and complex question. I can best illustrate it by describing the hazardous journey the average Tanzanian cow has to undertake on its way from the tribal 'boma'—the square or circular enclosure in which it is kept at night—into the tummy of the consumer.

Imagine, for a moment, that this average Tanzanian cow is one of, say, twenty or thirty cows belonging to a Gogo family somewhere in the heart of Central Tanzania. The dry season being what it is in these parts, the cow tends to resemble— when at last the rains come—a clothes-horse with an old hide slung in loose folds over it. Even when the land begins to blossom with green, the cow does not profit as it might by the change. Its Gogo master, a lazy farmer at the best of times, forgets to let it out of the 'boma' till mid-morning sometimes and shoos it back in by four in the afternoon, so its grazing time is shaved at both ends.

If the cow is not one of the 60% 'illiquid' cows, i.e. beasts who are being kept for counting or, in the case of tribes like the Masai, drinking (the mixture of blood and urine is said to be specially potent), it may eventually be taken to market. Now this word 'market' conveys—to Western ears at least—the impression of a busy organized place where, through a host of small discrete transactions, an overall balance between supply and demand is achieved.

In Tanzania, it is another story. Our average Tanzanian cow may not actually enter a market at all. It may simply be pushed into a ring formed by a lot of people standing round in a circle or at best by a line of push poles riddled with insect damage. Here it is a prime candidate for East Coast fever. Amongst numerous diseases affecting livestock, East Coast fever is the biggest killer. It can kill 60% of a herd of cattle without really trying. It is transmitted by ticks which fasten on to the cattle and swell with blood to the size of a thumb-nail.

The market itself may be attended by any or all of the following sorts of dealer: local butchers buying stock for the local meat demand; itinerant traders buying stock to be transferred to cattle-deficient areas and secondary markets; and Tanganyika Packers, who take about 50% of the cattle coming on to the market in Tanzania and are owned 51% by the National Development Corporation, a Government enterprise, and 49% by Brooke Bond Liebig.

The average Tanzanian cow does not, I am afraid, command a high price. The Arab dealers for years drove a hard bargain and the Gogo herdsmen went home from market with barely enough to get drunk on. The government in recent months has decided to oust the Arab middlemen, on the grounds that they were dunning the farmer. Effectively, it has declared them *personae non gratae* and has designated the local district councils as its official purchasers at the auctions. But the district council buyers are people who have never seen cattle nearer than from the top of a bus. They fail to make a profit themselves and they fail to give a good price to the farmer. So the Arabs, who know the game, are coming back into it—buying the cattle and reselling them to the district council buyer to keep the government happy.

But, whatever the price, the beast is bought and sold. It is transferred from one owner to another. The next step in the long progress is the quarantine area. Foot-and-mouth is endemic in Tanzania. It is to be found all over the country. Besides the

A and O varieties, which are the European kind, they have a peculiarly Tanzanian strain which specially attacks the bones of the cattle.

It is the foot-and-mouth problem which principally prevents Tanzania from entering the high price export market for frozen and chilled beef. A country like Britain, whose policy is to slaughter all foot-and-mouth infected beasts (and this can include blood-lines which have been built up over a century), could only accept frozen or chilled meat from Tanzania if it were satisfied that the most rigorous standards of inoculation and quarantine were being applied.

The logistics of an effective quarantine operation in a country like Tanzania are formidable. Some FAO experts have estimated that you would need a 60-foot high double-fence (the two strands would have to be thirty feet apart to prevent cattle sniffing through) encircling an area of some 500 square miles. The cattle would need to be brought from the market into this quarantine area and vaccinated. The vaccination is both preventive and curative. If the cattle are already incubating the disease, the vaccination will bring it on. The mouth will blister and the hooves may drop off. If the cattle are not incubating the disease, the vaccination should provide effective immunity but the veterinary requirement of dealing with large numbers of cattle in this way is of course enormous.

Quarantine arrangements in Tanzania are many years away from this sort of refinement. The average Tanzanian cow may spend its two weeks in the holding ground while all the time other animals, not subject to quarantine or observation, are moving freely in and out of the area.

The next step is the rail journey to the coast. The cow is fed and watered before the journey. It may then spend three or three and a half days on the train moving slowly towards Dar es Salaam. The weight loss, through stress and tissue shrinkage, is considerable. There will have been no light refreshments on the train. At a point not far from Dar, the cow is off-loaded. It is watered and it rests and grazes for a minimum of 24 hours. It is checked for foot-and-mouth again, goes through a spray race and finally walks the last few miles to the slaughter-house, operated by Tanganyika Packers.

At the time I was there, they were killing at the rate of 568 beasts a night, or two bays of 284 beasts each. The first cow—let us assume so as to make this brief history complete that it is our 'average Tanzanian cow'—walks or is driven up the ramp to the 'knocking' or stunning box at exactly 9.45 p.m. The bottom of the box is metal. A man sits up on a chair above the beast. He has an electrode in his hand with which he touches the animal, completing the circuit so that the animal is stunned.

The reason the animal is stunned, rather than killed outright, is that the meat has to be 'halal'. It is sold in the Persian Gulf and in Tanzania itself where there are a good many Muslims. The Muslims insist that the animal should be still alive when its throat is cut. Though stunning does not make for a good bleed, it is still the path of humanity.

If all goes to plan, the meat is hoisted on to the bleeding rail. It bleeds there for ten minutes before it is dropped on to a flaying bed. Zebu beasts are favoured because the hump fits neatly into a slot as it lies on its back. The brisket is slit, the skin is removed from the shanks, before the animal moves on to the dressing rail. Here the hide is peeled away with an electric flaying machine. The carcass moves on to the depaunching table, the paunch is washed down the chute, opened up as it goes and the manure hosed away. The stomach goes through a hasher and a washer. In view of the high protein content, there is a vigorous trade in fresh stomachs. If it is not sold as fresh meat, it forms the basis of meat meal.

Each carcass moves along with its own head and all the other edible offals. Inspectors will make incisions in the lymph glands and in other organs and it is important for them to know which organs belong to which beast. The conveyor belt is like an overhead railway. The inspectors can operate the points so as to shunt any carcass they want to examine more closely into a detention or inspection bay.

At about this point in its progress, your average Tanzanian cow is just a skeleton. The bones are dried and crushed and made into bone meal. The hooves and horns are chopped off and made into hoof and horn meal and then, after further processing, into hydrolised protein which is otherwise known as package soup. The trimmers trim out the glands, blood clots, unwanted tissues and fat. The rest is trimmed out as red meat. This represents about 35% of the original live weight.

What happens next depends on whether the cow is destined for corned beef or stewing steak. Tanzania Packers have built their economy on corned beef. The Fray Bentos line takes all the best beef. Three Bulls takes the rest. The lower the quality of the meat, the more it needs to be minced. Once minced, it is dropped into tanks and cooked for 20 minutes. The meat comes up through the hoppers onto the plastic tables, still steaming. The girls go over it again to remove any more gristle and then turn it over into a mixing bowl where sodium nitrate (which gives the pretty pink colour to corned beef), salt, fat and a certain amount of water are added.

An empty can comes down a chute, the meat is pressed into it by a device known as a 'podging unit', and the clincher clinches the lid. The can goes into a vacuum sealer which rolls the lid on tight. This is a difficult technical job. It is easier to seal a round can than an oblong can. But consumers first became used to (South American) corned beef appearing in oblong cans and there is resistance to a change in shape. Finally the cans are sterilized in a retort, remaining there for two hours at a temperature of 113°C and eight pounds per square inch pressure. Most of the cans are pre-lithographed with the appropriate emblem, Fray Bentos or Three Bulls.

One case, as exported from Tanganyika Packers slaughterhouse and factory, contains 48 cans of corned beef. Your average Tanzanian cow, shooed up the ramp before midnight, will have—long before morning breaks—filled up six cases of corned beef or a total of 288 cans.

*

July 14. I am driving up 'on safari' to the site where Alastair Hunter, who heads the UNDP/FAO team in Dodoma (it has been sent in to help the government with its cattle management programme), thinks they may establish a ranching association. The phrase 'on safari' seems to me rather grandiose, but it is one everybody uses. A man who is not at his desk is 'on safari'. In London or in New York, secretaries say that their employers are at a 'meeting' or have 'stepped out for a minute'. But it all amounts to the same thing.

When we stop for a few minutes *en route*, our driver rigs up the aerial for the radio. We learn that the House of Lords has rejected by 184 to 84 a Labour amendment seeking to continue the embargo on arms to South Africa.

At three o'clock we arrive at the project base camp, which consists of three round huts built at a cost of 50 East African shillings each in the shade of the sort of small hill South Africans would call a 'kop'. Hunter had insisted on the construction of the huts, because FAO was in the habit of docking project personnel 40 shillings a night from their safari allowance every time they used the FAO tent. In any event, the huts gave the base camp a kind of permanence which tents would not have had.

A man was finishing the thatching on one of the huts as we arrived. Near the entrance to the encampment, a circular fence concealing a six-foot hole in the ground, served at once as a field latrine and as a kind of gate-house.

The sun poured down. Occasional flights of bees passed overhead, making a rasping noise. I climbed up with David Thornton, the FAO Range Ecologist, until we reached a high rock, from which we could survey the whole 40,000 acres which had been selected for the proposed ranching association's area, and a good deal more besides. Inevitably, on the rough and ready maps which the FAO project had drawn up, the place was labelled Observation Rock.

We look out eight or ten miles across the plain. Below us we can see the huts of the Gogos. Here the bomas are square, not circular. They are only circular where the cattle are boma'd at night away from the homestead. Visibility is poor today because they are already burning the grasses. Over to the left are wet lands and grass lands. Too wet for trees. Thornton says that the trail through the plain may look easy from this height, but it will take three hours to go three or four miles in a Land Rover. As we sit on the crags looking out, two small birds go fiercely for a big bird who has been intruding into their air-space and put it to flight.

Thornton says to me 'Water is the key. Bring water down

into the valley—boreholes, tanks, or whatever it takes—and you stand a chance of having a good project. As things are now, the cattle have to walk so far for water that by the time they get back from having a drink they're dying of thirst!'

Thornton has to stay up at the camp for a few days, so I go back alone. Not far from the camp, still some way off the main road, is a small mission run by an Italian priest with the assistance of two nuns. As we pass it, the bell is ringing for the evening service. Already half a dozen African children are waiting outside. When the bell stops, they file into a small oblong chapel with a corrugated tin-roof which adjoins the mission. One of the children, older than the rest, leads the congregation in the Swahili prayers while the priest kneels at the back with the rest of us. I don't stay to the end but sneak out, rather guiltily, after about twenty minutes. The drone of the chanting pursues me to the car.

As we go back to Dodoma, the driver talks about the importance of education. His own parents, he says, sent him to the Arab school where he learned nothing useful. He was determined that his own children should have a better education than he had. 'With education,' he claims, in tones which suggest such things are the very summit of ambition, 'you can get a job in an office, maybe go to London. Someone a friend of mine knows has even gone to America.'

We see Masai on the road, long robes dragging in the dust and ornaments hanging pendulously from their ears. They run away as we drive towards them. Once a Red Cross team came, my driver tells me, and made the Masai give blood. Ever since then they have distrusted a white face. In 1957 or 1958, he says, two white surveyors working in the bush were hacked to pieces by angry tribesmen. Apparently some Masai women had seen the surveyors remove their shirts in the heat while they worked and, on the strength of this, had fled with stories of how they had been raped. Six people from the Masai were later hanged. Dodoma, he adds, is still a good hanging town. About three executions take place a month.

*

Alastair Hunter, who runs the UNDP/FAO Livestock Project in Dodoma, is nearly six feet tall and weighs—I should say—rather more than 15 stone. He is, in other words, a substantial figure. He has surprisingly long red hair and, with an unpublished novel in his desk, aspirations to be a writer. He has a farm in Perthshire, a chalet in Switzerland and intends to buy land in Apulia in Italy when he can find time to look for it. His children are at school in Scotland and fly out to Tanzania in the holidays. His wife's brother once was travelling reserve for Scotland at Rugby Football.

I spend most of the afternoon with him and in the evening we walk across Dodoma golf-course. The sun sets hugely behind Dodoma prison. We bump into shrubs and thorn which would never have been allowed on the course in the days when there were still a thousand colonial families in the town. On one or two of the tees, some pretence of raking and rolling has been made. But the general impression is one of decay. A maize patch has already been planted on one of the greens. What isn't taken will anyway revert soon enough to the bush.

We pass from the golf-course to the rugger pitch. The posts are still standing but the field is entirely overgrown. We come to the club house. Several panes of glass are missing in the windows of the snooker room. Two Indians, who work in government jobs, are engaged in a game of 'volunteer' snooker (an old favourite). They ring the bell for drinks, but more in hope than expectation. None appear.

We return to Hunter's house. It is a grand place on the outskirts of the town. It belongs to a Tanzanian politician who is the representative of his government at the headquarters of the East African Community at Arusha. Since he has an official residence in Arusha, he had had to give up his house here. President Nyerere has decreed that Ministers are to set an example to all by the simplicity of their life style.

Hunter pours me a drink. Our walk across the golf-course makes it doubly welcome. As we sit there I hear the sound of distant drumming. I ask what the drums mean. Hunter replies, in the classic manner, 'The natives are restless.' Then he says, 'Actually they're drumming to announce the imminent arrival of President Nyerere.'

Hunter explains that the President has come to make a tour of the 'ujamaa' villages in the region. The basic principle behind 'ujamaa'—which, literally translated, means 'familyhood'—is social. It means bringing people together into groups so that you can do something for them. Your average Gogo family lives on its own with its cattle in the bush. Their huts are widely scattered. Bring them together in some kind of co-operative village and you can put in a bore-hole, a dispensary, a road. If the land resource is only big enough to take a village of fifty families, you make a village of fifty families. Your ranching association becomes an 'ujamaa' enterprise, achieving economies of production and marketing and a social coherence which would otherwise be lacking.

The concept of 'ujamaa'—familyhood, self-reliance or however it is interpreted—goes back to the Arusha Declaration of January 1967 which Nyerere himself drafted. According to the Declaration, a 'regrettable emphasis on money and industry had made for a concentration on urban development'. Yet it is 'obvious that the foreign currency we shall have to use to pay back the loans used in the development of the urban areas will not come from the towns or the industries. Where, then, shall we get it from? We shall get it from the villages and from agriculture. What does this mean? It means that the people who benefit directly from development which is brought about by borrowed money are not the ones who will repay the loans. The largest proportion of the loans will be spent in, and for, the urban areas, but the largest proportion of the repayment will be made through the efforts of the farmers. . . . If we are not careful, we might get into the position where the real exploitation in Tanzania is that of the town-dweller exploiting the peasants.'

What 'ujamaa' stresses is the deliberate and planned development through self-help and self-reliance of viable rural communities. A well drilled here and there in the bush, a cattle dip installed, a more efficient market, an ox-plough to replace the hoe and panga—these may not appear to be dramatic improvements, yet, in Nyerere's view, this is the way to achieve a transformation in the lot of the 95% of Tanzanians who still live in the rural areas. It must be a process which emphasizes

rather than denies the rural character of development. Only
thus can Tanzania avoid the social, political and environmental
problems which have begun to plague so many other African
countries.

*

Next morning a Swedish Water Engineer called Homberg
takes me out into the bush in his Land Rover to meet up with
the Presidential party in one of the new 'ujamaa' villages.
Homberg is cross because 'ujamaa' villages are being designated
without anyone asking detailed questions about the water
supply. He says the authorities wanted to have 100 'ujamaa'
villages in the Dodoma region but there were only seventeen
drilling rigs in the whole country and the water-table could be
down 400 feet.
    'If I had four good rigs and three good drillers, then in a
year I could have 300 bore-holes.'
    After about an hour's drive, we stop in a village. There are
lines of official Land Rovers already waiting, all painted grey.
Homberg asks what time the President is arriving and learns
that he is expected at mid-day. It is only half-past ten, but the
school children are already lining the road and the villagers
are gathered beneath the baobab trees.
    We drive on and pass a Land Rover coming in the opposite
direction with a loudspeaker mounted on the roof. Clearly it is
there to announce the President's arrival and to make sure that
there is a decent turn-out.
    We pull off the road and wait for the President at Chungu
village in the Mwapwa district. There is a big crowd and the
drumming is intense. A police car comes through, followed
immediately by Nyerere's black Mercedes. Behind it a long line
of Land Rovers, belonging to the official party, concertinas to a
dusty halt. Doors open, men jump down and follow the President
towards the village. Nyerere walks to a flag-pole which has been
stuck in the ground in front of one of the village huts and
around which a circle of children has formed. They sing while
Julius K. Nyerere, leader of Tanzania since Independence,
translator of Shakespeare, father of his people and revered as
'Mwalimu', stands and watches in the shade of a baobab tree.

The singing goes on for some time. I can only recognize words like 'Tanzania', which recurs frequently. Later Homberg asks one of his Tanzanian students (he is teaching them how to dig wells without breaking the bit) to make a partial translation. The song apparently went something like this: 'Dr Banda has been mentally disturbed. He ought to go to Mirembe hospital before it gets too late. This is because he is claiming that Mbeya, Iringa and other areas belong to him and his country.' Mirembe is a mental hospital in Dodoma. They ended with the refrain 'Mzungu chaka Banda', which means, 'Death to Banda'.

I stayed with the Presidential convoy the whole day. Nyerere went from village to village. Sometimes he made a short speech; sometimes he stayed silent. Once a little boy stepped forward from the crowd and read out some welcoming words from a scroll. It is a marvel he can read at all, he is so small. Nyerere hugs him and drives off in a cloud of dust. Homberg, standing next to me, says: 'It is a big work to build up a country.'

We reach the camp at about half-past one. It has leap-frogged ahead, lorries loaded with tents and other equipment overtaking the President and his party as they stopped along the route. The equipment includes three mobile generators, four water-tankers, one lorry-load of petrol and diesel and the President's two caravans and portable latrine. It also includes Mr Arthur Knight, chief engineer for the Dodoma region and supervisor of the whole safari.

With his great white shorts and huge stomach, Arthur Knight stood out magnificently among the crowd at the camp-site. He said he was going south, to South Africa and greener pastures, when this job was finished. It was, in fact, his last major assignment. The year before he had handled the famine relief operations in Dodoma and he seemed to feel that that had been a considerably easier task.

We stand talking, while with half an eye Knight watches over the erection of the tents and the distribution of stores. He is full of praise for Nyerere: 'The only man on this safari that is anywhere near prompt is the President himself. At 8.30 this morning, he was completely ready. I had been watching for him because the last thing we knock down is the President's personal

latrine. Then I saw him standing outside, so I went up to him
and said "Permission to break, sir?" He grinned. He knew
what I meant. He stood there talking till nine o'clock, then he
said: "All right, fellows, let's go." The bugle went and we moved
out.'

By two o'clock the mess-tent is in place and lunch is ready.
We help ourselves to rice and stew and eat from billy-cans.
Nyerere sits a few feet away from me. On my right is a doctor,
one of many sent in by China as part of its large aid programme
in Tanzania. He is polite, but non-communicative. I ask him
how many Chinese there are in Tanzania and he says he doesn't
know.

Probably not even the Tanzanian government knows how
many there are. Now that the big railway project, the Tan-Zam
link, is going ahead, there will be more of them than ever—
driving along in their big grey trucks, with their peaked blue
caps and grey Mao suits with the red star on the collar.

Not long before my visit, the Chinese and the Americans had
what my friends referred to as a 'big punch-up' in the vicinity
of Mbeya, in Southern Tanzania. It wasn't reported in the
Press, but it happened. The incident took place when it seemed
as though the road the Americans were building and the
Chinese railway were both going to take exactly the same route.
Each side pulled up the other side's set of marker pegs and,
before long, it came to blows.

The Americans were larger, but there were more Chinese and
the final result was a stand-off. There must be a moral somewhere in this tale.

PART THREE

ASIA

November 16. Rome. I flew into the city last night on an Alitalia
flight out of London. Today, His Holiness Pope Paul VI visited
FAO as guest of honour at the special one-day conference
commemorating the 25th anniversary of the Organization. He
had, apparently, accepted the invitation only five weeks previously. Detailed planning for the visit began at that time.

The session started at 10 a.m. in the main Conference Hall.
The flags of the Member Nations of FAO were arrayed behind
the dais. They were also painted in miniature on the front of
the podium, four rows and thirty columns making a total of
120 flags, for the 120 Member Nations. Floodlight illuminated
the hall. Men with cameras stalked in and out of the rows.
Pretty multi-national girls distributed advance texts of the
Pope's speech and other conference papers. Seating was on a
country by country basis. I noticed that Bolivia and Botswana,
Cyprus and Dahomey were among those missing from the lower
reaches of the international alphabet. There were further gaps
in the L-R directory but I was not able to distinguish the absen-
tees precisely.

Some curtain-raising speeches filled in the time before the
Pope arrived. References were made to the recent cyclone
disaster in Pakistan and to the death of General de Gaulle.
Tribute was paid to the Prime Minister of Italy, Emilio Colombo,
who was sitting up on the dais and who, at the mention of his
name, rose briefly from his seat and made a short bow. Behind
Mr Colombo, the famous ear of corn—the FAO symbol—
sprouted and, surrounding it, the legend FIAT PANIS set the
tone for the Conference.

At 11 a.m. exactly the Director-General of FAO, Dr Addeke
H. Boerma and the President of the Conference, Dr Hernan
Santa Cruz, go down to meet Pope Paul VI, at the end of his
short but no doubt hazardous journey from the Vatican to the
FAO headquarters (once Mussolini's Ministry for Africa) near

the Terme di Caracalla. The Deputy Chairman takes the chair:

'In a few minutes we will have the privilege of listening to His Holiness' address. Thereafter, His Holiness will circulate through the various rooms of the buildings to meet the staff who are not present at this ceremony, though they are listening to and watching the proceedings on closed-circuit television. The afternoon proceedings will begin with a special message from the Secretary-General of the United Nations himself, delivered by his personal delegate. Then there will be speeches by representatives of each region of the world and the final act of the Conference will be a closing speech by the Director-General.'

Moments later the acting Chairman announces to the expectant hall: 'We have now been informed that His Holiness Pope Paul has arrived and is downstairs. He is on his way to the Conference Room which he will reach within the next few minutes. I would request that delegates remain seated until he arrives, when we shall all stand.'

Finally, His Holiness is here. The delegates stand and he walks down between the rows to take his seat on the dais. A special chair and a special microphone has been set up for him. He sits without moving as Dr Santa Cruz says a few introductory words. The Pope, we are reminded, was the author of the phrase 'the new name for peace is development.' It was his idea to establish a fund where money diverted from armaments could be put for the benefit of the world's poor.

The Pope himself is in white, with a scarlet cape and a white cap. Behind him sit a phalanx of Churchmen, mostly fat and elderly, all purple and vermilion and black. When Santa Cruz has finished, one of the phalanx gets up, removes the scarlet cape from His Holiness' shoulders and then brings him his speech to read out.

Paul VI spoke in French, his voice vibrant with love and suffering. Though the speech, like all such speeches, contained the expected quota of garbage, it was in a strange way moving and convincing. He spoke about environment and ecology (someone at the Vatican had clearly been doing his homework); he talked about the stupidity of the arms race; about the obstacles which stand in the way of development. Clearly he believed that in a world where men were unselfish, and where they loved one another, there could be an end to hunger and misery. He called for international law, based on justice and equity.

On the subject of the population explosion, he said he was aware of the opinions which were held in some international organizations, namely that birth control could radically transform the economic prospects of developing countries. But he could only reaffirm the teaching of John XXIII and the objections of the Church to methods of birth control, as these were defined, which the Church found intolerable. Admittedly he believed that 'rational couples' might find effective ways of planning their families. But this was cold comfort for those who had hoped for a reforming statement. Indeed, some observers saw this as the most powerful reiteration of official doctrine since *Humanae Vitae*.

The Pope made a special reference to the work of Dr Norman Borlaug and he ended with the quotation: 'I was hungry and you gave me to eat.' Then the minion came forward once more, took away the notes and gave His Holiness his cloak back again. Paul VI rose to his feet, shook hands with the Prime Minister and made the sign of the Cross above the heads of the standing, quietly clapping, delegates.

I went back in the afternoon and heard some of the statements made by the regional representatives. Finally, Dr Boerma made his speech, a powerful orderly presentation. In the course of it, he read out a letter from Dr Borlaug, in which Borlaug apologized for not being able to be present at the special one-day Conference of FAO. Borlaug noted that the Nobel Committee, who had seen fit to award him the Peace Prize this year, was reluctant for its nominee to make public appearances before such time as the Committee had had a chance formally to present the award in Stockholm. Borlaug had gone on to say that when the Committee awarded him the prize, it 'effectively awarded it to agriculture. The so-called "green revolution" is a result of a team effort, involving many different people.' Dr Boerma read out Borlaug's plea for more and better training in agricultural methods, for aggressive promotion of agriculture. The plea ended with these words: 'If we hesitate or falter, the monster—rapid population growth—will destroy the world.'

I could not help remembering the remarks of the Pope, a few hours earlier that day, and in the same hall. The delegates who had applauded one man, now applauded the other. But that was only to be expected. On these ceremonial occasions, applause is what the script calls for.

*

November 17. 1.30 p.m. I am just about to take off in a Pan-Am jet clipper for Ankara, Turkey. The plane was delayed and I have been sitting for the last hour in the International Departure Lounge at Leonardo da Vinci Airport. Over the past few months, as I have flown in and out of Rome, I have come to know the place well. The faces of the girls, who announce the times of the planes over the closed-circuit television, have changed more than once over the course of my project.

The flight time to Istanbul is one hour and fifty minutes. We leave Mount Vesuvius on our right and then turn to fly over the hills towards Brindisi, ancient Brundisium. We have to skirt Albania and cross over the Greek coast somewhere beyond Corfu; then we turn North and East again towards Thrace. From the air, one can clearly see the long thin fingers of land reaching down into the Aegean.

We stop for half an hour or so at Istanbul, then leave for Ankara. Ankara airport, when we arrive at about 7 p.m. Turkish time, is full of American servicemen. They are mostly air-force personnel who look as though they have been on leave in West Germany. They are laden with packages of all descriptions. One man staggers through Customs under the weight of an enormous colour television. When the Turkish customs official looks dubious, and begins to consult his papers, the serviceman pulls out a tin of Frankfurters from his luggage and thrusts it onto the counter. The official waves him on.

A UNDP driver meets me and takes me back to Ankara, 24 kilometres away. You know you are there when you round a bend and see the lights of the old city, blazing off the hill like a broad-based Christmas tree. I sign in at a hotel and walk out into the street. Dolmus taxis, loading on passengers at every corner. I haven't seen these for ten years. Crowds of Turks clustered round a lighted shop window where television sets

are displayed, and a sleek black-haired announcer is reading
the news. I only recognize words like Pakistan and Iran. It has
obviously been raining hard. There are great pools of water and
the streets are still glistening. I buy a big bag of roast chestnuts
for one Turkish lire, which is cheap since there are 15 lire to a
US dollar.

*

On average, Turkey has been importing 400,000 tons of
grain a year for the last twelve years. For the past two years,
the deficit has been particularly critical. A population growth
rate of 2·8% or more has meant that Turkey's inhabitants now
number almost 36 million, making her the 15th most populous
nation on earth. Drought has combined with a falling-off in
grain shipments from the U.S. under the Food for Peace programme to aggravate an already serious situation.

If Turkey uses foreign exchange to buy wheat, she has to cut
down on other imports. But in fact there is very little fat available in the import list. Luxury items account for less than 5%.
Her choice is, therefore, either to cut back on imports which are
essential for her modernization and investment programme or to
let people die of hunger. That is why, at this particular juncture,
it is vital for Turkey to achieve some 'green revolution' which
can transform the pattern of cereals production in the country.

In 1966, an agronomist who had been working with USAID
in India came to Turkey and brought with him a few kilogrammes of Mexican wheat. He happened to give them to a
farmer in the coastal region who grew them with some success.
His neighbours saw what he had achieved and the whole thing
blew up in 1967 when certain Deputies in the Parliament
demanded that their constituents be given Mexican wheat as
well. The government looked into the matter, decided to import
over 20,000 tons of seed and asked the U.S. Government to
finance the seed purchase. The seeds were brought in and
seeded in 1967.

Turkey has two entirely different environmental areas for
wheat. On the coast, i.e. those parts of Turkey which border
on the eastern Aegean as well as the southern coast by the Gulf
of Antalya, some 1·3 million hectares are planted to wheat. It

was in this region that the Mexican seeds—fall-planted spring wheats—were first introduced. In the first season, 170,000 hectares were planted. At the same time an intensive effort at agricultural extension was launched. The logistics of the operation were sound. Fertilizer, and other inputs, were available at the right time and at the right place. The average yield in that first season was 450 kilos per décare.

The next year, 1968, there was a five-fold increase in acreage. Two things happened. First, the Turks were unable to maintain the extension effort on the required scale. Second, the wheats were attacked by rust, particularly by stripe rust which Borlaug had not needed to pay much attention to in his programme, his main problems being leaf and stem rust. The wheats were also attacked by septoria. Overall, yields dropped by 50%. In 1969, the poorer farmers dropped out; acreage planted to the new varieties fell slightly—to 600,000 hectares; and yields improved.

Turkey devalued on August 12, 1970. The lire went from 9:1 to 15:1 in terms of the US dollar. The effect of this has been to make Turkey more competitive in a number of areas, such as cotton and forestry products. In the circumstances, any great expansion in the area under wheat in the coastal regions is unlikely.

The natural ecological region for wheat in Turkey is, in any case, not the coastal region but the Anatolian plateau. The plateau is the bread-basket of the country. Here, on the plateau, you have 6·7 million hectares planted to wheat compared with the 1·3 million on the coast. But the introduction of new varieties onto the plateau, which from the point of view of Turkey's food needs would be such a significant achievement, in fact presents a whole range of new problems.

These problems are interlocked. What the Turks need to develop for the plateau is a high-yielding winter wheat. Alternatively, they need a fall-planted spring wheat which has winter-hardiness built into it, so that it can withstand the cold which envelops the plateau through December and January. Next, they need a wheat of medium duration. The heavy rains fall in November, which makes planting difficult. If you plant before the rains, but with a short duration variety, the frost will hit the plant at a particularly crucial moment of its growth. If, on the other hand, you plant a medium duration wheat you can produce a wheat which has reached the five leaf stage (i.e. it is just beginning to tiller, but no more) at the onset of winter. The plant then hibernates through the cold months and you get maximum growth in early spring. The balance is a delicate one. If the plant is too big as you go into winter, you have winter-kill. If it is too small, you also have winter-kill.

For a medium duration wheat, planted *before* the rains, to be successful also requires far greater attention to the question of moisture conservation on the part of the Anatolian farmer. He will in essence be planting his crop on residual moisture. Similarly, much of the growth in the early spring will be on residual moisture. This places a heavy premium on the proper cultivation of land. And this in turn implies better ecological management of land and better cultural practices. It means a change in the patterns of grazing, where cattle stay on the land until the rains come, preventing moisture-saving cultivations. All of which argues that, even if you could develop a high-yielding winter-hardy medium-duration wheat for the plateau, there would still be a long way to go before Turkey's food deficit was eliminated.

Whether or not this paragon among wheats is in fact developed depends to a large extent on the work which is going on at agricultural research institutes, in Turkey and elsewhere. Perhaps the most important of these Institutes, in the Eastern Mediterranean region, is that which is situated outside Ismir, on the Aegean coast. It has been backed by UNDP, with specialist advice from FAO and has, for the last six or seven years since it was established, been collecting indigenous plant materials in Turkey and storing them for breeding purposes.

From the point of view of genetic resources, Turkey is one of the richest areas in the world. For centuries people have been moving east to west through Turkey, from Asia to Europe, or in the reverse direction. Some have settled in Anatolia and have brought their plants with them. Add to this the enormous diversity of ecological habitats. The climate can change tremendously within the space of three kilometres. So plants and insects, flora and fauna—all have a chance to find their own ecological niche. With its wild beet, its wild wheats and barleys, oats and fruits, Turkey probably contains one of the richest stores of germ-plasm in the world. The tulip first came from Persia and the Anatolian region. The Germans took it from Istanbul to Nuremberg and that was where the Dutch saw it to make it in due course into their national flower. Vamilov, the famous Russian geneticist, came through Turkestan and Caucasia in the 1930's and was astonished by the wealth and diversity of material. (Vamilov was later put to death under Stalin because, so my Turkish friends told me, Lysenko—the other famous Russian geneticist—'made propaganda against him'.)

Another reason for the genetic richness that is to be found in Turkey is that the spread of the new varieties across the face of the land is, as I have already noted, still relatively modest. The damage has not yet been done. But it is, even now, a race against time. These new varieties contain within them, in the most literal sense, the seeds of their own reversal. Every success breeds failure because the widespread adoption of a variety in itself destroys the genetic diversity and the range of ecological habitats, which is precisely what makes a vigorous and effective breeding programme possible. With the growing pressures of human and animal populations, we have, though we may be horrifyingly slow to recognize it, something of a crisis on our hands.

The Institute at Ismir—I flew down from Ankara for a short visit—is a belated response to this crisis. Its primary function is to collect and maintain a collection of seeds and plants which will represent in some manner the genetic wealth of Turkey even though that wealth may be destroyed or dissipated in nature. Because it is an emergency programme, the Institute has concentrated its energies first on forage crops and cereals. For the last few years staff of the Institute have been going off for eight- or ten-week expeditions in Toyotas, the Japanese Land Rovers. They take a trailer to sleep in but find, after all, that they sleep in the open because the trailer is soon filled with materials. They go into the eastern border regions, up to the Black Sea Coast, or even (with special permission) into Kurdish Syria.

They collect and label the plants at the same time. They take a rough harvest of mature seeds. They also make some herbarium samples, so they can put plants and seeds together. The material is given a CRIC number (CRIC stands for Crop Research and Introduction Centre) and then it is brought to the laboratory at Ismir for viability control.

If the seeds prove viable for long-term storage, the Institute is in a position to respond favourably to requests which may have been made by plant breeders from all over the world. The Institute runs a germination test. Even with low germination rates, most seeds will be retained rather than thrown away. Collection is an expensive business and to waste material is a heinous crime. The next step is to dry the seeds down to a constant level of moisture (for cereals 6% to 8% is most convenient for long term storage). Then the seeds are counted, by means of a special seed counter (a device which has 50 or 100 holes in it, through which the seeds are sucked in the number required). Once counted, they are put in paper envelopes for distribution. 200 seeds in general is enough for a breeder. Since the Institute cannot afford to be so generous, it will send a smaller quantity and rely on the breeder to do his own multiplication. This in turn presents problems for the breeder. Seed renewal is a difficult art and gene-erosion may occur.

For every seed that is despatched around the world, and for many that are not, a sample is stored. There are 25,000 different samples in the collection at Ismir and the majority of these have been gathered through exploratory expeditions. In the past the samples were all stored in old cardboard boxes in cold storage in some meat-shop in the town. Now, at last, a type of insulated tin has been devised and a refrigeration unit on the Institute premises itself has been constructed to house the containers.

This refrigerating plant costs the Turkish government 150,000 lire a year to run. The money is hard to come by. Some of the material is still in cardboard boxes on the floor of the refrigerating room, because there are insufficient funds for the containers. The UNDP, with FAO, will be providing 185,000 US dollars for the next two years. This is a start but it is not adequate. And two years is not a lifetime.

In the course of my time at the Institute, I visited every part

F *

of its operations. I put on furs and gloves to see round the cold-room, handled the samples in the tins. I visited the herbarium, saw how a multitude of wild plants had been dried and pressed and labelled. Here was a snow-flowering cyclamen; here was a forage plant which the Australians had recently been showing interest in; here were wild oats (the other kind) culled—so the label said—on the slopes of Mt Ararat. Had old man Noah left them there, his legacy to a distant generation which would one day recognize their genetic worth?

I talked to most of the men involved with the work of the Institute. They were serious dedicated scientists; Turkish nationals—yet performing an international service. It seemed to me strange that the world at large, which would profit so much from their endeavours, should be so reluctant to put up the modest funds they needed to carry on and to expand. For what is needed is a network of centres like Ismir and also a network of reserve areas, in field and prairie, mountain and forest, where nature's last resources can—for the benefit of man—be pre-served *in situ* from man's encroachment.

I remember sitting in the lobby of the Grand Efes Hotel in Ismir, talking to the Director of the Institute. He was an old wise man, a venerable scientist who had an almost poetic appreciation of the work he was doing.

'This old material we are collecting,' he told me, 'has wonderful potential. It has cold resistance, drought resistance, rust resistance—everything. We may need just one gene from one wheat—like, say, a dwarfing capacity. You can't put a price on it. It's worth the whole effort. But we have a very short time left. In 20 or 30 years it will be too late. In Europe or America there are few possibilities, genetic possibilities, for this kind of thing. But there is much money. In Turkey we have many possibilities but very little money.'

And the old man poured me some more Turkish coffee which, such is the complexity of agriculture, he assured me was not Turkish at all but imported from Brazil.

*

Friday morning, November 20. I cross by ferry to the Asiatic side of the Bosphorus, to meet Mr Romba who is driving up across the plateau from Ankara. It is a rendezvous we have arranged several days earlier, while I was still in Ankara before going to Ismir. Romba has told me that he will leave at four in the morning and will reach the ferry at exactly ten o'clock. Sure enough, as I wander back to the quay after a brief promenade through the local market, I see him—three minutes early, pacing up and down beside his car.

Romba swings round as I approach. He is watching the people disembark from an arriving boat. He clearly doesn't expect me to be early. His face lights up as he sees me and he utters a deep guttural exclamation. Romba is a tall Dutchman. He works as the Project Manager of the UNDP/FAO Hides and Skins project. He is a leather expert and, after so many years, his skin has begun to resemble the material. He has thin reddish hair and has worked in almost every country you can name—Indonesia, Malaya, Nigeria, Cambodia, India, Pakistan. He has at last, he tells me, bought a house in Holland so that his children, already aged 18 and 13 years old respectively, can say they have a home.

He talks about the UNDP/FAO Project. Later that afternoon, he says we will go to Istanbul—to the beautiful old section of the city by the walls where the tanners have their factories. He hopes I can bear the smell of it.

'At this time of the year,' he says, 'the fresh air keeps the putrefaction down. But it is still pretty bad. There is no waste disposal system; no water system. They're poisoning the soil. So much mess and chemicals is pumped out of the area and seeps down into the ground-water, that soon you won't even be able to use the water for industrial purposes, let alone for drinking purposes. Now this area, Kazliçesle, is a big tourist centre. Nearby is the Blue Mosque, Saint Sophia—all the beautiful sights. What the government plans to do is to move the tanners out, and build motels and hotels and so on.

'The tanners have to move. They can't go on doing what they're doing. And they know it. The business is too dirty. It's exactly the same as if your wife is not cleaning the kitchen any more. 350 years ago the first tanneries were in Kazliçesle and nothing has changed since then.

'It's not just the tanners we're going to move. We're also

going to move the shoe-makers, the leather-goods manufacturers, the fur-coat people—and all the ancillary industries. Last year Turkey exported 345,000 coats, either suede coats or hippy coats. You know, the things with goat hair sticking out and needlework all over. They're worth 120 million Turkish lire, and you can calculate that at the old rate of nine lire to the dollar.

'The government is going to relocate the tanneries—they number 104 altogether, big and small, but not all of them will be involved—over on this side of the Bosphorus, the Asiatic side. What the UNDP and FAO are doing is helping the government build an Institute which will be at the service of these people in their new site. It will offer the latest technical advances, in flaying, in curing, in transport, marketing, merchandising and so forth.'

Romba and I drive about 35 kilometres from the ferry, down the Ankara road, towards Pendik, a small town on the Sea of Marmara where the new Institute is being constructed. The building is half complete, though it will not be finally ready for another five months. Romba takes photographs from several different vantage points. This he does about once a month and then he compares one photograph with another to see what progress has been made. 'Sometimes,' says Romba, 'you cannot trust your eyes.'

The workmen who are laying the roof wave as Romba clicks away with his camera, then—in a gesture not hard to interpret —they blow their noses over the side of the building.

Romba assures me that the Institute is designed to help the tanneries, not compete with them. 'How to get someone's confidence if you kick him up under his pants! That is unreasonable!' says Romba.

The Institute will be one of the most modern in the world. There is another at Madras in India but that, says Romba, is more interested in research. He thinks it's better to give pure research to the universities and to concentrate on practical work and *applied* research.

We walk on round the site. The sun streams down. The Sea of Marmara, which Leander once swam seeking Hero, glints blue a few hundred yards away. It is hard to realize that in a few months time a whole new industry will be established here.

New factories. New slaughter-houses. New transport facilities. Hard for me, I mean. Not hard for Romba. This is a project he has lived with for years. He persuaded the Turkish government of the idea; then he persuaded the United Nations.

'These countries,' he says, 'are always thinking and talking about new Institutes. But there has to be someone to get the first line down on paper. I was here with UN Technical Assistance and pushed the project. So far UNDP has put up 800,000 dollars and two million will come from the government. But we will need more than that.'

Romba explains his vision of the Institute's function. 'I want to show these people how, using their own tools and their own dies and their own hides, they can make a better quality leather —or else make the same quality leather cheaper. Which is the same thing. Every bad tanner says he gets bad hides. But you can see two factories get skins from the same load and produce entirely different products.'

Not all hides, Romba admits, are the same quality originally. Many blemishes occur long before the tanner touches the leather. There is a certain kind of fly, for example, which lays its eggs on a cow's feet as it is grazing contentedly in the fields. The cow, as cows do, licks its feet. The larva is swallowed into the cow's stomach. Then it burrows up all the way through the cow's intestines and comes out into the open air, somewhere along the backbone, leaving a hole in the hide as large as a thumb nail and a great mound of pus as well. And then there are the tics which attach themselves to a cow's belly and suck the blood, leaving a scar on the skin. When the tics are replete, they drop off, but are picked up again by other cows.

We drive back to the Bosphorus to catch the ferry over on to the European side. We have glimpsed the future of the leather industry in Turkey; now we are to look at the past—at the old industry tucked up among the walls at Topkapi. We sit in line by the quay, waiting for our turn on the boat.

Romba is in a philosophical mood. 'The Turks are a very nice people,' he says. 'They're honest, straightforward people. Of course, if you are a careful government fellow, you try to do nothing. Since good you can never do, you try not to do bad. You sleep a bit in the office, so then you play cards at night. But if you really show them what is best for their country, they will try to do it. I will never disappoint them.'

To illustrate the point of his last remark, Romba tells me a story. He travels up and down the country, he says, and has friends in many parts. The tanning industry begins with the cows themselves grazing on the pastures of the plateau, and Romba likes to know his profession inside out (as indeed a leather expert should).

'Whenever I have time,' he says, 'I go to visit a mosque or a museum. One day I was in a little village, somewhere in the eastern part of the country, and the people there said to me "Do you want to see the mosque?" So I said yes, and I went in and looked around and then, when I had finished, someone came up with a box or something and asked if I would like to make a contribution. Well, you know, we Dutchmen are careful fellows, so I said "Contribution for what?" And the man replied "For the upkeep of the mosque." So I looked around and you know these places are all stone and tiled and really they don't need much upkeep. So I asked him "What kind of upkeep?" And he said, "Oh, this and that and oh, by the way, the Imam was hoping to get a new carpet because the one in the mosque was very old and worn." So I thought about it for a while and then I said to them, "Well, if I get you a new carpet, will you let me have this old one?" And they said yes. So I got them a new carpet—it cost a good deal of money—and now those people in the village think I am a kind of second saint. As for me, I have got a beautiful old carpet. It's probably the most valuable and lovely thing I have. They are happy and I am happy. Do you want me to return the old carpet to them and ask for the new one back and disappoint these people?'

And Romba, as the boat bumped against the shore on the Istanbul side, and as the cars began to roll over the ramp, repeated his remark as though it was a part of his professional faith. 'I will never disappoint these people.'

Romba and I spent the afternoon in Kazliçesle. We went from one tannery to another. It is hard to describe the scene. On the one hand you have the almost incredible beauty of this part of Istanbul. The ancient walls, breached by time and Turk alike, crumble into the sunset. The minarets aim off into the blue.

Sea-birds swoop over the Bosphorus. The Sultan rides in his palace. But lower the gaze by a few degrees of elevation and shorten the perspective of time by a few hundred years and you see, not a beautiful walled city, but piles of putrefying flesh scraped off the carcasses of cattle, rotting before the eye and quivering as each new shovelful is thrust out of the tannery door. Tailings from the sheep, scrapings of skin, hair and bones and gelatine—mire and blood indeed. And from it all rises an overwhelming overpowering stench, blighting the air and causing actual physical retching in the throat.

It may well be that, in spite of the efforts of men like Romba, the tanners will succeed in creating another Kazliçesle out of their new site in Asia. Perhaps this is the way they like it. But, at all events, the relocation of the industry will bring new light and life to this part of the Old City.

★

It is ironic that by far the most sensational outbreak of cholera, at least up until the time of the Pakistan disaster, should have occurred in Turkey. Turkey hasn't got a very efficient public health system but in the last few years they have been making very big efforts indeed in the fight against cholera. It has been a matter of national pride and, at the same time, a matter of economics. Nothing knocks foreign exchange earnings from tourism quicker than a dose of cholera.

Turkey concentrated her efforts in the border regions between herself and Syria, Iraq and Iran. These are the countries where the disease is endemic. This—or so the authorities thought—was where it would come from. They set up a network of laboratories along the borders, equipped with stoves, fridges, and electricity, and capable of doing serious technical work.

In August, two or three months before my visit, cholera outbreaks had occurred in a number of countries in the Middle East and Russia. However, very few countries—largely through political reasons—had notified the disease to the World Health Organization in Geneva and through WHO to the world. (WHO's epidemiological bulletin is released in Geneva every Friday evening and most public health authorities will have it by the following Monday or Tuesday.)

But Turkey thought she had nothing to hide. She was in the clear, and she wanted that fact made known. During the first week of September, at Turkey's request, WHO sent a two-man mission to the country. One of the men was from their regional office and had a very good knowledge of the south of Turkey. The other was a Czechoslovakian epidemiologist, specially recruited. (Czechoslovakia had its own problems with cholera at the time.) The team made a brief visit, to southern and south-eastern Turkey. The government, which in any case had been taking strenuous precautionary measures—with vaccination, chlorination of water supplies and environmental sanitation—opened all the doors.

The team found nothing. No evidence of cholera. They visited all the places which appeared to be menaced by infection from neighbouring countries. They did not, however, visit Istanbul.

At the beginning of October, some cases of diarrhoea appeared in Istanbul. Some were treated by doctors, some in hospitals. During the second week of October, the number of cases of diarrhoea reached alarming proportions. On October 13 and 14, the public health authorities went from Ankara to Istanbul and with them went the Chief Bacteriologist, Dr Alkis, from the Reifik Saydam Institute in Ankara. Dr Alkis specialized in cholera, had served on a WHO cholera panel and had developed a culture which had been named after him. He it was who isolated and identified the cholera vibrio, bio-type eltor, serotype Inaba.

At the same time, epidemiologists—by plotting the foci of the outbreaks against maps of the city's water system—were able to determine that there was water-borne transmission. The infection had not come from the source of the water itself, but had somehow infiltrated into the supply somewhere along the route. Further investigation revealed how. There had, it appeared, been an interruption in the water-supply. Pressure within the pipe had dropped with the result that, instead of repelling seepage from outside—as is normally the case when a pipe is under pressure—it had in fact served as a kind of suction device. In this case what the pipe had sucked in had been cholera-infected sewage.

The authorities are still reluctant to specify exactly whose sewage it was. They will say only that it is possible that a touring company of players, who had been in Istanbul on their way to Syria earlier in the summer and who had come back to the city on the way home, may have been responsible. The group apparently found the Istanbul hotels too expensive and settled instead in the city's somewhat insalubrious Sagamalcilar district.

The Turkish authorities, once they knew what they had on their hands, took vigorous measures. They vaccinated population around the foci and super-chlorinated the water. They kept a complete record of all movements into and out of the area. And, of course, they treated those who were sick, and probably a good many who weren't sick at all but who thought they were or else were just hoping for some free square meals in hospital.

By the time of my visit, with the outbreak totally controlled, things were getting back to normal. There had been no surface mail for weeks in or out of Turkey (mail could come in but since the Turks had nothing to put in the mail trucks to send back, they soon stopped accepting it). But at last the trains through Bulgaria were running again.

Cars and trucks were still only permitted through Bulgaria in convoy and the Turkish border with Greece remained cut off. A WHO man, wanting to leave Istanbul for Rome, had to fly by Ethiopia. Turkish migrant workers, bound for West Germany, found the way barred.

In all, some 474 cases of cholera were registered in Turkey between October 13 and 23, 1970, with a confirmed diagnosis. There were 46 deaths. I was interested, though not unduly surprised, to learn that several of these deaths had occurred in the tannery district of Kazliçesle.

2

DR GLENN ANDERSON is a Canadian. He looks like a Canadian. He talks and acts like one. He strode into his office in the Rockefeller Foundation building on Kautilya Marg in New Delhi with mud on his shoes and a deep red tan on his face. He wore a blue check shirt with an open collar, had broad shoulders and a broad smile. He apologized for being a bit late. He had been out in the fields, sowing.

We sat talking for the best part of four hours. I have never talked about wheat for four hours at a stretch before and I can't readily imagine a situation when I will do so again. That afternoon in Delhi was, in its way, a unique experience. Sometime I hope some enlightened despot will shut Dr Anderson away in a dark-room with only a recording machine for company. He should not be released until he has dictated for posterity all that he knows of the story of the 'green revolution' in India. For it is, truly, a remarkable story; a fascinating story. All I can give here is the bare, amateurish outline—a hint and a promise.

When, a few weeks earlier, I had visited the CIMMYT field-station outside Mexico city, I had inspected material which would, in one form or another, find its way around the world. Both for wheat and for maize, CIMMYT runs an 'international nurseries programme'. Under this programme, promising lines are subjected to the widest possible international screening and testing under a range of different climatic and ecological conditions. One of the countries where CIMMYT material has been tested over the years is India. With ten major breeding stations and eighteen substations, India has in fact the biggest wheat-breeding programme in the world.

Back in 1962, Government of India scientists, working in the wheat breeding programme, became interested in some of the material that Norman Borlaug was sending them out of Mexico. In 1963, the Rockefeller Foundation sent Borlaug on a mission to India, at India's request. Borlaug spent a month in the country and his assessment was that conditions in India were very similar to those in Mexico. He went back to Mexico and despatched 100 kilogrammes of seed which was planted in the 1963/64 season. The principal lines involved were Mayo 64, Sonora 63, Sonora 64 and Lerma Rojo 64A.

The results of the first plantings were good enough to convince the Director of the Indian Agricultural Research Institute, Dr M. S. Swaminathan, of the value of the new material. And his advocacy was in turn crucial in persuading the then Minister of Agriculture, Dr Subramanian, to give support to the venture. It was no small matter for a Minister of Agriculture to say to his scientists in effect: 'Look, you fellows are barking up the wrong tree, and I propose to go and buy wheats in Mexico for India, rather than Indian wheats.' A good deal of national and professional pride was involved, on the part of both politicians and scientists.

In the spring of 1964, Dr Anderson came to India to take up his duties as joint co-ordinator of the all-India Wheat Improvement Programme. With Dr B. A. Krantz of the University of California, who was in India at the time spending a sabbatical year with the Rockefeller Foundation, Anderson worked on a series of agronomic trials for the new dwarf wheats.

In 1965, with a year of learning and experience behind them, the Government of India ordered from Mexico 200 tons of Sonora 64 and 50 tons of Lerma Rojo 64. Pakistan ordered some wheat for testing at the same time. Both consignments were shipped out of San Francisco on the same vessel (narrowly escaping destruction in the riots which gripped the Watts area of the city at that time.) While the ship was still at sea, war broke out on the sub-continent and the cargo had to be divided at Singapore so that each country's consignment could be handled separately.

The 250 tons was seeded and grown in the 1965/66 season. Germination was poor. Nevertheless the yield exceeded that of the traditional varieties. Though the stand initially was not especially good, the wheat managed to tiller and catch up. In that same season, there were the first national demonstrations. Swaminathan instructed his research personnel to demonstrate the new wheats right on the farmers' fields, rather than merely on the research station.

In the summer of 1966, the Government of India ordered 18,000 tons of Lerma Rojo and 2,000 tons of Sonora from Mexico. This was the largest single seed order ever placed anywhere in the world up to that time. Dr S. P. Kholi, co-ordinator of the all-India Wheat Improvement Programme, himself went to Mexico to take charge of the purchase arrangements. He and his team met with the Mexican Secretary of Agriculture and gained his permission to deal with the farmers directly for the seeds rather than having to work through the national seed production agencies. In this way, they saved themselves and India money, perhaps as much as 50%—and money, especially foreign exchange, was particularly scarce at that moment. They also saved time, which was crucial. The team was so late in getting to Mexico that the Yaqui valley was already harvested and they had to buy the seed in the Hermo-sillo area in the state of Sonora. Moreover the team had to get the seeds back from Mexico in time for the new growing season when already the failure of one harvest had created a crisis situation and the very real threat of famine.

In the 1966/67 season some 700,000 acres was seeded to the dwarf wheats which had been imported from Mexico. At the same time, work was continually going on—at breeding stations all over India—on the other lines Borlaug had originally sent from Mexico. Besides the four principal lines I have already mentioned, Borlaug sent smaller samples of over 600 other selections. The Indian wheat breeders found that under Indian conditions some of the lines were superior to the commercial Mexican varieties. In the same way as the CIMMYT people used two growing seasons, in Toluca and Obregon, so the Indians were able to advance a generation by breeding both in the plains and at higher altitudes in the hills.

In 1966 the first selection from this indigenously tested material, named PV 18, was released for commercial cultivation. One of the prime movers in this enterprise was D. S. Athwal who was then at Punjab Agricultural University. (Subsequently he went to the International Rice Research Institute in the Philippines, and I was able to meet him there

at the end of my trip through Asia.) PV 18 outyielded both
Lerma Rojo and Sonora 64 by 10 to 30%. In extensive trials
conducted in 1965/66 on farmers' fields, PV 18 produced yields
which occasionally exceeded eight tons per hectare.

It is hard to describe the sheer excitement that can be
involved in this wheat-breeding business. Many people may
not realize that there *is* any excitement. Yet if Crick and
Watson's story of how they found the double-helix structure
of DNA became an international best-seller, the search for the
'miracle' wheat is surely worth a paragraph or two.

PV 18 is a two-gene dwarf variety with a height of about
95 cm. It has profuse tillering capacity, thick straw and broad
dark green leaves. The ear-head is broad with about 70 grains
as compared with the 50 grains which are to be found in the
improved indigenous wheats of the Punjab. (It is important to
realize that research on wheat improvement had been going
on in the Punjab since the early 1900's—what was new was the
Mexican material.) Grains of PV 18 are variable and smaller
in size than those of indigenous wheats such as C 306. PV 18
is resistant to all three rusts (i.e. leaf rust, stem rust and stripe
rust), has a high response to heavy doses of fertilizer and
resistance to lodging.

But PV 18 has a red grain and even hungry Indians do not
like red-grained chapattis. This is a matter of taste and
tradition. Forty years ago, I was told, everyone ate red chapattis and it wasn't until the famous Punjab wheats, C 518 and
C 591, were developed in the early 1930's at the College of
Agriculture and Research Institute, Lyallpur (now in West
Pakistan) that amber-seeded wheats came to predominate, and
preferences changed to the yellow chapatti. So the question
was: could an amber-seeded wheat be developed with good
chapatti making characteristics but which still had the agronomic properties of PV 18?

PV 18 had been developed from the progeny of a multiple
cross attempted in Mexico. The precise label was $(Fn \times F58 - N)$
N_{10-B}-Gb66118156 $-$ I.M24 $-$4M. From this same cross
(which has been abbreviated in popular literature to No. 8156)
a sister strain to PV 18 was derived known as Kalyan Sona
which, literally translated, means 'golden saviour'. Kalyan

Sona is also a two-gene dwarf wheat. Plant height, like that
of PV 18, is about 95 cm. Like PV 18 it has profuse tillering
capacity, thick straw and broad and erect dark green leaves.
In fact, the principal difference between the two varieties is
that Kalyan Sona has an amber grain. (In Mexico, this amber-
seeded plant is known as Siete Cerros and I had seen it weeks
before growing in the fields at Toluca.)

Three other leading Indian varieties came from that first
shipment from Mexico back in 1963. The most important of
these is a wheat known as Sonalika ('gold-like'), which is the
only near rival to Kalyan Sona. It is a semi-dwarf wheat,
genetically diverse from PV 18 and Kalyan Sona. Its plants
attain a height of about 105 cm. The grains are fewer (about 55
to an ear) but larger. It yields less than Kalyan Sona but
matures earlier, a fact which may be important for a farmer
trying to raise two crops a year.

Besides Sonalika, wheats known as Safed Lerma and Chotti
Lerma have been important. The first is like the original Lerma
Rojo 64, but it has a white kernel not a red one. Chotti Lerma,
also called S 331, does well in central and southern India as
well as in the wheat areas in the northern plains.

Finally, mention should be made of Sharbati Sonora, a
wheat which Dr Swaminathan produced from the original
Mexico Sonora 64. He irradiated the plant with gamma rays
and produced a mutant with an amber kernel as opposed to
a red one.

The area under the new wheats increased from about three
quarters of a million hectares in 1966/67 to nearly three million
in 1967/68. In 1969/70, out of a total wheat area of 16 or 17
million hectares, dwarf wheats occupied over 10 million
hectares. In 1964, the best year till then, the wheat harvest
had been 12·3 million tons. In 1965 and 1966, years when the
monsoon failed, the harvest had fallen to 10·4 and 11·4 million
tons respectively. But by the harvest of 1967/68 it had built up
to 16·5 million tons, which was 40% higher than the previous
record. In 1968/69, production increased to 18·7 million tons.
The following year, as the acreage under dwarf wheats rose,
production exceeded 20 million tons.

This, in summary, is the story of the wheat revolution in

India, at least as far as the bare facts and figures are concerned. Under-lying the successes that have been achieved are several factors which tend to be overlooked in a quick overall review. As we sat in his office, Anderson listed them for me.

On fertilizer: 'The economists said that 120 pounds per acre of fertilizer would give maximum returns *per acre*, but if you put 40 pounds per acre over three times the acreage you would get more wheat in absolute terms. But the Rockefeller Foundation stood by the full dose because this would be the psychological clincher in demonstrating the value of fertilizer.'

On price: 'The decision of the government to keep a floor price for wheats was all important. This could not be geared to the world price of wheat. Conventional economics breaks down. It's much better to grow and help keep the agrarian economy busy than to go and buy food. Ten dollars per quintal was guaranteed in peak delivery periods after harvest. The government performs a buffer-stock function. It hopes to build stocks of food-grains up to seven million tons. It's better to pay the price for the grain instead of a whole range of subsidies here and there. The farmer may be illiterate but he's not necessarily unintelligent. He is subject to change as long as you can show him he is going to make more money.'

On credit: 'Predominantly credit is still dispensed by the private lender. If you go through the bureaucracy, you may get the money but it's there at the wrong time. Time will show how good the repayment rate is for official credits. Credit is given in kind rather than in cash. There is a great temptation to use cash credit for the marriage of daughters and so forth, rather than for agricultural purposes.'

Looking to the future, Dr Anderson seemed especially concerned about the disease problem. 'There is a danger—I don't want to overdramatize it—of yellow or stripe rust. It occurred last year in the Middle East, in Morocco and Turkey. It attacks Kalyan Sona. What we have to do is to take the major breeding lines and put them back into a screening nursery. We have already got one going. It includes Lebanon, Turkey, Pakistan—all the wheat-growing countries. The idea would be to take the principal commercial varieties and put these into a trap nursery and grow them in the principal disease centres across the world. Each country could add on its own commercial varieties, so you'd have about 60 varieties in the base list altogether.

'We have identified pretty well the epidemiology of stem rust, leaf rust and stripe rust. Stem rust starts in Mysore and moves north, following the temperature gradient. It slows down because of the elevation. Also there is less moisture (for any of the rusts to attack a plant the spore has to germinate in moisture). The rust arrives quite late in the season in the Indo-Gangetic plain, maybe two or three weeks before harvest. Epidemics in the upper plain are almost unknown. But you have had epidemics in Madya Pradesh in years of high moisture, also in Bihar.

'Brown rust or leaf rust comes out of the Himalayas, establishes itself on the new seedling crops in December, then around February it starts to build up. Brown rust in Mysore also follows the temperature climb as the temperature rises with the advance of the season, so you have two populations coming out each year.

'Stripe rust is a cold-loving rust. It comes out of one area up in Punjab, one in U.P. and one in Bihar. The rust from Bihar doesn't attack wheat, only barley. The other two tongues come out and advance on the plains, spreading south. The damage will extend a bit north of Delhi, then follow an east-west line, moving out in parallel to the Himalayas as it generates spores. Then it meets the heat advancing from the south, so that cuts it off. The rust that attacks Kalyan Sona has come from Africa, following varieties that are susceptible.'

Dr Anderson, at the time of my visit, was in a reflective mood. He was leaving India after six years in the country to go to Mexico, to CIMMYT. It was a good moment to look back at some of the achievements and shortcomings.

'The most important thing in my view,' he said, 'has been the change in the attitude of the farmer. This has been brought about by his ability to get yields. And this in turn has meant that the farmer is going after consumer goods whereas before he was living on a subsistence basis. The tractor population is going up, after 5,000 years when agriculture in India meant a wooden plough which was really a spear with a bit of iron on it.

'In the first year, in my personal experience, the farmer didn't know what a variety was. In the second year, he knew it and he knew what he had to do with it. People write articles implying that the masses should starve and die slowly and peacefully and gracefully. Those who are actively involved just don't have time to write about it. You're out there in the field, getting your hands dirty. You have to, if you're going to be effective. Hell and twenty, there's room enough for everybody. But you have to approach it with a missionary zeal. You've got to believe that you'll beat the problems. When I first came here, Ralph Cummings, who was Director of the Rockefeller Foundation's India programme till 1966, said to me: "You may be wondering what the job is. All I can tell you is that India doesn't grow enough wheat. Then it's in your hands."'

That they were indeed capable hands is borne out by the evidence of history.

*

I first saw Dr Subramanian in Mexico City, when he was attending the annual CIMMYT Board meeting in the Hotel Aristos. He had been singled out to receive, on the occasion of the meeting, a special gold medal for his work in making the 'green revolution' possible in India. In the course of a short speech of commendation, Robert Osler—the Deputy Director of the Institute—mentioned Dr Subramanian's courage and vision in giving backing to his agricultural people, and in authorizing large purchases of seed from Mexico, at a time when there was considerable opposition in India to such a move.

One afternoon during my time in New Delhi I called on Dr Subramanian in his home and asked him to relate, as he saw them, the principal highlights of the wheat story in India.

'There is an impression,' Dr Subramanian began, 'that India emphasized industry more than agriculture. But this is not altogether true. The First Plan stressed agriculture—that was 1952 to 1957—but in rather a complacent way. In the Second Plan period, 1957 to 1962, the food deficits began. In the Third Plan, the importance of agriculture was fully realized and the doubling of the budget estimates for agriculture took place.

'A 2·5% annual increase in agricultural production took place over those 15 years. But 1·8% of this came from expanding the area under production. At the same time, the population was increasing, not at 1·9% or 2% a year, but at 2·5%. I was haunted by the deficit, and the food imports we were receiving under PL 480 contributed to a false sense of security.

'Another factor which inhibited agricultural development was price policy. Our great concern was to contain the inflationary trend, given our large investment plans. So the PL 480 imports were used to permit a cheap food-grains policy. This influenced procurement prices from the farmers. Agriculture was not a paying concern.

'I was called on to be Minister of Food and Agriculture in 1964 when Jahawarlal passed away and Lal Bahadur formed his administration. I came from a different area—from mines and heavy industry. But this was an advantage. I came to it fresh. I set up a survey, to try to see what had gone wrong in agriculture, what was the missing link. When I analysed it, I found that diminishing returns had set in. I came to the conclusion, after consultation with experts, that we had been intensifying our efforts on the basis of traditional technology. But what we required was a new technology in agriculture.

'Our research workers—in collaboration with the Ford and Rockefeller people—had been made aware of the possibilities of Mexican wheat and new hybrid maize and new sorghums and so forth. The new varieties meant more fertilization, more plant protection measures. We had to evolve a new strategy. But how were we to make our farmers take to the new technology? The experts were sceptical. They said we would need at least a generation. Another set of advisers said we would need collectivisation.

'This is where you need to take a political and social view of these things. No doubt in the USA the improvement of agriculture has been a long gradual change. But here we were introducing technology which had been fully developed, which gave 200% to 300% increases in production. The stakes were so high, it was just like gambling.

'So I said, let us have national demonstrations on a large scale. The first year was 1965/66. We had 1,000 demonstrations on the farmers' fields. Amidst all the other traditional crops, these new wheats were the outstanding crops. I have seen these farmers come from hundreds of miles. For them, it was like going to a temple to witness a miracle.

'We had 250 tons of seed and we estimated the demand for the next year at 5,000 tons of multiplied seed. But the demand picked up and that was how the Mexican purchase happened —over 20,000 tons of seed. But even that wasn't enough to meet the demand.

'The second aspect was price. Soon after I took over, I made a recommendation to the government that unless we changed our price policy we would be in trouble. The government agreed and reversed its decision on the cheap grain policy. The new technology also required chemicals and fertilizers, and pesticides for plant protection measures. They either had to be produced within the country or imported. So the foreign exchange was earmarked, while domestic production was being built up.

'In retrospect, it was historical compulsion, compulsion of circumstances, which enabled me to force through in one month critical decisions which might otherwise have taken years. The food situation was desperate. The sheer volume of PL 480 imports at the time demonstrated how critical the situation was. But I told President Johnson that by 1972 we would become self-sufficient with regard to cereals. After March 1972, if we needed food, we would make commercial imports.

'In the 1950's, with best monsoon conditions, we were producing at a maximum 55 million tons of food grains. During 1964/65, under the most favourable conditions, we produced 87 million tons. But now our basis is 100 million tons and, besides what we have achieved in wheat, a rice revolution is in the offspring.

'Progress means change, change means new problems. If you're afraid of problems, you can't have change. From the technological point of view, modernization itself requires land reform. New agriculture means new investment. These will only take place if people are going to profit from investment. This means that a man must be certain that, yes, this is my land. If a man holds land above the permitted ceiling, he won't invest because he knows it may be taken from him. If he is a tenant, security of tenure becomes very important.

'Also the new agriculture is completely changing the agricultural operation. It is more intensified agriculture, it needs more intimate management. Two crop areas become three crop areas. The five-acre family-managed unit has great potential. Japan demonstrated this. The USA is a completely different production pattern. Japan also developed small farm implements. For a country like ours, we can't have mechanization throwing thousands of people out of work. Production would be useless if it meant that people were unemployed and they had no income.'

*

Punjab is the bread-basket of India. Traditionally, it has always led the country as far as agriculture is concerned. Punjabi farmers recognized the potential of the 'green revolution', and acted accordingly, before other states had even heard of it. A few figures make the point. Between 1964/65 and 1968/69, Punjabi farmers had planted 80% of the land with 'miracle' varieties; consumption of fertilizers increased four-fold; yields doubled; the number of tubewells for irrigation rose from 7,000 to over 100,000; the number of tractors rose from 5,000 to over 13,000. By 1969/70 Punjab was producing almost one-quarter of India's total wheat tonnage.

If Punjab is the cream of India, Ludhiana district in the Punjab is the cream of the cream. More figures. The dwarf wheats were planted on 75 hectares on 100 farms in Ludhiana district in 1965/66, on 8,093 hectares in 1966/67, on 93,000 hectares (about 55% of the total wheat area) involving about 32,000 or 80% of the district's farmers in 1967/68 and by about 90% of Ludhiana farmers in 1968/69.

I first travelled through the Punjab (on both sides of the border) in the summer of 1961. I wasn't in those days especially concerned with agriculture and I dare say I failed to notice a good many things which, on this more recent trip, I would have been anxious to observe. What I remember most clearly about that drive from Peshawar through Rawalpindi, then on into India via Lahore and Amritsar, was the number of Persian wheels. To me the sight of a camel plodding round and round a hole in the ground while water came up on an endless chain of buckets and was tipped into a rough irrigation ditch, was in some way symbolic of the land itself. An endless round. Elemental; timeless and unchanging. Or so I thought. Yet, only ten years later, the scene was quite different. If the wells were still in use, they were fitted with electric or petrol/diesel pumps. The camels had padded off, with their great slow strides, into oblivion. The chain of buckets had been pulled up and lay rusting on the earth beside the well.

More often than not, the old wells had been replaced altogether. Tubewells now thrust far deeper into the earth to extract its vital juices. Higher profits from shorter wheats made capital investments possible on a scale which would not have been dreamed of in earlier years.

I fly up to Ludhiana from New Delhi. The plains below show a shimmer of green, for sowing is virtually finished and much of the wheat has already begun to sprout. An hour or so after landing at Ludhiana, I am out in the fields looking, at close range, at the 'green revolution' in action. My guide and mentor is H. S. Bains, whose full title is Assistant Professor Extension (Farmers' Training), Punjab Agricultural University, Ludhiana.

Bains is a Sikh. Though the practice is common among many of his co-religionists, he refuses to wear his beard in a net. Instead it blows free in the wind, white and immense. He has a wild look and a driving energy. When farmers see Bains, Assistant Professor Extension (Farmers' Training), heading their way in one of the grey jeeps belonging to Punjab Agricultural University, they buckle down to the job in hand in no uncertain manner.

Bains believes in driving fast. His face set in a ferocious scowl, he weaves out of Ludhiana with one hand on the horn and the other holding his turban against the wind. From time to time he releases his grip long enough to be able to jerk the steering wheel to the right or left.

All roads in India are overloaded with humanity, and human

impedimenta. The roads in Ludhiana district in the Punjab
are overloaded to bursting. For to the normal traffic of Indian
daily life has been added the additional traffic generated by
the 'green revolution'. We pass oxen, moving like tanks down
the very centre of the road, pulling loads of busa (wheat straw)
that are literally as tall and as wide as pantechnicons. We pass
lorries bearing the kharif crops to markets; wait at level cross-
ings for trains to pass bulging with grain and heading for
different parts of the country. Punjab, as the economists would
say, is in the middle of an 'export-led boom'.

We turn off the main road and bounce a few miles down a
sidetrack, the dust rising behind us. We come to a village.
Bains says: 'This is the village Jhandi. It is the first village in
our programme.'

Jhandi is a village like a hundred, a thousand, other villages
in the Punjab. A cluster of flat-roofed mud houses, a cluster
of women around a well or washing clothes by a stream, a
cluster of animals lazing in whatever narrow shade the noon-
day sun permits. At first sight it does not seem so much different
from all the other mud villages I have seen over the years,
across half of Asia.

We jump down from the jeep and stride around. 'Here',
says Bains, 'is a field of wheat, shared between two brothers.
It is all irrigated. Not a single piece of land will be left fallow.
They have 24 acres altogether and they rent another two. They
have installed two tubewells. The demand for electric power
in the Punjab is such that there have had to be power cuts.
That means that the farmers who installed diesel, instead of
electric, tubewells will benefit.

'Last year,' Bains continues, '22 out of the 24 acres on the
farm were under wheat. They planted Kalyan 227—that's what
we call Kalyan Sona here in Punjab. They got 12½ quintals
per acre.'

We walk to the edge of the field where a tractor has been
backed up to a tubewell. Its motor is running and a belt runs
from the power take-off point to the well-head. Water gushes
out into an irrigation ditch. One of the brothers joins us. Bains
asks him some questions in Punjabi, then informs me:

'The tractor is consuming one litre of petrol an hour. The

man is irrigating every ten or fifteen days. He irrigates first
before planting, then he rotates the water around. He is applying fertilizer at the rate of one quintal per acre of ammonium
and the same amount of phosphate. He is also using one quintal
per acre of calcium/ammonium/nitrate. He'll dose it with more
fertilizer if he thinks he needs it.'

Bains and I go in with the man to have the first of the many
cups of tea we drank that day. Bains points out to me signs of
growing prosperity. 'See, here he has a pukka floor. Here is a
colour photograph of the man's family.' We sit on a sofa and
I notice in the corner of the room a radio set. Women move in
and out of the room, but there is no sign of their permanent
presence.

Bains says: 'The general practice in India is that the ladies
sleep aloof. They are up at five in the morning, they do all the
cattle and all the housework.'

We go back to the jeep and drive on to another village.
'This', says Bains, 'is the village of Hissowal. Here we will
talk to Mr Ram Singh. You will probably be quite confused
with all the Singhs before the day is out. The point is that the
Sikhs are some of the best farmers, so these are the people we
are going to.'

Ram Singh, it turns out, is a small farmer. He has eight acres
altogether, of which six are under wheat. His son works at
Punjab Agricultural University and is known to Bains. Ram
Singh is achieving yields of 15 or 16 quintals. He has kept back
two acres for fodder. He mixes Napier grass with the wheat
straw and feeds it to his seven milking cows. He uses the same
five horse-power motor for driving the tubewell and for cutting
up the fodder. He uses the cow-dung on the fields and saves
money on fertilizer.

Bains believes that the extension service should be concerned,
as a matter of priority, with the small farmer. 'Let us apply
our minds to the small cultivator,' he says. 'Let us help him
with a small ten horse-power tractor. Design bins for storage
so he does not lose so much from the rats. Modest improvements.
That is what we are needing.'

More tea with Ram Singh. We sit outside his house. An old
woman, Ram Singh's mother (or perhaps it is his mother's

mother), spins away at the gandhi wheel, making a cotton blanket to add to her grand-daughter's (or great grand-daughter's) dowry.

Bains says we must be on our way. We have seen a medium farmer, we have seen a small farmer. Now we must see a large farmer. So we drive on for 20 miles to visit Jaghit Singh who has about 100 acres, of which 75 are under wheat.

Jaghit Singh was a living embodiment of what the prosperity of the 'green revolution' has meant to those who can lay their hands on 100 acres of good Punjab earth. He was Ram Singh multiplied by 20, the epitome of the young progressive Punjabi farmer. We walk around his land and, as we go, he tells us how he did it. He says he started in 1951 with 20 acres.

'I am the son of a small farmer. We were refugees from Pakistan. Nothing was with us. We lost everything in Pakistan. It pinches me that now the government wants to interfere and split up our holdings.'

Jaghit Singh says that: 'the common man's fate changed in 1966/67. People were actually hungry in those days. Three years back they were paying one rupee for a single grain of triple dwarf wheat. UP 308 sold for 250 rupees a kilo. I obtained seed from a friend and multiplied it out. I used to sell it for 100 rupees a quintal. There was more money to be made of course in those days from selling for seed purposes, than selling food-grains. Everybody wanted the new seeds.'

Jaghit Singh was a powerful advocate of the importance of fertilizer. He split his fertilizer applications into three, giving one-half at the time of sowing, one-quarter before the first irrigation and the last quarter at the fifth or sixth irrigation. He used 90 to 100 lb of nitrogen per acre, 50–60 lb of phosphate and about 60 lb of potash. He attempted to take account of the need for micro-nutrients and trace elements as well, though he recognized that at the moment there were practical limitations to this level of sophistication.

He had a new combine harvester and he showed it to us, standing in a new concrete yard. 'Old people', he said, 'didn't believe that the same machine could do cutting and threshing and bagging.' Use of the combine gave him an important price advantage over other farmers. He could market his crop while others were still threshing. This meant he could command a scarcity premium before the price fell to its support level, as the great glut of wheat from the rest of the Punjab came on the market.

Singh was building a new house; he had hired an architect from Chandigarh; he had dug a swimming pool and, when the tubewell was finally electrified, he would probably use the machine to fill up the pool besides irrigating the crops. He had been in Montana, in the United States, on an International Farm Exchange Programme; had a daughter five years old and a son one year old. Modern farmer, modern man. Huge radiogram in the sitting-room; cassette tape-recorder, new record albums. Seeds of change indeed.

Bains has one last category of farmer to show me: the demonstration farmer. The demonstration farmer is a man who has a national or state demonstration plot on part of his land. He is provided with seeds and fertilizer by the extension service. In return, he holds 'field days' which (in theory) will be attended by farmers from neighbouring areas who want to learn at first hand what to do and not do with the new technology. The theory, as often as not, has been realized in practice. Men have walked 100 miles to visit demonstration plots and have gone home to their villages to spread the story of the small miracles they have seen.

The last Singh Bains took me to—a Mr Bachat Singh— prided himself on achieving record yields in Ludhiana district. He had fifteen acres and leased six acres more. The national demonstration plot consisted of one acre of this land. Had I come a few weeks earlier I would, no doubt, have seen some spectacular growth. But the kharif crops had all been harvested and the rabi crops had not yet grown. But there was, even so, no mistaking the nature of the enterprise in which Mr Bachat Singh was engaged. He had moved out of the village and had built himself a house actually on his fields. Instead of walking out each day to his land, he lived among his crops and breathed the same air as they did. What he lost from the point of view of communal village life, he gained in income and—so it seemed—in personal satisfaction.

This new house was, unlike most village houses, a two-storey

G

affair. It stood out on the flat plains of the Punjab like some kind of lighthouse. On top of the upper storey, as a result of some strange architectural brain-storm, a tower had been constructed—thus heightening still further the effect of prominence. On the sides of the tower, in huge Punjabi letters, slogans had been painted. I asked Bains what they meant and he in turn, after consulting with Mr Singh, explained their significance. Farming in Mr Singh's eyes was, Bains said, part of the religious life. The slogans were expressions of this belief. And Bains translated some of them for me. One of them said: 'No smoking' (a typical Sikh injunction). Another said: 'The young may prosper and the farmer may prosper.' Yet another said: 'The industrious or hard-working farmer is the real guardian of this country. The sluggish farmer is the enemy of his country.'

★

My second afternoon in Ludhiana I sat in on a lecture for young farmers at the Agricultural University. Bains explained that a three-month course was in progress. All the participants were young men who were already farmers and who were temporarily absent from their farms, or else youths who showed some desire to become farmers. They had three such courses a year and so far had trained some 400 people. The course was advertised in the newspapers. Participants were provided with free board and lodging and paid a stipend of 50 rupees a month.

When we entered the room, the lecturer appeared to be explaining by means of diagrams how fertilizer could be applied so that the plant received maximum benefit. Though he was talking in Punjabi, he used enough key words like 'nitrogen' and 'yield' for the gist of his remarks to be reasonably clear. In front of him, six deep and ten across, sat serried rows of Sikhs in their various turbans. They listened intently and, once they had recovered from the momentary surprise caused by our visit, asked keen lively questions. Bains interprets for me. One man, he says, wants to know whether urea fertilizer should be applied before or after watering. Another asks when the first irrigation should be applied, so as to most facilitate the tillering stage of the wheat.

I realize as I listen that education, especially agricultural education, is vital if the momentum of the 'green revolution' is to be sustained. My mind went back to Tanzania and the efforts of Professor Vishnyakov. Tanzania was different from India and the problems of agriculture in Africa are not the same as those of Asia. Yet the fundamental concept of creating literate farmers was common to both continents and their diverse cultures.

That same evening Bains drove me out about 40 miles from Ludhiana, to a small village in the Samrala tehsil. We had been asked to observe a functional literacy course. Since Professor Vishnyakov had, through circumstances beyond his control, been unable to oblige in this respect, I looked forward to the evening with double interest.

The class we were to attend was in fact part of a national programme instituted by the government and supported by UNDP and UNESCO. This programme, known as 'Farmers Training and Functional Literacy', reached into every section of the country. One hundred districts throughout India had been selected for intensive experimentation. Through the Farm and Home Units of All-India Radio, the Ministry of Information and Broadcasting was presenting special programmes about the 'new farming'. Sixteen thousand radio sets had been supplied for discussion groups up and down the land. The anticipated audience would ultimately total five million families. The Ministry of Food, Agriculture, Community Development and Co-operation was responsible for training programme officers and convenors of discussion groups in the agricultural aspects of their job. The Ministry of Education was responsible for the Functional Literacy Component.

At the time of my visit, substantial progress had already been achieved. The programme had begun with five districts in 1966/67. By 1970, it covered 70 districts and the hope was that by the end of 1971 this coverage would have been extended to the full 100. Men and women were being exposed to practically every known extension method. Demonstrations, field days, tours, pictures, films, posters, discussion groups, radio programmes—all these, and more, were involved in the effort to inform and educate a mass audience about the whole 'package of cultural and agricultural practices' needed to implement the 'green revolution'. In India, when anything happens, it happens on a gigantic scale. Already 300,000 farmers had attended Production-cum-Demonstration Camps organized under the UNDP/UNESCO Project. Six hundred short courses had produced training for more than 20,000 participants. Another 100,000 had been enrolled in discussion groups.

The figures themselves give some indication of the sheer size of the project. Though the percentage of literacy in India is now estimated at 33, the absolute number of illiterates grows year by year with the overall growth of the population. If the UNDP/UNESCO Project can indeed reach out to five million farm families, it may make a significant contribution to the 'food deficit' and the 'literacy deficit' at one and the same time.

There are 60 Functional Literacy Centres altogether in the Samrala tehsil of Ludhiana district. The class to which we were invited was to take place in Nagra village about ten miles from the town of Samrala itself.

We arrive in the village by about 8 p.m. But it is still early and the men have not yet come in from the fields. The teacher takes us to his house and serves us with *roti*, which is a mixture of maize and flour and mustard leaves, and *sag*, a form of buttered spinach which is eaten with the flat unleavened bread of the Punjab. The teacher explains to us that this is the busy season. 'Even if a man's mother dies, he will keep her for ten days because he doesn't want to bury her. He is too busy.'

Finally word arrives that the class is assembled. We follow the teacher out into the night towards the communal meeting room. Inside the room about 25 men of all ages assembled. In the doorway or at the windows the children have crowded to watch the proceedings. Most of the people there have wrapped blankets about their shoulders since the night chill has already descended.

The teacher, who is a farmer himself, stands in front of the group and talks. This is functional literacy in action. The examples he uses are all meant to have a basis in real life. If the teacher writes '28 plus 28' on his slate, he is teaching the use of fertilizer (28 lb of ammonium phosphate plus 28 lb of nitrogen) as well as arithmetic.

He calls for volunteers from the class to come to the board. There is a momentary pause, then a very old man rises from the floor (we are all sitting cross-legged), takes the chalk and slowly and carefully writes his name in Punjabi: K. M. Singh. Then, after the name, he writes the letters BDO, which Bains tells me means 'Block Development Officer'. Then he puts the tips of his fingers together, turns to the group, bows and says— this old man of at least 80—'I have been practising'. So the group smiles and he returns to his place.

Bains stands up and asks permission to speak. He tells them he would like to start a discussion group here in the village and that a man from the university will come to talk to them about their problems. He explains that he will appoint a convenor of the group and that they will talk about seeds and manures and fertilizers. Bains sits down and a heated discussion takes place. The main issue seems to be whether the University should come and establish a demonstration plot somewhere in the village.

The attendance book is being passed round. Looking at it, I see that classes started at the beginning of the month but that attendance has fallen off because this is the busy season. When the book arrives back at the teacher, the lesson begins in earnest. The teacher has himself written a manual for the group and he goes through it. Today the subject is manure; tomorrow it will be pesticides and plant diseases. Posters on the wall repeat some of the key illustrations from the book so that those who have poor eyesight can follow the lesson.

The group works through the story for today. 'Dal Ghosh and Bhindi Ghosh go to the fields together. Dal Ghosh talks to Bhindi Ghosh about agriculture. Dal Ghosh and Bhindi Ghosh discuss how to produce more wheat in their fields. . . .'

The group reads, and tries to write. For some of them writing is clearly difficult. The teacher explains to us how he simplifies the intricate Punjabi characters so as to make it easier for the old people whose hands are stiff with age.

'It will do for a start,' he says, 'they can come to the others by and by.'

*

G *

Journalists have amused themselves in recent years by attacking the 'green revolution'. They have pointed to social and political by-products of the new agriculture and, sometimes, have seemed to argue that these by-products are so serious that it might have been better if the 'green revolution' had not taken place at all. This, frankly, is rubbish. Of course, there are second and third generation problems. Some of them are important and need to be taken into account by politicians and agricultural strategists and aid-giving agencies. But these second and third generation problems would not exist if the first generation problems were not solved, or near solution. A sense of perspective is required.

Inequality of land ownership, inadequacy of credit facilities for the small farmer, insecurity of tenure on the part of tenants and share-croppers, landlessness, the growing disparity between irrigated and rain-fed areas—all these are subjects which demand the urgent attention of the Centre and the States. India cannot afford for the 'green revolution' to become the prerogative of the Jaghit Singhs of the world, while ignoring the needs and the potential contribution of the Ram Singhs. India cannot afford the displacement of her rural population, through mechanization of agriculture or amalgamation of holdings, at rates which exceed the ability of the urban centres to absorb the inflow. Journalists have made great play of the 'green revolution turning into a red revolution'. It would be tragic if an emotive slogan were taken as an expression of the inevitable.

Another subject of criticism has been the relative lack of progress in rice, as compared to wheat. Rice comprises about 40% of the total food-grain crop in India and perhaps 80% of the rice crop is grown under monsoon conditions. The vital need is to develop a 'package of agricultural practices' for increasing rice production and profitability under monsoon conditions (progress is greater with rabi-grown rice).

Those who follow these things, like the Ford and Rockefeller Foundations in India, believe that today a revolution in research is taking place which can in the course of time transform the outlook for rice. They believe that there is a good chance of evolving 'dwarf, profuse-tillering, erect, dark green

varieties of medium to short duration which are not season-
bound, and which have good fertilizer response and pest
resistance'. If, to these new varieties, a new agronomy can be
added and a new marketing structure evolved for what remains
at the moment a predominantly subsistence crop, we may hope
to see a genuine rice revolution in India. At that point the
target of 'self-sufficiency in food-grains' (which effectively
means a harvest of 130 million tons in 1973/74 and an annual
increase thereafter at least matching the 2·5% growth in
population) would presumably be quite firmly in the bag for
a few years at least.

THE STORY of rice in the Philippines does not begin in the Philippines. It begins in Taiwan in 1945 when, with the restoration of Chinese rule to the island, local breeders began to pay attention to the improvement of native (indica) rice. The Taichung District Agricultural Improvement Station began making crosses among the indica varieties. One of the plants they used for this purpose was known as Dee-Geo-Woo-Gen which, literally, means 'brown-tipped, short-legged'. No one is precisely sure of the origin of Dee-Geo-Woo-Gen. It was first discovered as a single plant growing in a farmer's field in Taiwan, though its original provenance may have been Southern China. At all events, Dee-Geo-Woo-Gen was mated with Tsai-Yuan-Chung, a tall drought-resistant variety and from the match resulted the famous Taichung Native 1. Taichung Native 1 was named (an important event in the life of a variety)in 1956. It showed good response to fertilizer but was not immediately adopted on a widespread basis. At that time, the export of rice to Japan was still a prime objective of Taiwan's agricultural policy and the Japanese preferred *ponlai* (or japonica) rice rather than indica.

However, by 1964, the popularity of Taichung Native 1 had increased rapidly. One-third of the area under indica was planted to the variety. It became clear that a breed of indica had been developed that was no less responsive to fertilizer than the modern japonica varieties which had been grown in temperate regions, and systematically improved, since the beginning of the century. In short, a fertilizer-responsive rice suited to *tropical* climates (and the great hungry areas of the world are typically tropical or sub-tropical) was in prospect.

In 1962, the International Rice Research Institute (established jointly by the Ford and Rockefeller Foundation in cooperation with the Republic of the Philippines) had begun work at Los Baños in the Philippines on rice production in the tropics. The scientists who came to the Institute believed that one of the fundamental reasons for the low yields of rice in the tropics was the lack of a variety which could absorb heavy doses of fertilizer without lodging, or falling over. The traditional tropical varieties were tall and leafy and tended to lodge under any form of heavy fertilization or intensive management.

IRRI's geneticist, Dr T. T. Chang, had originally come from Taiwan and he returned to the island almost as soon as the Institute began work in the hope that the semi-dwarf indica varieties from Taiwan might prove useful in the Institute's breeding programme. He saw Taichung Native 1 and brought it back to Los Baños, together with its parent Dee-Geo-Woo-Gen and some other Taiwanese specimens, of which the most important was I-Geo-Tse.

The breeders at Los Baños made 38 crosses in 1962. Twelve of these involved either Dee-Geo-Woo-Gen or I-Geo-Tse as one of the parents. The most successful cross was between Peta, a tall Indonesian variety, which had disease resistance and heavy tillering, and Dee-Geo-Woo-Gen, the dwarf Chinese variety. The story goes that the particular cross, an outstanding line, IR8-288-3, in the F4 generation, was nearly missed by the IRRI plant breeder, Henry Beachell and IRRI Director Robert Chandler (who is for rice what Borlaug is for wheat), as they inspected the plots. But they went back to take another look and decided to give IR-8-288-3 another chance.

Less than three years after the original cross was made, IR-8-288-3 was planted in its first yield trial. The date was March 1965. The computed yield was 6,600 kilograms per hectare. What made this result even more surprising was that it was obtained in the cloudy monsoon season, when plant performance is supposed to be limited by insufficient solar radiation. Put in agricultural language, the result showed that IR 8 was not photoperiod sensitive. It would thrive whether the days were long or short, sunny or cloudy, i.e. in a variety of climates and latitudes.

From experiments conducted in the 1966 season, the Institute was convinced of the superiority of IR-8-288-3 to Taichung Native 1. It had proved to be more resistant to disease, more responsive to fertilizer. It was more adaptable and had stiffer straw. Seeds were sent to 60 locations throughout the world. In November 1966 the last four digits were lopped off the cross-number and it was given the variety name IR-8. That the popular Press promptly re-christened it the 'miracle' rice was hardly surprising. Its potential was staggering. The lack of photoperiod sensitivity meant that it could be planted more or less any time of the year. With a 120-day growing season this, in turn, meant that under ideal conditions three crops a year could be grown. In addition to this, IR 8 possessed crucial differences in plant architecture as compared to the traditional varieties. IR 8 had a grain/straw ratio of about 1·0 compared with a ratio of about 0·5 for Peta. In other words, at harvest half of the dry matter of IR 8 is grain. Thus 'miracle' meant a potential yield (expressed on an annual basis) of well over 20 tons per hectare per year.

Even if the 'potential' was drastically scaled down to take account of local conditions (such as work preferences, labour availabilities, provision of 'inputs' etc.); even if allowance was made for the fact that what happens on the research station in a totally controlled situation is a far cry indeed from what happens in the field, the development of IR 8 still represented —technologically—a quantum leap. The base for rice production in the tropics was so low, broadly speaking (in India it is still today around 1 to 1·5 tons per hectare), that even modest improvements in yield seemed 'dramatic'. Improvements such as those promised by IR 8 were indeed 'miraculous'.

Another variety, IR 5, was released by the Institute in 1967. IR 5 is more resistant to leaf blight than IR 8, though its plant type is inferior. In December 1969, two new varieties were released, IR 20 and IR 22. These new varieties are similar to IR 8 in plant type and yielding ability, but have better grain quality. The emphasis of the Institute's work had shifted to producing a rice which was more acceptable to Asian consumers than the original IR 8.

In a hungry world, devoting a lot of attention to questions of flavour and grain quality and cooking characteristics may at first sight seem an unnecessary refinement. In fact, these considerations are often crucial. In subsistence economies, where 80% of the rice is eaten in the place it is grown, the production of rice is far more than a nutritional matter. It is an integral part of the culture. A man who eats with chop-sticks needs sticky rice. A man who is used to aromatic food needs *basmati* rice. IR 8 has a white belly and 'dorsal chalkiness' and some consumers may prefer the clear translucent grains of traditional varieties. Rice is not a single homogeneous product. There are a thousand different rices for a thousand different cultures. Once he has made some progress towards increasing absolute yields, the job of the plant-breeder is to see how, within the genetic strategy he has adopted, he can 'maximize consumer preference' in other aspects as well.

*

On June 3, 1966, President Marcos came out to IRRI to look at the work of the Institute. Two days later Dr Robert Chandler, the Director of the Institute, was called by the President's Office. He and his team from Los Baños were to come into Manila on June 11 to meet with the Cabinet. That meeting inaugurated the most successful national rice-growing programme the world has yet seen. In less than three years, the Philippines (which typically had imported at least 10% of the rice it consumed annually) turned into a net exporter. The Philippines showed the world that—with determined leadership and appropriate policies—the promise of the new varieties, as demonstrated at the research station, could be realized in practice on a nation-wide scale.

That it happened at all was in large measure due to one man, Rafael Salas. Salas had once run the *Manila Chronicle*; he had been Assistant Vice-President of the University of the Philippines; he had been Executive Director of the National Economic Board. He was a member of the Philippines Cabinet at the age of 37 and, as the Executive Secretary of the Cabinet, was known in the Philippines as the 'little President'. More than any other person, he enjoyed the delegated authority of the President.

Marcos asked Salas to be Action Officer for the rice programme, in addition to his normal duties. Salas agreed on condition that he could have full control over the budget resources of the government. This he obtained. As Executive Secretary of the Cabinet, he was also Executive Secretary of the

Interior. He could give directions not only to the other Cabinet officers, but also to provincial and local authorities throughout the Philippines. Thus from the outset of his work Salas had both financial and legal authority. It was a formidable combination.

To this must be added Salas' remarkable single-minded energy. He was probably the only Cabinet officer who had more flying hours than the average pilot in the Philippines Air Force. There were times when he worked 18 or 20 hours a day, for three months at a stretch, on the rice problem.

Salas worked through the Rice and Corn Production Co-ordinating Council (RCPCC), which had succeeded the National Food and Agricultural Council. He recognized from the start that the co-operation of all sectors of the community would be required and that the involvement of traditional 'leaders' in the community would be crucial. It was felt that the most effective way of proceeding was by pilot projects. Salas chose 12 out of the 63 provinces in the Philippines and the RCPCC, looking for some 'demonstration effect', concentrated its efforts there. The strategy worked. The Philippino farmer, blessed with a natural propensity to envy his neighbour (especially if his neighbour is making money), was impressed by the pilot projects. He redoubled his efforts. Priests, lobbied discretely by Salas, stressed in their sermons the merits of the high-yielding varieties. The area planted to the new varieties rose to 13% of rice-growing area in 1967/68 and 27% in 1968/69. The rice programme had started in February 1967. By the end of 1968, self-sufficiency and an exportable surplus had been achieved. That was the measure of the achievement.

Salas stayed with the Programme for three years and seven months. (He left the Philippines in November 1969 to become Executive Director of the newly established United Nations Fund for Population Activities). He himself is the first to recognize that, for a permanent agricultural revolution in the Philippines (or anywhere else), you must have a constellation of changes going far beyond the 'crash-programme' approach, however successful this may be on a short-term basis.

The provision of credit and of fertilizer was stressed by the RCPCC, but there were inadequacies in both respects which were to become marked with Salas' departure for New York.

The extension of the programme beyond the paddy areas into the upland areas, where a large proportion of Philippines rural population lived, was technically complex (high-yielding upland varieties had yet to be evolved). Above all, slow progress on land reform and in correcting the maldistribution of income for which Philippine society is renowned, hampered the achievement of a sustained and steady growth in agricultural production. At the time of writing, the Philippines had once again become a rice importer. In March 1971, the government had decided to buy 300,000 tons of rice from Japan.

There is no doubt that the exceptionally severe typhoons of late 1970 had something to do with this decision. The more significant reason is that a programme which is built, virtually, around the efforts of one man cannot long survive his departure unless the required structural and administrative reforms are put in train and vigorously prosecuted.

4

To go from the Philippines, where the 'rice revolution' has been in full swing for a number of years, to the north-east of Thailand is to pass, within the space of a few hours' flying time (including a change of planes in Bangkok), from one world to another. Why is it, I wonder, that of all the points on the compass the north-east seems the most ill-favoured, by nature and circumstance alike? North-east England, north-east Brazil, north-east Thailand—these are all depressed areas where men and women in their several ways have to struggle to keep alive. Perhaps it is something to do with the motion of the earth as it spins on its axis.

I arrived at Khon Kaen airport at 9.20 a.m. on December 5, the birthday of his Royal Majesty, King Bhumibol Adulyodej. I was met by Rudolf Leuenberger, a German-American who was the Project Manager of UNDP/FAO's Kalasin Project. We drove into town along the new paved road built to specifications laid down by the US army, which likes to move tanks and other heavy vehicles around in a hurry. Leuenberger tells me that he hopes the place won't go communist for at least another five years, i.e. until his tour of duty ends.

Kalasin is three hours further on along the road to Laos and, since there isn't much of a market there, Leuenberger stops the jeep and does his shopping in Khon Laen. These local markets are the same the whole world over. A mush of rotten fruit and vegetables under foot; women squatting behind their stalls; bowls of dried fish; bowls of live fish which the old women prod from time to time so that they twitch and kick.

Fish are one of Leuenberger's problems. Over the years the Royal Thai Government, through its Irrigation Department, has built a network of reservoirs and canals in an attempt to bring water to this drought-stricken region. But to persuade the people to use the water, is another matter altogether. These fish-loving folk knock holes in the concrete of the canals at the first opportunity; let the water out of the reservoirs; block up the channels. Instead of growing rice, they fish. They will make ponds at the slightest excuse and they will spend their days squatting waste-deep in the muddy water, arms outstretched beneath the surface and a happy smile on their faces.

It is poetic, but it is not farming. If they are happy, does it matter? The answer, I am afraid, is 'yes, it does matter'. Even though there may be a rough balance today between production and consumption in the north-east of Thailand, this state of affairs will not long endure unless urgent steps are taken to improve the agricultural situation. The population of Thailand is growing at well over 3% a year, which means it will double in 20 years; and one-third of the population lives in the north-east. There was a time, admittedly, when the great rice-bowl around the Delta provided an exportable surplus of food-grains, both within and outside the country. But that surplus has dwindled over the years. The north-east has to look after its own future.

The full title of the UNDP/FAO Kalasin Project is 'Experimental and Demonstration Farm for Irrigated Agriculture'. The object is to teach farmers, through experiment and demonstration (as the title suggests) how to use water for the production of crops. In theory irrigated diversified crop production will take place on the so-called 'lowland areas', where previously the only crop grown was rainy-season rice. The rice, of course, will still be grown in the rainy season but (hopefully) yields will show a dramatic increase (at least three times the present level) as a result of using better crop varieties, proper fertilization, improved cultivation methods and supplementary irrigation where rainfall is insufficient. Conceivably, double-cropping of rice could take place along classic 'green revolution' lines.

Kalasin is on the Nam Pong river, which is a tributary of the Mekong. The reason the Project is located at Kalasin is because back in 1957 the Thai Government built a dam there with a storage capacity of five billion cubic metres, not to speak of a network of canals and laterals. To this day the system has remained virtually unexploited. If you drive out into the country, you can see the effects of disuse and disrespect—great gaping holes in the concrete lining of the channels; some

laterals left half-finished; others finished but empty and overgrown. Here was a case where men failed to understand that
water is wealth.

The Government is rehabilitating the irrigation network and
it has called on UNDP and FAO, and tall serious German-
Americans like Rudolf Leuenberger, to help in a kind of parallel
psychological rehabilitation of the Thai peasant. As we drive
through the countryside on the road from Khon Kaen to
Kalasin, we see men and women pushing through the fields of
rice in long lines abreast, getting in the harvest. We stop the car
and watch them. They are a happy people, surely. People, who
sing as they swing their short hand sickles; who bend and weave
among the plants, wide coolie hats shading their faces.

But Leuenberger tells me about the kind of yields they obtain
in this care-free casual way, and how much is lost even after the
crop is harvested, and I have to agree with him that the days of
pastoral bliss are over. With the birth-rate being what it is,
there is no land left to subdivide. The only option is to intensify
and this inevitably implies a new way of farming and a new
style of life. It means that the Thai peasant will have to forget
about the patch of kenaf he used to grow on the uplands for the
small cash income it gave him. It means he will have to concentrate all his attention on growing rice and other crops in an
organized systematic way. There will be less singing and dancing,
and much less fishing. There will be a lot of running, mostly to
stand still.

The Thai Government hopes to develop irrigated agriculture
over 400,000 hectares in north-east Thailand. And this is purely
relying on tributary projects. If the possibilities of a dam on the
main stem of the Mekong (e.g. at Pa Mong) are realized,
another two million hectares of potentially irrigible land
could probably be added to that figure. This is a measure
of the importance of the work which is today going on at
Kalasin.

The Mekong, like the Amazon, is one of the world's great
rivers. It is South-East Asia's largest single natural resource.
Each year an average of more than 475 billion cubic metres
flows, almost completely unutilized, through the mouths of the
Mekong Delta into the South China sea. Its lower basin covers

more than 600,000 square kilometres, comprising almost the whole of Laos and Cambodia, one-third of Thailand and two-fifths of the Republic of Vietnam. This lower basin is inhabited by a population of 30 million, representing half the total population of these four countries. It is about 2,500 miles in length, of which 1,100 is in China and 1,400 in Laos, Cambodia and Vietnam.

Back in 1957, a United Nations Technical Assistance Mission headed by Lt.-Gen. Raymond Wheeler reported: 'The Mekong is a majestic river. . . . Wise conservation and utilization of its waters will contribute more towards improving human welfare than any other single undertaking.' The Mekong Committee, which was established at the same time, identified Pa Mong as one of five priority projects submitted for examination. In 1961, the United States agreed to carry out the overall feasibility investigation of the Pa Mong project. In mid-1963, a team from the US Bureau of Reclamation arrived in the field and began work.

In January 1969 (South-East Asia having undergone a sea-change in the interval with the escalation of the Vietnam war) the United States submitted its Pa Mong project Stage I, Interim Report to the Mekong Committee. The heart of the project, as envisaged, is the combined reservoir created by constructing dams on the Mekong river at Pa Mong, about 20 kilometres upstream from Vientiane, and on its tributaries, the Nam Mong and Nam Lik. The reservoir thus created, with a total capacity of about 100 billion cubic metres, would enhance downstream development and navigation, in addition to regu-lating the river for flood control, irrigation and an annual generation of 20·4 billion kWh of electrical energy.

Whether Pa Mong ever gets built remains a matter of speculation. The political problems are probably as important as the financial and the technical problems. Pa Mong would require a degree of regional collaboration—before, during and after construction—among the riparian countries which on present form they have shown themselves unable to achieve. It is this aspect, no doubt, which accounts for the powerful attraction the Pa Mong project has exercised over successive US admini-strations.

At the time of writing (June 1971) it looks as though South-East Asia may indeed achieve the kind of unity which would make the construction of a main-stem Mekong project feasible. But the unifying force will be Peking, not Washington. The world being what it is, this fact may tend to diminish Western enthusiasm for the project. We do not, I have heard people argue, want to 'spend 20 years building a dam for the benefit of the other side'.

I wonder if the people of Kalasin, when they see the water flow through the canals to the water-courses, and from the water-courses to the ditches in the paddy-fields, would really know the difference.

5

SOMEWHERE EAST of India and south-west of China (more precisely between latitudes 28½ and 16 degrees N) lies Burma. It is today's forbidden land. Until very recently it was hardly worth even applying for a visa. None were being granted. The Burmese saying: 'When we are cleaning house, we don't invite many guests' was strictly applicable. The few who were able to visit Rangoon, usually on their way to somewhere else, reported a strange sense of seclusion, of isolation. Burma was turning its back on the world and its face to the wall.

At the beginning of the Asia leg of my trip, while in Rome, I applied for permission to enter the country. I had with me the requisite seven passport-sized photographs (taken in the machine in Baker Street Underground) and a letter of introduction from FAO. I said I wanted to see as much of the country and its people as I could. Having examined other forms of agricultural development in other parts of the world and having heard a great deal about the uniqueness of the Burmese approach, I wanted to look and to learn. It took the Burmese Embassy in Rome's Parioli district less than an hour to decide to let me in. Heinrich Harrer had seven years in Tibet; Burma allowed me seven days.

Journalists who have written about Burma recently (and they have been few enough) have tended to take a hostile attitude. This, of course, is the nature of journalism. You fly into a place. You pick up the telephone to call a friend or a contact and you say 'Where's the trouble? What is it?' No trouble is no news.

The visitor in any case usually arrives via Bangkok and the contrast overwhelms him. Bangkok is a bustling Western city; packed with tourists and 40,000 US Servicemen; spawning bars and massage-parlours by the street-load; riddled with venereal diseases of the most virulent sort; polluted, congested, filthy beyond belief—in short, Bangkok has everything that can

possibly be needed to make the average Westerner feel com-
fortably at home.

Rangoon, on the other hand, is a sleepy little town which
hasn't been painted for 15 years. First impressions, unless you
are prepared for them, are liable to prejudice you against the
place in advance. Moreover, the visitor who makes it to Burma
finds, unless he is lucky enough to have other sources, that his
range of contacts is filtered through the old colonial middle-
class which has been alienated by the new form of government.
He hears the criticism and so he relays it, sometimes without
being willing or able to put it in perspective.

*

I check in at the Union of Burma Airways counter at Bangkok
airport. A smiling Burmese girl at the desk says, 'Gentleman,
how many baggage you want check? Okay, you follow him.
Gentleman, don't forget your pen.'

The flight is UB 226 from Bangkok to Rangoon. It had arrived
early, and I could see the plane—a Boeing 727—standing
quietly on the runway. Originally Burma had chartered a 707
from North-West Airlines, along with its crew of nine. That
became too expensive so they acquired the 727 from Eastern Airlines. Under IATA rules the plane would probably have been
retired and scrapped. But Burma isn't a member of IATA and
doesn't want to be. The UBA fleet also comprises Dakotas,
given by the British government after the war, some Fokkers
and a Viscount or two. There is a daily flight to Calcutta and a
twice-weekly flight to Katmandu. The Russians once presented
an Ilyushin to U Nu, but no one has heard of it since.

At 12.40 p.m. UB 226 comes up on the screen, boarding at
12.55 hours. By the time I reach the cabin, there isn't a window-
seat left in the tourist class, so a steward tells me I can go into
the first class section. Music, canned in the United States, masks
the preparations for take-off. Coca-cola is brought round and
little scented paper towels in tinfoil wraps. We are given two
Rangoon papers published in English: *The Working People's
Daily* and *The Guardian*, both 25 pyas per copy.

1.15 p.m.; we have crossed over the rice bowl and are over
drier country. There are fairly rough roads below and a good

deal of wood and scrub. We are issued two sets of currency control forms in duplicate. It takes a good 20 minutes to complete them.

1.20 p.m; we are over thick forest. It is mountainous and impenetrable. This range of hills runs all the way up to the Shan plateau and the Chinese province of Yunnan, forming Burma's eastern boundary. A tray of lunch is brought, sandwiches and cake in cellophane wrappers. Also an orange. One of the hostesses offers us Burmese cigarettes.

The steward distributes an envelope, pre-addressed to the Chairman, Union of Burma Airways Board, 104 Strand Road, Rangoon. A form inside says, 'if you think that there is anything more that we could have done to add to your comfort and have any criticism of the way you have been looked after, or if there is any feature of our service which you particularly appreciated, please tell us. We shall value your comments which will be treated confidentially and will not be used for press or publicity purposes.'

1.45 p.m.; the western edge of the Gulf of Martaban comes into view. The water of the bay below has a reddish tinge. We are beginning our descent into Rangoon. The pattern of fields is not unlike that of the Bangkok delta. In the distance, through cloud, I have a glimpse of a large river which must be the Irrawaddy, or rather one of its several mouths. . . .

*

Most of whatever small insights I acquired during my time in Burma I owe to P. K. Ghosh, the UNICEF Representative. Erskine Childers and his wife Mallika (both of whom worked for the UN—in Bangkok) had provided the original introduction. It was one of the most valuable I have ever had. Ghosh—'please call me "P.K." '—looked after me hour by hour during my stay. He came with me to meetings, accompanied me to Pagan and Mandalay, invited his numerous Burmese friends (including some very high officials of the government) to the house so that we could talk freely and without restraint.

His hospitality was phenomenal. I have seldom consumed so much whisky in so short a time. He knew Burma as well as he knew his own extensive wardrobe. He had fought, like so many

Indians, with the British army during the war and had got
roaring drunk the night Rangoon was finally liberated from the
Japanese. He had returned after the war for UNICEF, then—
following a spell in New York—the government has asked for
him back. In all, he directed a massive operation. UNICEF had
a fleet of 800 vehicles, working in every corner of the country.
Ghosh was spending nearly a million and a quarter dollars a
year—principally in health, education and social welfare.
UNICEF was also involved in youth-training programmes, the
production of medicines and vaccines and in nutritional
research.

★

The Union of Burma came into existence as an independent
republic at 4.20 a.m. (the hour was chosen by astrologers) on
January 4, 1948. That U Nu became the first leader of the new
state was largely due to the accident of history. A few months
earlier, in July 1947, Aung San, the 'Liberator', and several of
his closest associates were mown down by two gunmen at a
cabinet meeting. The assassins were found and publicly hanged
and U Nu, who happened to be out of the room at the time, took
Aung San's place. Since 1948 the story of Burmese politics
centres around the personality and rivalry of two men, U Nu
himself and General Ne Win. They have ridden the last 20
years like a see-saw. When one is up, the other is down.

By repute U Nu is a kind-hearted, very devoted man who,
during his term of office, made the mistake of surrounding
himself by a bunch of crooks. When there was serious trouble—
and with the Karen uprising, the fall in the price of rice and
internal dissensions within the AFPFL this was most of the
time—he would go up into the mountains and pray for 15 days.

Perhaps the high point of his rule came when the sixth great
Buddhist Council (the first had been held shortly after Buddha
died) met in Rangoon from May 1954 to May 1956 to recite
and review the Pali texts and to celebrate the 2500th anniversary
of the death of Gautama Buddha. For this great event U Nu
had the World Peace Pagoda constructed. He dreamt one
night that Buddha had come to a place outside Rangoon not
far from the Inya Lake hotel. At a cost of some 900,000 kyats

(currently five kyats—one dollar), he built on the site a replica of the famous Sarnath Cave in India. (The rocks themselves came from India.) He brought two landscape gardeners from Yugoslavia to build gardens on the roof. In spite of this, the cave leaked badly so he summoned an engineering firm from California to fix it. The 2500th anniversary celebrations were held inside this cave. The seats and the public address system can be seen today, as well as the portraits of the patriarchs.

In 1958 U Nu voluntarily resigned in favour of General Ne Win, the army Chief of Staff, who pledged himself to clean up the mess and to restore internal peace. Ne Win's first intervention is known as the 'caretaker government'. At the end of 18 months (a good deal of which time U Nu spent meditating in the mountains) elections were held and U Nu once again became Prime Minister. But things were no better than before. On March 2, 1962, the military under the leadership of Ne Win engineered a coup. All the members of the government were arrested along with the key leaders of the minorities. The constitution was set aside and the self-chosen Revolutionary Council began to rule by decree.

There is no doubt that Ne Win acted with a good deal of finesse. His armed guards took the Chief Justice at five o'clock in the morning. They entered the secretariat so that when the high civil servants came to their desks at the usual leisurely hour, they found them already occupied. One or two nasty things happened to the students, but—for students in a modern world—this tends to be an occupational hazard.

Nor is there any doubt that the personality of General Ne Win dominates Burma today. He is very much in the saddle, a strong man who knows it. He is Chairman of the Revolutionary Council and also Chairman of the Revolutionary Government. He plays golf each day. The whole course is surrounded, some 200 to 300 soldiers being deployed. There is walkie-talkie communication from green to green. No one else plays while the General is playing. (In any case, no one else would want to be within 200 yards in case of some shooting incident!) The General is also a horse-racing man; his father-in-law was chief steward of the club, but he closed down the Royal Rangoon Turf, saying it was 'making the poor poorer'.

An American magazine reported that he had been seen in cut-aways, silk hat and white gloves at Epsom for the Derby and had lost £50,000. The magazine has been banned since then in Burma, though this is probably more a question of economics and foreign exchange availability than petty vindictiveness.

The General sometimes goes to England for medical treatment, but he takes good precautions before leaving. Once he sent a possible rival to Japan to be in charge of Burma's pavilion at Expo '70, even though the man protested he knew nothing about trade. More recently, before coming to England for his latest visit, he brought all the top regimental commanders from their regions where they were becoming little lords, made them all into Deputy Ministers, so that they would be stationed in Rangoon where he could keep an eye on them and appointed new commanders in their place.

A few months ago, when there was a severe earthquake, he moved out of the President's house which used to be the residence of the British Governor, back to his old house, just across Inya Lake from the hotel. This is where he lives today, surrounded by anti-aircraft guns, anti-tank fences and the loyal army.

But Ne Win is not a conventional dictator, relying on force and little else to sustain him in power. What makes Burma such a fascinating and important country today is the basic philosophy which underlies every act of the Ne Win regime and which, for better or for worse, has made Burma almost unique among the nations of the world. She is not a 'developing' country, at least in the sense that word is usually understood. Whereas Thailand and Mexico, the Philippines and the Ivory Coast—to give a few examples—all have common features in that they are pursuing the conventional growth patterns which characterize industrial (or industrializing) economies, Burma is different from all of them. She doesn't necessarily want to go that particular route or, if she does, she wants to do it in her own way and at her own pace.

As Erskine Childers of the United Nations Development Programme put it to me in Bangkok: 'What crops up all the time is the absolutely dominant motive of self-reliance. People say it's taken so far that they have deprived themselves of assistance they actually need. The Burmese answer "Thank you very much, this may be so—but we decide." The Burmese view is: "Yes, we want to advance science and education in our schools. But no, we do not want from UNESCO and USAID science kits which go out of repair and then we have to ask you for more. Show us how to make the materials so we can manage for ourselves." '

It is all tied up with Buddhism, the middle path. The Buddhist when he sits in front of his little shrine beside the Shwe Dagon pagoda in Rangoon isn't asking anyone to do anything for him. This is not a case of community worship with the priest interceding on behalf of a passive congregation. On the contrary, the Buddhist is saying 'Let me be more like Buddha, so I can manage in my own way'.

Ne Win and his associates at the same time have recognized that a good many undesirable things come into a country on the back of aid. Non-alignment is the cornerstone of the foreign policy of the revolutionary government, yet it is almost impossible to maintain such a posture if you are a major recipient of international assistance from either East or West.

Aid often creates a psychological dependence on getting still more aid. It saps initiative and enterprise. Or again, aid may foster—as it has in so many countries—a type of development wholly inappropriate to the circumstances. Coca-cola plants are constructed instead of improvements being made to basic water-supply systems. Aspirations are created which can never be fulfilled. The Western 'expert' generally wants to bring his whole cultural baggage with him and this can include utter myths about what happens and what is possible in his own country.

Effectively Burma has over the years since the 1962 revolution, become virtually independent of external assistance. USAID was about to sign a 35 million dollar road contract for the road to Mandalay, with motels, rest-houses—the lot. Ne Win said 'Out. We don't want your road. We don't want your money.' And the same went for all the other aid-giving agencies except those who operated under the aegis of the United Nations and the Colombo Plan. Burma won't even have volunteers. No Peace Corps, no VSO, no nothing. 'If volunteers are needed,' they say, 'we have plenty of our own.'

This is not ingratitude. It is straightforward logic. If you invite a Burmese for dinner, he may come or again he may not. The Burmese philosophy is that you are gaining merit for feeding them, and that the dinner is largely for your benefit, not theirs. They take the same view of international assistance.

*

If you start from certain premises, you tend to arrive at certain conclusions. Some of the steps on the road may be unpleasant and difficult to take. Pressures, hard to resist, may build up as entrenched interests mobilize against you. Judged by conventional yard-sticks, the great experiment may seem to be a failure.

The foreign visitor steps out from the lobby of Inya Lake hotel and snaps his fingers for a taxi. But there aren't any taxis or precious few. If he wants a roll of lavatory paper, his best bet is to go to a friend in one of the embassies. They can bring it in in the diplomatic bag. If he needs a loaf of bread, he will find there is only one breadshop in Rangoon known, quaintly enough, as the People's Pătisserie. There will be a long queue at six o'clock in the morning. There are one or two restaurants but, if you do choose to eat out, eat early. They tend to be out of food by 7 p.m.

All this may at first sight seem discouraging. Burmanization has also meant nationalization on an unparalleled scale. When the Indians and the British left the country, the government took over their businesses and all other business as well. By the end of March 1964 most commercial enterprises in Rangoon including wholesalers, brokers, department stores, timber shops and the entire export trade were nationalized. By January the following year, Burmah Oil, Burma Corporation and Burma Unilever had been taken over, thus virtually eliminating all foreign investment. Nationalization was extended to private schools and private hospitals. Foreign missionaries were asked to leave.

But first impressions are not always necessarily right. Of course, there have been shortages. Inexperience alone would account for that. Nationalizing virtually overnight such a major chunk of the economy is a massive undertaking. For some,

particularly those who owned businesses and who now find the
best they can do is work for the government at a subsistence
wage, the process has been cruel. For almost everybody, it has
been frustrating. To have to produce the old light-bulb before
you can buy a new one would try anyone's patience.

Controls are always irksome and in Burma the controls are of
a most stringent nature. If you choose to leave the country,
you have that privilege. You may take with you what you
stand up in and an airline ticket purchased in Burmese currency. But you may never return, not even as a tourist or in
transit. As far as Burma is concerned, you are an un-person.

But the sufferings of the middle class, poignant as they may
be, are not the whole story. What Ne Win has done is to shut off
the supply of inessential consumer goods, those luxury items like
light-bulbs and lavatory paper not to speak of Mercedes Benzes,
which absorbed so much of the country's scarce foreign exchange. Instead, he has freed resources for the import of essential commodities, like medicines and high priority investment
items, which (in theory) should lead to improvements in the
living standards of *all* sectors of the population.

I never saw, during all my time in Burma, anyone who
looked hungry or unhappy. I never saw a beggar who looked
as though he meant it. The 'longyi' may be a simple enough
garment, worn by men and women alike, but it is a good deal
cleaner and more efficient than the gunny-sacks they used to
wear in the 'good old days'. Frankly, compared to India, Burma
seemed like paradise.

*

The Burmese Way to Socialism, the base on which the whole
edifice is built, is a difficult enough tract to read. The ideas, to
the Western mind at least, are obscure and the language con-
torted. Yet in practice it has proved a workable manifesto. It
presents, to my mind, a viable alternative to traditional patterns
of economic development in the Third World, an alternative
which may be relevant far beyond the shores of Burma herself.

Even now, of course, evolution is still going on. The return to
civilian rule envisaged in the setting up on a country-wide basis
of Workers' Councils and Peasants' Councils has yet to be

achieved. National solidarity is a hard concept to interpret; political cadres remain overworked and undermanned. But the outline, the action-programme is there and that is more than half the battle.

Perhaps the best way to describe what Burma wants to be is to describe what she does *not* want to be. She does *not* want to turn into a country where the capital city swells up like an infected gland, attracting to itself manpower which cannot conceivably be employed in any productive capacity. In other words she wants to avoid the horrors of rampant urbanization as these are found in Africa, Latin America and other parts of Asia. She wants, incidentally, to avoid some of the pollution and environmental problems that go hand-in-hand with this hideous process.

She does *not* want to be a Western Society if this means the constant pursuit of materialistic goals and the social divisiveness produced by the differential accumulation of wealth. (Anyway, accumulation is not a part of Buddhist philosophy. Hardly anyone makes a will; yet there are very seldom any quarrels over inheritances.)

She does *not* want television and she doesn't (really) want tourists. She may accept a few for the foreign exchange they bring with them. But it will be a carefully regulated business. The cultural steamroller, whether it is fuelled in Madison Avenue or Gorky Street, will be stopped in its tracks long before it can do any real damage.

What then is she aiming for? As far as I can see, the object of the Ne Win regime is to create not so much wealth, but a certain quality of life.

*

Burma is a land of proverbs. The one that dominates their political philosophy is 'man matters most'. And they give the proverb an explanatory gloss by saying 'He is the one who makes things good and he is the one who makes things bad'. Materially they know they are not very rich. But spiritually, they believe they are very rich.

Their strategy, if one may use that overworked word, is fairly simple. They start with the idea that Rangoon is not Burma.

Rangoon, even if you add in all the whole of the Greater Rangoon area, has not much more than one and a half million people. Burma as a whole has about 27 million people in its 269,000 square miles.

Ne Win's government wants to take development to the countryside in a planned systematic way. This is where well over 80% of the population lives. The approach has a three-fold emphasis; health, education, agriculture.

It is almost moving how great an importance the Burmese attach to the health service. Not for them the cold calculations of the cost/benefit economists who see every life saved as another mouth to feed. Health, as they see it, is a humanitarian imperative. Expenditure on health in 1968/69 was 186% higher than that for 1961/62. They have reduced infant mortality from 300 per 1000 live births down to 70. If they realize the demographic consequences of this achievement, they show no sign—at the moment—of being unduly worried. Family planning and population control are notions which belong to a distant tomorrow.

There is a system of National Service for doctors, who spend two or three years in the villages. Medical students will also spend time in the villages. They are building up a health network—centres, sub-centres, midwives, dispensaries—all over the country. A major effort is being put into leprosy control (the disease affects almost 12% of the population); also into the control of trachoma (especially prevalent in the drier zones) and elephantiasis.

The philosophy throughout is 'bring the services to the villages, otherwise the villagers will come to the town to look for them'.

It is the same story with education. Burma, like India, was bequeathed Macaulay's educational system. In India today, the moment an arts student is issued with his admission certificate, he might as well be issued with an unemployment certificate as well. In Burma, there is actually a chance that—if he is admitted to a degree—he will get a job. The number of students who are allowed to graduate in any particular discipline is carefully tailored to manpower projections.

Formerly 60% of university students took liberal arts degrees. Now this is changing to 70% doing science and engineering and agriculture. In 1962 when Ne Win came to power there were only two agricultural engineers in the whole country. But there were literally hundreds of lawyers and classicists who couldn't get their hands dirty if they tried.

They are developing technical and vocational education and, at a more basic level, putting an enormous effort into literacy campaigns. The secret here is the way in which youth—in so many countries the source of disaffection and disillusion—has been harnessed and mobilized for development.

There are night schools in the villages all over the country. Youth workers hold classes, teaching adult illiterates alongside their children. They won't leave the village until 100% or 95% literacy has been achieved. The slogan is 'each one, teach one'. Teach a man to read and then he will go and teach his friends.

So far quite a small proportion of Burmese youth is involved on these voluntary projects, perhaps not more than 10%. There are budgetary and administrative constraints which means that for every successful application, ten are turned away. But the number is steadily growing and already it represents a tremendous resource. It looks as though Burma, with its 'Youth in Development' programme, has de-fused the Youth Bomb.

Nowadays there is no such word in Burma as extra-curricular. The word is co-curricular. One school decides 'We will look after cleaning, keeping the local hospital tidy, etc.'. Another school decides 'We will look after irrigation, keeping the canals clean'. The use of one's hands is taught as having dignity and worth on its own. This is decolonisation of education on a fantastic scale. The jettisoning of English as the principal medium of instruction was only a part, though a necessary part, of this process.

All this can be seen as creating the rural infrastructure for genuine agricultural progress. The 'green revolution' has reached Burma, just as it has reached India and Thailand. There is every chance that the Burmese Way (which in any case emphasizes agricultural rather than industrial development) will permit a genuine transformation of agricultural production, while avoiding some of the social and political pitfalls to which the 'green revolution' has so far proved susceptible.

The new techniques, the new technology require healthy literate farmers. If we are not to see a process of large-scale mechanization with all its consequences it also requires farmers in whom the spirit of collaboration is deeply inured.

If men and women are to remain happily on the land, they must have farms of their own. Given population pressures, even in Burma, these are bound to be small farms, perhaps not much more than an acre or two per family. There is nothing intrinsically bad about this—indeed the story of the 'green revolution' to date is that some of the highest per acre yields have been achieved on the smallest farms.

But it does mean that certain operations will need to be conducted on a co-operative—if not a communal—basis. Credit and marketing lend themselves most readily to the co-operative approach, but more than this may be necessary. Co-operation may also be needed on the production side—for example, in land-clearing, sowing, harvesting, threshing and such like.

If the Burmese Way can achieve a revolution in the *mental attitude* of the peasant farmer, permitting through co-operative action the creation of a type of farming pattern that is both small-scale yet technically efficient, it could without exaggeration prove to be a tool that can change the world.

I have absolutely no doubt that Burma is a country with tremendous possibilities. It has vast forest resources, especially of teak; vast mineral resources—lead, gems, coals, oil, antimony; vast fishery resources—both sea and freshwater. It has a population which, thanks to the efforts of the priests and an enlightened government, comes second only to Japan in the Asian literacy stakes. What is more its volume of external debt is insignificant. It has not sold its soul for a mess of pottage in the form of loans, grants and suppliers' credits from aid-giving agencies and commercial enterprises. As a result, it is one of the very few countries I have visited in the so-called developing world that still has a soul.

*

You won't see any flying fishes on the road to Mandalay today, if there ever were any. If you go to Mandalay (assuming you can get permission) you go by air. To drive, you need security trucks, carrying Bren guns and nine or ten men, who will travel ahead and behind. You stop when they stop and you don't move after nightfall. It's a dangerous business and expensive, since you have to pay high wages to the guards.

Even if you go by boat, you never know when to expect the 'insurgents' to ambush you. The river narrows at several places and you are an easy target from the banks. Besides it is uncomfortable. The boats don't carry food and the toilet facilities (which tend to be important on a five-day journey) beggar description.

Burma has had an 'insurgent' problem as long as anyone can remember. One of the by-products of the Burmese Way is that self-contained racial groups have jealously husbanded their cultures and identities. During the war one of the problems was to stop the Shans and the Karens, the Mons, the Chins and the Kachins from going after each other and the dominant Burmese and to persuade them to concentrate on the Japanese instead.

When politics is added to race and old-fashioned banditry thrown in for good measure, it is not surprising that at any point of time fairly large chunks of territory are outside the control of the central government. Some insurgents fall into no discernible category, so a special one has been invented. They are called 'multiflag insurgents'.

Today a new element has been injected into this always fluid situation. In 1968 U Nu, after being in prison for six years, was allowed by Ne Win to go to India for 'ayurvedic' treatment, i.e. treatment by the indigenous doctors. The Indian government built him a house; U Nu said he wouldn't take part in politics but would teach Buddhism. Instead he went to the States and somehow—so it is said—raised three million dollars. Then he set up in Bangkok and began talking about a glorious return.

Undoubtedly he had made some impact. I was told that some 40 or 50 people a day were going, with insurgents' help, from Burma into Thailand to join their former leader. The guerillas and the tribesmen have elephants and for a fee will escort them through the jungle. The other day it was reported that U Nu had moved camp into Northern Burma itself and was intending to launch the counter-revolution from there.

It is almost impossible to believe U Nu has any chance of success. Could anyone, barring certain embittered members of the middle class, really want to return to the shambles of the Fifties? Yet politics is a strange business. Who knows what promises U Nu may give to potential supporters and be believed? Or perhaps U Nu and Ne Win will finally join forces and exercise a condominium over the country, signing official papers and documents of state with the composite and ambiguous title: U Win.

On my last afternoon in Burma I climbed up the steps to the top of the hill at Mandalay. From the summit one looked out over the town, capital of the Buddhist World. Here, in 1871, King Mindon convoked the Fifth Buddhist Council. Here, in 1885, came a British force to dethrone Mindon's son Thibaw and his wife Supayalat and deport them to India. Here, not much more than half a century later, the Japanese and the Allied armies fought a ping-pong battle over the swirling mud-brown waters of the Irrawaddy, destroying and rebuilding Ava Bridge (which connects the Mandalay and Sagaing divisions) several times in the process.

I could see that the inside of the great palace, several hundred feet below, had been totally obliterated in the fighting. But the walls still stood and the moat which surrounded them still drew its water from the river.

*

Mandalay, as far as I was concerned, was the end of the road. This was it, folks. There was nowhere else to go, or—even if there was—it would keep for another year. At home, there were still two shopping days left before Christmas. With luck I could make it before the stores closed. So I flew back to Rangoon and, that same night, caught a BOAC flight back to London. It was a long journey—over 24 hours, I believe, though it was hard to be sure because the clock kept on changing as we flew west and north.

Though the stewardesses did their best to ensure that passengers were distracted at all possible moments when they were not actually sleeping or, for whatever reason, unconscious—that long flight through the night provided me with the occasional moment for reflection. I was able to look back, not just on the Asia leg of my trip, but on the African and Latin American legs which had preceded it.

The 'green revolution' has—I believe—given the world ten or fifteen years breathing space. Food production for a while may catch up with or even keep ahead of population growth. But if the momentum of population growth itself cannot be checked, the triumph of men like Borlaug and Chandler and Anderson, and of all those who work in the field of agricultural development, will be hollow indeed.

The 'breathing space' theory will be shown to be a nonsense. For—without massive and effective programmes of population control, initiated in parallel with development efforts—any temporary reprieve will merely increase the price to be paid at a later date. Thus the population 'crunch' when it comes, will be greater inasmuch as the population base itself is greater—thanks to the 'green revolution'.

INDEX

Abome, 117-18
Accra, 75, 77, 79, 80, 99, 100, 103, 117
Addis Ababa, ix
Aden, 90
Adulyodej, King Bhumibol, 192
Afghanistan, 6
Africa, ix, xiii, 28, 74, 75, 85, 87, 94, 110, 111, 117, 119, 128, 131, 181, 206; North, 62; North-west, ix; South, 6, 138, 143; West, 78, 94, 103
Aguilar, Roberto, 37-40
Akatani, Kan, 94
Alfalfa, 62
Algeria, 5
Alkis, Dr, 162
Alvarez, Dr Edouardo, 22
America, 76, 97, 117, 139, 156; Central, see Central America; Latin, see Latin America; North, 68; South, ix, 36, 55, 117; see also USA
Anderson, Dr Glenn, 164, 165, 169-70, 212
Ankara, 150, 154, 157, 158, 162
Appiah II, Nana, 95-6
Argentina, 6, 22, 40
Arizona, 9, 63
Asia, ix, xii, xiii, 5, 153, 161, 167, 181, 197, 206; South-east, 195, 196
Athwal, D. S., 166
Aung San, 200

Bahadur, Lal, 172
Bains, H. S., 175-83
Baker, Desmond, 76
Bananas, 48-54, 124, 126

Banda, Dr Hastings, 77, 143
Bangkok, ix, 192, 197-8, 199, 202, 210
Barber, Anthony, 73
Barley, 6, 170
Beachell, Henry, 187
Beans, xi, 15, 18
Belefougou, 106-7
Belgium, 75
Bennett, Erna, 10-11
Besuk, Steve, 58
Bilharzia, 80, 90-1, 122
Boerma, Addeke H., ix, 147, 148, 149
Bogota, 44-5, 55
Bolivia, 147
Borlaug, Dr Norman Ernest, 5-9, 12, 61, 149, 152, 164-5, 166, 187, 212
Botswana, 147
Brasilia, 65
Brazil, 6, 7, 23, 55, 58-9, 62, 63, 65-7, 68, 156, 192; SUDENE, 59, 67, 68-9
Britain, 74, 122, 135; see also England
British Council, 119-22
British Guiana, 90
Bulgaria, 163
Burma, 197-211
Burundi, 28
Butcher, Dave, 93-4, 95, 99

California, 6, 37, 62, 201
Calli, 22
Camarra, Dom Helder, 64-5
Cambodia, 74, 157, 195
Cardona, Ramiro, 46
Carpenter, Bob, 29, 31, 32, 33

Caruso, 57
Cattle, xi, 117, 160; Argentina, 40; Brazil, 62, 64, 67, 69; Dahomey, 103-4, 105, 108, 113-14; rabies in, 22-6; Tanzania, 130-140
Central America, ix, 28, 32, 33, 34, 37, 50
Central American Fisheries Project, 28-9, 31, 33
Ceylon, 57
Chandler, Robert, 187, 189, 212
Chang, T. T., 187
Chapingo, 16
Childers, Erskine, 199, 202
Childers, Mallika, 199
China, 78, 144, 186, 195, 197
Cholera, 161-3
Chungu, 142
CIAT, 22
CIMMYT, 3-4, 11-15, 20-1, 164, 166, 170, 171; India, 164-74; Puebla Project, 15-19
Clark, William, xiii
Cocoa, 49
Coffee-growing, 41-2
Colombia, 30, 36, 44, 45, 55; bananas, 49, 50-4; cocoa, 49; land reform, 46-8, 53-4; maize, 21-2; wheat, 6
Colombo, Emilio, 147, 149
Columbus, Christopher, 21, 76
Congo, 103
Costa Rica, 28, 50
Cotonou, 100, 101, 102, 105, 108, 109, 110, 116, 117, 118
Cotton, 107, 124, 126, 152
Crick, Dr Francis, 167
Crossman, Richard, 73
Cummings, Ralph, 171
Cushing, Cardinal, 40
Cyprus, 147
Czechoslovakia, 162

Dahomey, 79, 101, 102, 104, 106, 107, 108, 110, 112, 118, 147; Oueme Project, 110-16; tobacco 116-17

Dar es Salaam, 119, 129, 135
De Gaulle, President, 147
Denmark, 103
Devlin, Bernadette, 109
Dodoma, 128-31, 137, 139, 140, 142, 143
Douglas-Home, Sir Alec, 74
Duran, Dr Sergio, 53, 54
Dutch East Indies, 57

East Coast fever, 134
Ecuador, 29
Elephantiasis, 207
El Prado, 48-50
El Salvador, 27, 28, 29, 34, 47; coffee, 41-2; land reform, 35-7
El Triunfo, 27, 28, 29
England, xi, 74, 81, 100, 120, 121, 192, 202; see also Britain
Ethiopia, 6, 9, 163
Europe, 9, 75, 117, 153, 156
Evans, Jim, xiii

FAO, 10, 11, 20, 23, 24, 27, 28, 29, 41, 48, 49, 53, 81, 98, 103, 110, 112, 123, 126, 129, 135, 137, 138, 140, 197; Fifteenth Session, ix; IWP, ix-xi; Kalasin Project, 192-6; Pope visits, 147-50; San Francisco Valley Project, 60-4; Turkey and, 153, 155, 157-9; Volta Lake Project, 78-84, 86-92; Far East, ix
Fish/Fishing, xi, 29-33, 74, 78, 124, 193, 194; Dahomey, 114; Ghana, 81-6, 91-2, 98; protein, 32, 34
Foot-and-mouth disease, 134-5
Ford Foundation, x, 172, 184, 186
France, 27, 75, 100, 117

Geneva, ix, 161
Germany, 75; West, 150, 163
Ghana, 75-80, 87, 88, 91, 92, 94, 99, 100, 102, 103; Volta Project, see under FAO
Ghezou, King, 118
Ghosh, P. K., 199-200

Gilbert, Mike, 80-1, 85-8
Grapes, 64
Greece, 11, 27, 163
Guatemala, 28, 34, 37
Guinea, 98

Haiti, 34
Hammarskjöld, Dag, 103
Harrer, Heinrich, 197
Harris, Kenneth, 73
Hawaii, 11, 41
Heath, Edward, 73, 121
Hermosillo, 7, 9
Herring, 31
Holdgate, Les, 122
Holland, 157
Homberg (engineer), 142, 143
Honduras, 27, 28, 34, 35, 40
Hunter, Alastair, 137-8, 140-1

Iceland, 32
INCORA, 46-9, 52-4
India, x, xi, xiii, 76, 151, 157, 158,
    181, 197, 201, 205, 207, 208, 210;
    rice, 184-5, 188; wheat ,5, 6, 7,
    14, 164-79, 184
Indonesia, 157
Iran (Persia), 6, 151, 154, 161
Iraq, 9, 161
Ismir, 154, 155, 156, 157
Israel, 92
Istanbul, 150, 154, 157, 160, 162,
    163
Italy, 30, 115, 140

Jackson, Sir Robert, 79
Jamaica, 34
Japan, 36, 174, 191, 202, 209
Jhandi, 176
John XXIII, Pope, 149
Johnson, Charlotte, xiii, 100
Johnson, Leo, 55
Johnson, Paul, 73
Johnson, President, 173
Jones, Cen, 90

Kalasin Project, 192-6

Katmandu, 198
Kenya, 6
Kenyatta, President, 119
Kholi, Dr S. P., 166
Klatt, Art, 12-15
Knight, Arthur, 143-4
Koerber, Charles, 104, 108, 109,
    116
Kofi, Mr and Mrs, 97
Krantz, Dr B. A., 165
Kubitschek, President, 65
Kumasi, 99

Langostino, 32
Laos, 192, 195
Latin America, xiii, 6, 22, 27, 37,
    59, 206
Lazarev, Grigori, 112-16
Leather industry, 157-61
Lebanon, 169
Leprosy, 207
Leuenberger, Rudolf, 192, 194
Lind, Lars, xiii
London, 57, 73, 85, 119, 137, 139,
    147, 211
Los Baños, 186, 187, 189
Lucas, 63
Ludhiana, 174, 175, 179, 180, 181,
    182
Lysenko, 154

McKenzie, Bruce, 119
Macleod, Iain, 73
Madras, 158
Maize, 20, 39, 41, 74, 111, 112, 117,
    172; improvement, 4-5, 11, 15,
    20-2, 164; Puebla Project, 15-19;
    protein value, 19, 21; varieties,
    10, 17, 20-2
Malaria, 88
Malawi, 77
Malaya, 57, 118, 157
Manaus, 56-7
Mandalay, 199, 203, 209, 211
Manila, 189
Marcos, President, 189
Marques, Gabriel, 49

Marseilles, 27
Marshall, Judith, 94-7
Martin, Monsieur, 116-17
Maudling, Reginald, 73
Menzies, Gordon, 77-8
Mexico, x, 3-5, 7-8, 12, 13, 14, 16, 22, 23, 24, 25, 26, 61, 62, 164-6, 167, 168, 170, 171, 202
Mexico City, 3, 5, 9, 11, 12, 16, 20, 23, 164, 171
Middle East, 121, 161, 169
Milk, xi, 18, 23, 105, 106
Mitro, 114-16
Morocco, 6, 169
Moscow, 123
Mussolini, 147
Mwanza, 119, 120, 121, 122, 123, 125, 127
Myren, Delbert, 16, 19

Nagra, 182-3
Nairobi, 119
Nasser, President, 98
Navarette, Dula, 7-8, 61-3
Navarette, Mrs Dula, 8, 9
Near East, ix
Nehru, Jawaharlal, 172
New Delhi, 7, 164, 171, 175
New York, ix, 5, 57, 137, 190, 200
Nicaragua, 28, 34
Nigeria, 157
Nile perch, 82
Nkrumah, Gamal and Yaaba, 98
Nkrumah, President, 97-9, 103
Nkwakubew, 95-7
North Africa, 62
North America, 68
North-west Africa, ix
Norway, 31
Nu, U, 198, 200-1, 210-11
Nuremberg, 154
Nyerere, President, 140-4

Obregon, 8, 11, 14, 166
Ohenewa, Nana, 96-7
Oil-palm, 117, 118
Oil seed, 62

Oklahoma, 12
Onions, 62, 64
Osler, Robert, 4-5, 171
Oueme Project, 110-16

Pacheco, Rafael, 48, 49, 53, 54
Pacheco, Mrs Rafael, 53
Pagan, 199
Pakistan, 147, 151, 157, 161, 178; West, 167; wheat, 5, 14, 165, 169
Palo Alto, 23, 25
Panama, 28, 50
Parakou, 104, 105, 108, 116
Paris, ix, 57, 115
Paul VI, Pope, 147-50
Pawley, Walter, x
Peas, xi
Peking, 119, 196
Penalosa, Dr Enrique, 52
Pendik, 158
Peron, President, 40
Persia (Iran), 6, 151, 154, 161
Peru, 55, 58
Petrolina, 7, 60, 61
Philippines, x, 166, 202; rice, 186-92
Pickett, Doug, 120-2
Pigs, xi, 18, 19, 22
Pineapples, 68
Piraeus, 27
Pork, xi
Powell, Enoch, 121
Protein, 4, 95; fish, 32, 34; maize and, 19, 21; petroleum molasses, xi; vegetable, x-xi
Puebla Project, 15-19
Puerto Rico, 34
Pulses, xi
Punjab, 166, 167, 170, 174-80, 181, 182

Rabies, 22-6
Rangoon, 197, 198, 199, 200, 202, 203, 204, 206-7, 211
Rao, Dr, 7
Recife, 7, 58, 64, 67
Rentjens, Jan, 103-4, 105, 106-9
Rhodes, Mr and Mrs, 12

Rhodesia, 6
Rice, x, xi, xiii, 68, 124, 184-5; Dahomey, 111, 112, 113, 114; Philippines, 186-92; Thailand, 193-4
Rio de Janeiro, 64
River-blindness, 89-90
Rockefeller Foundation, x, 3, 8, 11, 16, 164, 165, 169, 171, 172, 184, 186
Romba, Mr, 156-61
Rome, ix, 11, 63, 75, 84, 112, 115, 147, 150, 163, 197
Rosetti, Bruno, 28, 29, 30
Russia, 6, 161

Sagittario (ship), 27, 28, 29, 30
Salas, Rafael, 189-90
Santa Cruz, Dr Hernan, 147, 148
Santiago, ix
São Paulo, 64
Scotland, 140
Shrimp, 27, 32
Sierra Leone, 90
Singapore, 165
Singh, Bachat, 179-80
Singh, Jaghit, 178-9
Singh, K. M., 183
Singh, Ram, 177-8
Sleeping sickness, 89
Sorghum, 74, 105, 172
South Africa, 6, 138, 143
South America, ix, 36, 55, 117
South-east Asia, 195, 196
Spain, 21
Spiny lobster, 32
Stalin, 154
Subramanian, Dr, 165, 168, 171-3
SUDENE, 59, 67, 68-9
Swaminathan, Dr M. S., 165
Switzerland, 140
Syria, 6, 76, 154, 161, 163

Taiwan, 186, 187
Tanzania, 119, 121, 122, 123, 127, 128, 130, 131, 133-7, 141-2, 144, 181

Taylor, Bill, 82-3, 87, 91
Tegucigalpa, 34
Texas, 12
Thailand, 192, 202, 208, 210; rice, 193-4
Thant, U, 103, 148
Thornton, David, 129, 138-9
Tibet, 197
Tobacco, 116-17
Toluca, 11-12, 166, 168
Tomalin, Nicholas, 73
Tomatoes, 62, 64
Trachoma, 207
Trinidad, 23
Tucson, 9
Tunisia, 6
Turkestan, 9, 154
Turkey, 10, 150, 153-4; cholera, 161-3; leather industry, 157-61; wheat, 10-11, 151-6, 169

UN, 28, 78, 94, 103, 112, 116, 159, 190, 199, 203; Ghana and, 76-7, 79, 80, 87, 88; Tanzania and, 122-8; Secretary-General, see Thant, U; see also FAO, UNDP, UNESCO, UNICEF, WHO
UNDP, 4, 7, 20, 23, 24, 27, 33, 41, 48, 49, 60, 79, 102, 104, 110, 112, 123, 125, 137, 150, 153, 155, 158, 159, 181, 182, 192, 202
UNESCO, 123, 125, 181, 182, 203
UNICEF, 199-200
United Fruit Company, 49-54
USA, 6, 28, 117, 151, 172, 174, 179, 195, 198, 210; see also America

Vamilov, 154
Venezuela, 23
Vietnam, 74, 195
Vishnyakov, Professor Yuri, 123-8, 181
Volta Project, see under FAO

Washington, 196
Watson, Dr James D., 167
Wellhausen, Dr, 4, 8

West Africa, 78, 94, 103
West Germany, 150, 163
Wheat, x, xi, 20, 187; improvement, 3, 4-6, 11, 12-13, 15, 164; India, 5, 6, 7, 14, 164-79; Turkey, 10-11, 151-6; varieties, 8, 9, 10-11, 13-14, 165-8
Wheeler, Lieutenant-General Raymond, 195
WHO, 78, 90, 91, 161-2, 167
Wilson, Harold, 74

Win, General Ne, 200-2, 203, 205, 206, 208, 210-11
World Bank, xiii, 79, 112
Wright, Carl, 102-3
Wright, Mrs Carl, 103

Yugoslavia, 201

Ze Doca, 67, 68
Zei, Mr, 98-9